Colorado

An Altitude SuperAmerica Guide

by **Patrick Soran and Dan Klinglesmith**

Publication Information

Altitude Publishing Ltd.
Unit 521, 12445 East 39th Avenue
Denver, Co 80239
(800) 957-6888

Extreme care has been taken to ensure that all information presented in this book is accurate and up-to-date, and neither the author nor the publisher can be held responsible for any errors.

Cataloging in Publication Data
Klinglesmith, Dan, 1955
Colorado: an Altitude SuperAmerica Guide
Includes index.
ISBN 1-55265-014-6
1. Colorado—Guidebooks. I. Soran, Patrick, 1953-
II. Title. F774.3.K54 1998 917.8804'33 C98-910089-8

We acknowledge the financial support of the Goverment of Canada through the Book Publishing Industry Development Program (BPIDP) for our publishing activities.

Front cover photo: Wilson Peak, San Miguel Mountains, Uncompahgre National Forest

Insets, front cover: right: Western horseback riding, Steamboat Springs;
left: Bald Eagle

Frontispiece: Pawnee Buttes, National Grasslands

Back cover photo: Crystal Mill

Design and Production Team

Concept	Stephen Hutchings
Art direction/design	Stephen Hutchings
Design/layout	Kelly Stauffer
Editor	Sabrina Grobler
Index	George Stacey
Financial management	Laurie Smith
Maps	Mark Higenbottam

A Note from the Publisher

The world described in *Altitude SuperAmerica Guides* is a unique and fascinating place. It is a world filled with surprise and discovery, beauty and enjoyment, questions and answers. It is a world of people, cities, landscape, animals and wilderness as seen through the eyes of those who live in, work with, and care for this world. The process of describing this world is also a means of defining ourselves.

It is also a world of relationship, where people derive their meaning from a deep and abiding contact with the land–as well as from each other. And it is this sense of relationship that guides all of us at Altitude to ensure that these places continue to survive and evolve in the decades ahead.

Altitude SuperAmerica Guides are books intended to be used, as much as read. Like the world they describe, *Altitude SuperAmerica Guides* are evolving, adapting and growing. Please write to us with your comments and observations, and we will do our best to incorporate your ideas into future editions of these books.

Stephen Hutchings
Publisher

Altitude GreenTree Program
Altitude Publishing will plant twice as many trees as were used in the manufacturing of this product.

Printed and bound in Canada by Friesens

Contents

Maps

The ***Colorado SuperAmerica Guide*** is organized according to the following color scheme:

Introduction .....
Highlights of Nature .....
Highlights of History .....
Recreation .....
The Front Range .....
The Rocky Mountains .....
The Western Slope .....
The Eastern Plains .....
Reference .....

Introduction

Crystal Mill

In 1893, a Massachusetts English professor, Katharine Lee Bates, was standing atop Pikes Peak admiring the vistas of Colorado when she wrote poetry that was to make her, and Colorado, famous: *Oh beautiful for spacious skies, For amber waves of grain. For purple mountain majesties*

Above the fruited plain.
America! America
God shed His grace on thee.

Indeed, the broad flanks of the Rockies and the sweeping swath of Colorado's high plains were the inspiration for *America the Beautiful.*

Bates wasn't the first to admire the region's many delights. Humans have been enjoying Colorado for generations. While we tend to think of Colorado as having been settled during the gold and silver rushes of the mid- to late 1800s, the fact is that nomadic hunters stalked bison on the plains and in alpine meadows 12,000 years ago. Ancestral Puebloans—inaccurately called the Anasazi—thrived in the Four Corners area from the time of Christ until about 1300 A.D. The Arapaho, Ute and Cheyenne enjoyed the bounty of the mountains and plains for several hundred years. Hispanics settled the San Luis Valley as early as 1830, a mere twenty-five years after Lt. Zebulon Pike wandered the state, as lost as any tourist ever got.

Colorado's Native American heritage quickly vanished with the discovery of gold. Prospectors and miners came by the thousands along with shopkeepers, ministers and ladies of both good and ill repute. Gold and silver were their common bonds as they wrestled this western stretch of the Kansas Territory into the United States.

Although mineral moguls got all the glory, thousands of families settled the Eastern Plains and Western Slope. These hard-working, patient people converted thousands of acres of land into bountiful ranches and farms, somehow overcoming the natural and supernatural impediments that obstructed their pastoral paths.

To some extent, the state still depends heavily on mining and agriculture to fuel the financial future, but the booms and busts of more than 100 years have taught Coloradans a valuable lesson—diversify.

left: Garden of the Gods

Today, tourism pitches in a healthy portion of the state's economy. And the state greeted the information age like an actress embracing a bouquet of flowers. The nation's largest television cable company—TCI—is headquartered south of Denver. Situated only one satellite "bounce" between Europe and Asia, Colorado is perfectly located to receive and process the information gathered by twinkling satellites. Information-age mega-companies such as Quark and US West also call Colorado home.

Historically, the state has been politically conservative, nearly always electing a Republican legislature. Equilibrium-minded voters have often balanced this with a Democratic governor.

State politicians are beginning to play on the national stage. Senator Gary Hart had a real chance at the presidency in 1988. Governor Roy Romer recently headed the Democratic National Party. Ben Nighthorse Campbell was the first Native American ever elected to the Senate. Denver's ex-mayor, Federico Peña, held two cabinet posts (Transportation and Energy) in Bill Clinton's administration.

Perhaps because of its extraordinary scenery, excellent economy and wonderful weather, as well as Coloradans' come-on-in hospitality, the state has said "howdy" to some quarter-million new residents since 1990. Colorado is appropriately shaped like a welcome mat.

Pikes Peak from the Garden of the Gods

How to Use this Book

This book is loaded with recommendations, maps, photos and commentary. The text, while sometimes brief, has a definite philosophy; these are the state's "must-sees." Even if you can't visit everything mentioned here, you'll know what you missed, and will have a list of things to do for your next foray into the Centennial State.

The first chapter, Highlights of Nature, covers the lay of the land. The information provides a brief summary of what to expect from the state's geography, weather and geological makeup. Space has also been devoted to describing the state of Colorado's ecology. Descriptions of flora and fauna identify plants and animals you might expect to spot during a visit.

Next comes Highlights of History. Colorado's past is replete with cowboys and Indians, miners and farmers, Ancestral Puebloans and modern-day technological history-makers.

Chapter four, Recreation, describes some of the activities you might want to enjoy during a stay. While it is by no means exhaustive, this chapter will guide you to a good starting point.

When Coloradans talk about any area of the state, they invariably refer to it as being in one of its four regions: the Front Range, the Rocky Mountains, the Western Slope, or the Eastern Plains. For that very reason, the core information about Colorado is presented here in exactly the same way. Chapters five through eight take in-depth looks at these four domains.

The Front Range is the swath of territory—both foothills and high plains—that sweeps north and south along the Rocky Mountains' eastern flank. The state's major cities lie here: Denver, Boulder, Colorado Springs, Pueblo, Greeley and Fort Collins. So too do some of its more famous "mountain" attractions: Central City, Royal Gorge and Rocky Mountain National Park.

The Rocky Mountains form a backbone right down the middle of the state, interrupted here and there by immense inter-mountain valleys such as South Park or the San Luis Valley. They offer countless day and nighttime activities, lodging that runs from budget to budget-busting, no-star to five-star dining, and more scenic vistas than any one state ought to be allowed.

Draping down to the west from these mountains lies a series of plateaus called the Western Slope. It is arguably some of the state's most dramatic scenery and contains some of its most interesting diversions. In the Central Plateau is the Colorado National Monument, a mini version of Utah's beckoning Canyonlands. The Four Corners region boasts many fascinating remains of the Ancestral Puebloans. Up north, near the intersection of Wyoming and Utah, is Dinosaur Country—the state's paleontological treasure trove.

To the east, encompassing nearly half the state's acreage, are the Eastern Plains. They are hardly plain. In the southeast is a famous stop on the Santa Fe Trail—Bent's Old Fort. To the northeast stand Pawnee Buttes, elegant vertical stone formations rising from the prairie and sacred to the Plains Indians.

Finally, extensive practical information about Colorado is in a reference section at the back of the book. Here you will find restaurants, hotels and contact numbers for dozens of tourism agencies.

Colorado Facts and Superlatives

- Population: 3.8 million.
- Size: 104,247 square miles.
- Called the "Centennial State" because it entered statehood in 1876–100 years after the Declaration of Independence was signed.
- State flower: Columbine.
- State song: *Where the Columbines Grow* by Arthur Flinn.
- State fossil: *Stegosaurus.*
- State bird: Lark bunting.
- State animal: Rocky Mountain bighorn sheep.
- State motto: "Nothing Without Providence" (*Nil Sine Numine*).
- State gemstone: aquamarine.
- World's largest underground mine: Climax, Colorado.
- World's highest auto tunnel: Eisenhower Tunnel, 11,000 feet, which crosses under the Continental Divide.
- World's highest railroad: Pikes Peak Cog Railway, which climbs to the top of Pikes Peak.
- World's highest suspension bridge: Royal Gorge Bridge, which hangs 1,053 feet above the Arkansas River.
- World's largest open-air hot springs swimming pool: Glenwood Springs.
- World's largest laundromat: Smiley's on East Colfax in Denver.
- World's highest continuous paved road: Trail Ridge Road in Rocky Mountain National Park.
- The state features 54 peaks over 14,000 feet; the highest being Mount Elbert at 14,433 feet above sea level.
- The state's lowest point is in the Arkansas Valley at 3,350 feet above sea level.
- The 18th step on the state's capitol building in Denver is exactly one mile–5,280 feet–above sea level.
- The dome of the state's capitol building in Denver is covered with 200 ounces of 24 karat gold.
- The cheeseburger was invented–and patented–in Denver by Louis Ballast in 1944 after he grilled a slice of cheese onto a hamburger.
- Christmas lights were invented in Denver when D. D. Sturgeon, an electrical contractor, dipped bulbs in paint and strung them around a tree outside his sick son's window.
- Katharine Lee Bates was inspired to write *America the Beautiful* during an excursion up Pikes Peak in 1893.
- Colorado averages 300 inches of snow and 300 days of sunshine per year.
- Geographically, Denver is exactly halfway between Tokyo, Japan and Munich, Germany.

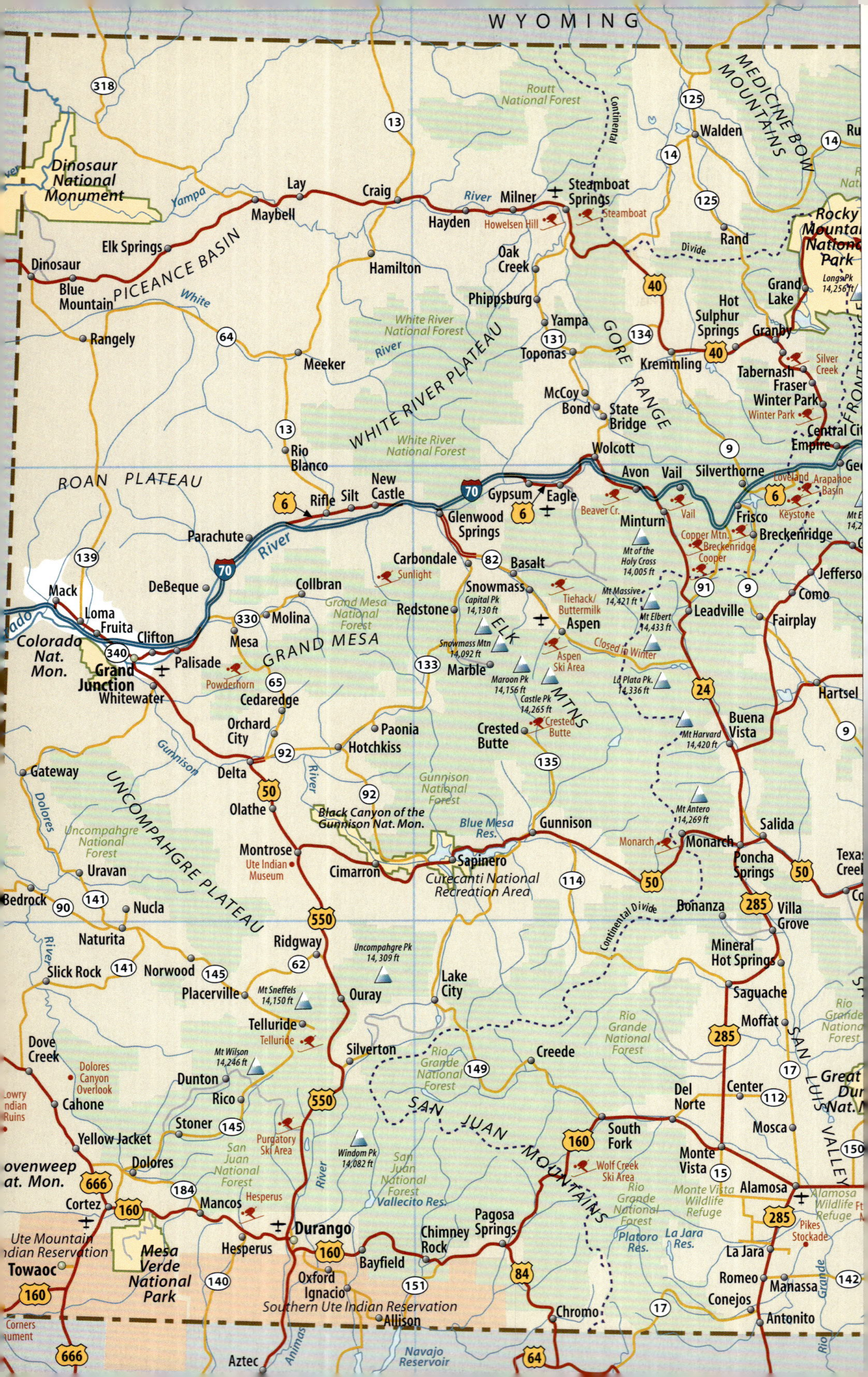

WYOMING
Dinosaur National Monument
Yampa
Lay
Maybell
Craig
River
Milner
Steamboat Springs
Steamboat
Hayden
Howelsen Hill
Routt National Forest
Continental Divide
Walden
MEDICINE BOW MOUNTAINS
Rand
Rocky Mountain National Park
Longs Pk 14,256 ft
Grand Lake
Granby
Hot Sulphur Springs
Elk Springs
PICEANCE BASIN
Dinosaur
Blue Mountain
White
Rangely
Hamilton
Oak Creek
Phippsburg
Yampa
Toponas
White River National Forest
Meeker
GORE RANGE
Kremmling
Tabernash
Silver Creek
Fraser
Winter Park
Central City
Empire
FRONT RANGE
McCoy
Bond
State Bridge
WHITE RIVER PLATEAU
Rio Blanco
ROAN PLATEAU
Rifle
Silt
New Castle
Gypsum
Eagle
Wolcott
Avon
Vail
Silverthorne
Loveland
Arapahoe Basin
Keystone
Frisco
Breckenridge
Copper Mtn.
Cooper
Beaver Cr.
Minturn
Mt of the Holy Cross 14,005 ft
Parachute
Glenwood Springs
Carbondale
Sunlight
Basalt
DeBeque
Collbran
Grand Mesa National Forest
Molina
Mesa
GRAND MESA
Mack
Loma
Fruita
Clifton
Colorado Nat. Mon.
Grand Junction
Palisade
Powderhorn
Whitewater
Redstone
Snowmass
Capitol Pk 14,130 ft
Tiehack/Buttermilk
Aspen
Aspen Ski Area
Closed in Winter
Mt Massive 14,421 ft
Mt Elbert 14,433 ft
Leadville
Jefferson
Como
Fairplay
Snowmass Mtn 14,092 ft
Marble
Maroon Pk 14,156 ft
Castle Pk 14,265 ft
ELK MTNS
La Plata Pk. 14,336 ft
Hartsel
Cedaredge
Orchard City
Paonia
Hotchkiss
Crested Butte
Mt Harvard 14,420 ft
Buena Vista
Gateway
Gunnison
Delta
Olathe
Gunnison National Forest
Black Canyon of the Gunnison Nat. Mon.
Blue Mesa Res.
Mt Antero 14,269 ft
Salida
Monarch
Poncha Springs
Texas Creek
UNCOMPAHGRE PLATEAU
Uncompahgre National Forest
Dolores
Montrose
Ute Indian Museum
Cimarron
Sapinero
Curecanti National Recreation Area
Uravan
Bedrock
Nucla
Naturita
Bonanza
Villa Grove
Ridgway
Uncompahgre Pk 14,309 ft
Slick Rock
Norwood
Placerville
Mt Sneffels 14,150 ft
Ouray
Lake City
Mineral Hot Springs
Saguache
Telluride
Moffat
SAN LUIS VALLEY
Rio Grande National Forest
Dove Creek
Dolores Canyon Overlook
Mt Wilson 14,246 ft
Silverton
Creede
Dunton
Rico
Del Norte
Center
Great Sand Dunes Nat. Mon.
Lowry Indian Ruins
Cahone
Stoner
Purgatory Ski Area
SAN JUAN MOUNTAINS
South Fork
Mosca
Yellow Jacket
San Juan National Forest
Windom Pk 14,082 ft
Wolf Creek Ski Area
Monte Vista
Hovenweep Nat. Mon.
Dolores
Hesperus
Vallecito Res.
Monte Vista Wildlife Refuge
Alamosa
Alamosa Wildlife Refuge
Cortez
Mancos
Durango
Pagosa Springs
Chimney Rock
Platoro Res.
La Jara Res.
Pikes Stockade
Ute Mountain Indian Reservation
Mesa Verde National Park
Towaoc
Hesperus
Bayfield
La Jara
Oxford
Ignacio
Romeo
Manassa
Conejos
Southern Ute Indian Reservation
Allison
Chromo
Antonito
Four Corners Monument
Aztec
Animas
Navajo Reservoir

Cheyenne
Sidney
80
Julesburg
Virginia Dale
287
Rockport
85
25
Pawnee National Grassland
Pawnee Buttes
71
Peetz
Sedgwick
76
138
385
Proctor
River
Poudre Park
Wellington
Fort Collins
Ted's Place
Roosevelt National Forest
Ault
14
Briggsdale
Stoneham
Sterling
6
Fleming
Haxtun
Amherst
23
Holyoke
New Raymer
Atwood
Merino
Windsor
Eaton
Greeley
Kersey
Jackson Reservoir
Riverside Reservoir
52
71
Platte
61
59
Clarkville
34
Estes Park
Loveland
Evans
South
Goodrich
Weldona
Snyder
36
7
Lyons
66
Gilcrest
Masters
63
Longmont
Platteville
76
Wiggins
Fort Morgan
Brush
Akron
Otis
Yuma
Eckley
Ft. Lupton
Keenesburg
52
Boulder
Lafayette
Hudson
Prospect Valley
Woodrow
Eldora
119
Nederland
72
Louisville
Brighton
Westminster
79
Abarr
Idaho Springs
Golden
71
Aurora
Bennett
Lindon
Anton
Idalia
Georgetown
Lakewood
DENVER
Byers
36
Last Chance
Joes
Cope
Littleton
470
70
Deer Trail
GREAT
Republican
Evans 14,264 ft
Conifer
Parker
285
85
Grant
Bailey
Sedalia
Elizabeth
Kiowa
59
385
Seibert
24
Stratton
Burlington
Castle Rock
86
Genoa
70
Flagler
Pike National Forest
Deckers
Westcreek
Limon
Hugo
25
PLAINS
Lake George
Woodland Park
Peyton
24
Calhan
Ramah
71
40
24
Divide
Colorado Springs
Punkin Center
Wild Horse
Kit Carson
40
Firstview
Arapahoe
Cheyenne Wells
Florissant Fossil Beds Natl. Mon.
67
Pikes Pk 14,110 ft
94
Rush
Yoder
Aroya
Big Sandy Cr.
287
Cripple Creek
Security-Widefield
Fountain
Sand Creek Massacre
Fort Carson Military Res.
Cañon City
Parkdale
Royal Gorge Bridge
Penrose
Eads
Brandon
Chivington
96
Florence
Pueblo West
Nee-So-Pah Reservoir
385
Cotopaxi
67
Boone
Adobe Cr. Reservoir
Wetmore
96
Pueblo
Ordway
Avondale
78
Kornman
Westcliffe
Fowler
L. Meridith
Arkansas
Bent's Old Fort
Fort Lyon
Hasty
50
196
Silver Cliff
165
Beulah
Rocky Ford
Las Animas
John Martin Reservoir
Lamar
Granada
69
San Isabel Nat. Forest
Colorado City
Rye
Huerfano
Hawley
La Junta
101
SANGRE DE CRISTO MOUNTAINS
25
71
Purgatoire
385
Great Sand Dunes Nat. Mon.
Gardner
Timpas
Toonerville
10
Comanche National Grassland
69
Delhi
Two Buttes
Walsenburg
116
Thatcher
109
Ft. Garland
160
La Veta
350
Springfield
Walsh
Ft. Garland Museum
Cuchara
Model
Pritchett
Cuchara Valley
159
12
Kim
160
Utleyville
San Luis
Stonewall
Segundo
Trinidad
160
Comanche National Grassland
Campo
San Luis Cultural Center
Trinidad L.
389
Branson
NEW MEXICO
Raton
OKLAHOMA

Highlights of Nature

Black bear cubs

Why are millions of visitors compelled to venture to Colorado each year? In a word, "nature." While the Coors Brewery draws 300,000 beer lovers per fiscal annum, Vail Mountain ushers 1.5 million skiers down its slopes each winter. The Denver Mint may call out to 200,000 penny-pinchers, but Rocky Mountain National Park hosts three million binocular-holders. In fact, of the state's top ten attractions, which draw about eleven million site visits annually, only two are not intimately involved with the enjoyment of Colorado's great wide open.

It's no wonder; the square-cut state's 104,237 square miles (the nation's eighth largest state) teem with parks, lakes, streams, game, fish and forests, not to mention vistas, views and panoramas.

In Colorado's various elevations above sea level, five ecological life zones flourish. Plains Grasslands make up nearly half the state's area; these acres of wild sagebrush, alive with jackrabbits and prairie dogs, are beautifully preserved in the Pawnee and Comanche National Grasslands. On the flanks of the mountains themselves rolls the Piñon Juniper or Foothills zone. This area is characterized by blue-berried Piñon trees, the "where-are-you" call of mourning doves and mule deer rustling in the grass. The Montane areas cover the lower elevations of the state's central spine—the Rocky Mountains—with Ponderosa pine parklands along with Douglas fir and aspen forests. Higher in altitude lies the Subalpine forest, atwitter with gray jays and timbered with Engelmann spruce, lodgepole pine and aspen. Above 11,400 feet, wind washes the Alpine Tundra, keeping plants and animals close to the ground.

A popular place to explore three of these areas—the Montane, Subalpine and Alpine—is Rocky Mountain National Park. The park straddles the Continental Divide and is bisected by one of the highest automobile courses in the world: Trail Ridge Road. Unfortunately, during July and August, Trail Ridge can resemble an L.A. traffic jam which, Coloradans argue, is all the more reason to get out of the

left: Bugling bull elk

Topography

Tundra Trail rock formation

Picture Colorado as a state with the approximate proportions of a flag. Divide it approximately into thirds with two wiggly vertical lines and you have a topographical map of Colorado.

The left or western third is called the Western Slope because it drapes down as rough-cut plateaus stepping from the height of the Rocky Mountains.

Down the middle—a band running anywhere from 100 to 140 miles wide—run the Rocky Mountains themselves, a jumble of some three dozen mountain ranges. These chains are punctuated here and there with enormous valleys left low as the mountains rose around them—North, Middle and South Parks. The peaks dominating the southwest corner are the San Juans.

The Rockies we admire today are actually the third mountains to dominate this region. During the Paleozoic era and again in the Mesozoic, the earth's crust heaved up to great heights. These uplifts, exposed to wind and water for eons gradually wore down, their silt forming layers of sedimentary rock.

Around 65 million years ago a new chain arose, with peaks as high as 25,000 feet, which have eroded to what we see now. Ice sheets or glaciers carved many of the valleys and cirques.

More than 1,000 Colorado pinnacles top the two-mile-high mark and 53 of them climb above the 14,000-foot marker. The state's highest point is atop Mt. Elbert at 14,433 feet. Along the top of the remarkable Rockies dances the Continental Divide, the line that separates water heading for the Pacific or Atlantic oceans.

Wind and water are wearing these Rockies down at a rate of about one foot every 9,000 years. Much of that sand, gravel and topsoil piles up along the mountains' bases, forming the High Plains—to the right on that imaginary flag-map.

This vast acreage, thousands of miles of fields and farms, spreads east. Colorado's lowest point is out on the eastern border, where the Arkansas River sneaks out of the state at a mere 3,350 feet above sea level.

car and into the backcountry. And with hundreds of miles of trail weaving through the 265,727 acres of parkland, this certainly isn't difficult.

The state offers a broad sampling of wildlife. Properly aimed binoculars will almost certainly spot herds of elk. Almost everyone who comes sees a mule deer, a Clark's nutcracker and a squirrel or two. Above timberline, watch for elk as well as yellow-bellied marmots, pikas and ptarmigan. Coyotes are heard howling on many evenings. You might also hear the chirping of Steller's jays.

Much of this wildlife lives in Colorado's two national parks, eight national monuments and historic sites, 48 wilderness areas and 42 state parks and recreation areas. Denver's park system alone covers more than 20,000 acres—an area nearly 25 times the size of New York City's Central Park. Add 14 million acres of national and state forest and a new image of the "Wild West" emerges, one centered on wilderness and wildlife.

About 65,000 miles of stream and more than 2,000 lakes and reservoirs are open to public fishing. Smallmouth and largemouth catfish, as well as walleye and bluegill swim in the lower elevations. In the higher reaches, lakes burst with brown, brook, rainbow and lake trout. The luminously beautiful greenback trout, nearly extinct here in its home waters, is making an encouraging comeback.

If it's fishing you dream of, your fantasy is likely to come true. The Colorado Division of Wildlife stocks 18,000,000 trout and 8,000,000 warm-water fish into the streams and lakes. Nearly 150 miles of stream and 600 acres of lake have been set aside as Wild Trout Waters; no stock in these waters, just nature at her best. The so-called Gold Medal streams are those where you're likely to catch a record

Colorado's State Parks

Over the years, Colorado has created 42 state parks, ranging from the postage-stamp-sized Picnic Rock at 13 acres to the 70,708-acre State Forest State Park. These parks are meant to be used for recreation: most provide picnic sites, boat ramps, hiking and biking trails and camping facilities. A nominal fee is charged for park use and annual passes are available. The parks are open to the public year round, and some even allow winter camping. Day-use areas are generally open from 5 a.m. to 10 p.m. Camping reservations may be made up to 90 days in advance by calling 800-678-CAMP. For more information on state parks, contact the Colorado State Parks office at 303-866-3437.

Following is a chart of several of the state's most popular state parks.

Park name	Nearest city	Land acreage	Water acreage	Campsites	Hiking trails	Biking trails	Boating	Fishing	X-country skiing	Elevation
Arkansas	Leadville	5,000	148	40			•	•		4,000
Bonny	Idalia	5,000	1900	201			•	•	•	3,700
Boyd Lake	Loveland	197	1750	148	1/4	1/4	•	•	•	5,000
Chatfield	Littleton	3,768	1550	193	18	18	•	•	•	5,430
Cherry Creek	Aurora	3,305	880	102	12	12	•	•	•	5,550
Eleven Mile	Lake George	4,075	3405	265	1-1/2		•	•	•	8,566
Golden Gate Canyon	Golden	14,000	20	168	60	30		•	•	9,100
Lory	Bellvue	2,479		6	25	15	•	•	•	7,015
Mueller	Divide	12,103	15	90	85	25		•	•	9,500
Pueblo	Pueblo	9,045	4646	401	18	18	•	•	•	4,800
Ridgway	Ridgway	2,200	1000	187	7		•	•	•	6,870
Roxborough	Littleton	1,620			12				•	6,500
Spinney	Lake George	3,400	2520				•	•		8,686
State Forest	Walden	70,708	130	110	50	112	•	•	•	10,000
Trinidad	Trinidad	2,000	700	62	9		•	•	•	6,300

State of the State's Ecology

For decades, clean water, fresh air and wide-open spaces have made Colorado seem to many like the perfect place to plant roots. Certainly, that's the image Colorado wishes to project—pristine wilderness offering itself as a flawless playground for four-wheelers bouncing jauntily through babbling brooks while elk look on rapturously. Unfortunately, the facts weave a slightly different tale.

"I would have to say," says Kirk Cunningham, Conservation Chairperson for the Rocky Mountain Sierra Club, "that Colorado's ecology is a picture of "green" bleeding into brown. And the Front Range, from a scenery and wildlife standpoint, is barren and black."

The mission of the Sierra Club is to preserve and protect the wild places of Colorado, to safeguard its natural resources and to shelter the human environment by means of public education, lobbying, litigation and political action.

Development along the Front Range and its accompanying traffic have forced out animals, dried up native rivers and created a smog problem (locals call it the "brown cloud") so troublesome that in the past, the U.S. government has threatened to pull the state's highway funding. What has spared Colorado that ax are technological advances in the automobile industry. "Up till now, Detroit's cleverness has overcome Colorado's development numbers," says Cunningham, "But sooner or later it's going to catch up with us."

A beyond-healthy growth rate is covering tens of thousands of Colorado acres a year with houses and highways, but several bits and pieces brighten the scene according to Cunningham: Boulder's green belt, the Rocky Mountain Arsenal Wildlife Refuge, several stunning national parks and monuments, national forest wilderness areas and protected BLM desert land.

Water quantity, too, is an issue in this largely dry-as-a-desert state. "If we keep sticking straws in the ground and sucking out water," insists Cunningham, "we're going to dry up our underground water resources."

The real water problem is in the mountains themselves, where mine tailings, sewage treatment effluent and septic run-off contribute to brooks (which look to all the world as brilliant as beer ads) that are dosed with metals and ammonia.

Cunningham says development in mountain valleys and riverbeds, particularly ski areas, is the hardest thing of all on natural environments. "Seventy percent of the state's wildlife depends on these riparian habitats for some part of their life cycle," Cunningham says. He adds, "The only eco-friendly ski resort is one without any building at its base." Those are hard to find. Tearing down acres of trees for ski runs doesn't help the situation, but Cunningham believes that smaller ski areas come closer to an eco-friendly ideal.

To make matters worse, bike paths, hiking trails and jeep tracks fragment animals' daily routines and migration paths. The noise caused by all-terrain vehicles, snowmobiles and motorcycles can devastate naturally nervous animals.

And while moose have made a return to the state—and for this, the Colorado Division of Wildlife deserves a big pat on the back—the grizzly bear and the wolf are still in exile.

What's a person to do? Cunningham offers several ideas. First, get off the beaten path to spread the land use around a little. Stop in at the Bureau of Land Management or the forest service offices to get information about visiting seldom-used areas of the state. Next, learn the ground rules about camping and back-country use. Learn how to treat the land, how to impact it as slightly as possible, how to handle the waste created. Finally, Cunningham suggests staying away from ski areas. "There is nothing scenic about them," he insists. "They have altered the scenery. They're nothing but motels and shopping malls."

Strong words. So where is the wilderness in Colorado? "It's all over," says Cunningham. "The San Juan corner in the southwest still has intact wild areas, and the Flat Tops up north near Steamboat Springs, though increasingly popular, is still lovely. The West Elk Wilderness and the Sangre de Cristo Wilderness are terrific. The Rawah area in the northern Front Range is also beautiful."

Cunningham should know. A retired chemist with the U. S. Geological Survey, he migrated to Colorado in 1975. "I moved here to be in a state with an impressive backyard."

breaker. The state has 158 miles of Gold Medal and to keep them pristine, the state allows only catch-and-release fishing in these watery wonders.

One of these rivers, the Gunnison, flows through the deepest chasm in the world. The Black Canyon of the Gunnison is a mere 50 miles long, yet its proportions—1,300 feet wide by 2,600 feet deep—makes it proportionally the deepest gash on the planet.

The state sports a few other deep gouges as well—hard rock mines full of mineral bounty. Colorado plays a sequential-numbers game when it comes to mining: Colorado is the nation's leading producer of silver, second in gold, third in lead, fourth in zinc and fifth in copper. Colorado boasts the only active diamond mine in the country.

It seems certain that the late John Denver, a singer and former Snowmass resident, was thinking of Colorado when he sang, *Sunshine on my shoulders makes me happy*. With 300 days of sun a year, Colorado regularly outshines even San Diego and Miami. Yet the wedgewood-blue skies cloud over long enough to drop 300 inches of fluffy flakes per year on those world-renowned ski resorts. It's not uncommon at all to experience blizzard conditions in the high country while Denverites ride bicycles in shirtsleeves.

Bighorn sheep

But is Colorado ever *dry*. Much of the state is technically a desert, receiving less than 15 inches of moisture per year. And with an average relative humidity of less than 33 percent, Coloradans lather on lip balms and skin creams daily.

The wind kicks up now and again, too. Along the Front Range, particularly near Boulder and Golden, winds can whistle by at 60 to 70 miles per hour. Luckily, some are "chinooks" or air masses much warmer than the surrounding atmosphere, which raise the temperature as much as 20 degrees in the winter.

In fact, variety is the operative word when it comes to Colorado weather. Thirty-degree temperature swings within a day are as common as cottonwoods on streambeds. Winter heat waves on Thursdays and Fridays regularly freeze into ski-on-fresh-powder weekends. There's an old saying here: "If you don't like the weather, wait a minute, it'll change."

left: Columbine

Animals

Black bear

Mule deer

Bald eagle

Most visitors hoping for a glimpse of Colorado's wildlife won't be disappointed. In fact, on many days elk still pose roadside in Rocky Mountain National Park, seemingly modeling for photographs. To help visitors locate wildlife, Colorado has developed a number of viewing spots that are popular with visitors precisely because they are near places that are also popular with animals.

Some tips: Animals are most active in the morning and evening; be quiet and still. Binoculars are a big help. Lastly, patience pays off.

Bald Eagle
Colorado's eagle population is thriving. Look for large birds with white heads.

Best locale: Morrison Hogback Hawk Watch near Morrison.

Beaver
Beavers, with their broad tails and hard-working habits, are found in mountain valleys.

Best locale: Rocky Mountain National Park.

Black Bear
Give these animals a wide berth; they can be aggressive. There are no grizzly bears in Colorado.

Best locale: Black Canyon of the Gunnison National Monument

Coyote
Look for scurrying reddish-brown figures low to the ground.

Best locale: Colorado Headwaters Scenic and Historic Byway near Kremmling.

Elk
Colorado has one of the largest populations of this majestic animal in the country.

Best locale: Rocky Mountain National Park.

Golden Eagle
Regal hunters and graceful fliers, these birds seem to enjoy the hunt as much as the meal.

Best locale: Rocky Mountain Arsenal Wildlife Area.

Moose
These large mammals were re-introduced to the state in the 1970s. They enjoy wet areas clogged with willow bush. Look for large brown masses among the green foliage.

Best locale: Silver Thread Scenic Byway from South Fork to Lake City.

Mule Deer
Abundant in grassy areas throughout the state, best seen in the morning and evening. The name is derived from their mule-like ears. The males have horn racks which they shed each year.

Best locale: Maroon Bells Wilderness Area.

Pronghorn
Quick as lightning, these graceful herds move through wide-open sage flats at up to 80 miles per hour. The black, fishhook-shaped horns and white belly are definitive markings.

Best locale: Kremmling Pronghorn Viewing Site.

Rocky Mountain Bighorn Sheep
Gray with characteristic curly horns, bighorns like the rockiest parts of the Rockies.

Best locale: Georgetown Bighorn Viewing Site.

Sandhill Crane
Thousands of these graceful birds flock to transition feeding locations during spring and fall migrations.

Best locale: Monte Vista National Wildlife Refuge.

Plants

Alpine sunflower

Aspen stand

Prickly pear cactus

Layered like a wedding cake, Colorado enjoys five life zones that vary according to elevation above sea level. They rise from the lowest elevations in the state to high above timberline—the elevation above which trees will not grow—at 11,400. While the zones intermingle at their edges, each has its own spectrum of plants and animals as well as its own delicate ecology.

Plains and Arid Zones

3,500 to 5,000 feet
The Arapaho, Cheyenne and the great American Bison, now mostly gone, once roamed on this dry land. This zone stretches from the state's foothills out to the east and into the Four Corners area of the southwest.

Cottonwood
These massive trees with shiny, serrated leaves prosper in groves along creek beds. In early June, their seeds create blizzards of snow-like seeds.

Sagebrush
Fragrant, pale green plants cover hundreds of square miles of Colorado.

Foothills Zone

5,000 to 6,000 feet
The foothills separate the plains from the mountains themselves. Great rolling hills act as a backdrop for free-standing juniper.

Colorado Juniper (Red Cedar)
These symmetrical trees usually only reach 20 - 30 feet tall. They have dense, scaly, fragrant leaves and blueberry-blue berries growing in dry areas of the foothills and mesas.

Montane Zone (Lower and Upper)

6,000 to 9,000 feet
This broad zone supports several different ecologies from grassy Ponderosa parklands and moist willow-choked river beds to cool forests.

Ponderosa Pine
These relaxed evergreens with reddish bark and a rounded crown tend to be widely spaced, allowing for open park-type areas where grasses thrive.

Douglas Fir
Tall, straight-as-nails and gray-trunked, these trees like north-facing, moist slopes.

Quaking Aspen
These members of the willow family, with white trunks and paddle-shaped leaves, grow in vast thickets.

Colorado Columbine
These spectacular purple and white flowers bloom from early June through mid-August. Blossoms rise up on slender stalks from bushy plants that prefer moist, sun-dappled locales.

Subalpine Zone

9,000 feet to 11,400 (timberline)
This dense forest zone is below timberline. Aspen groves thrive in moist areas and valleys.

Englemann Spruce
Straight-trunked and finely crowned with bark-like small plates, these grow in dense forests.

Lodgepole Pines
These tall, slender pines gather in dense forests. Native Americans used their trunks as teepee or "lodge" poles.

Alpine Zone

11,400 feet and above
Plants form a tight system close to the ground, dozens of wildflower species bursting out in July and August.

Alpine Avens
Large areas of these tint the mountainsides yellow from June to August.

Highlights of History

Humans first ventured into Colorado thousands of years ago. The grassy Eastern Plains lie in great migratory paths of game, which early nomadic hunters stalked. Primitive campsites containing stone tools and remains of mammoth kills have been dated to 10,000 B.C.

Over time, agricultural communities settled in Colorado. Ancestral Puebloans inhabited the extreme southwestern corner of the state as early as 1 A.D. They thrived in the canyons and windswept mesas until 1300 A.D., when they mysteriously abandoned their cliff dwellings and disappeared into history. Their architectural legacy, in addition to finely crafted baskets and pottery, bear testimony to a gifted society.

By the 16th century, descendants of Shoshone and Algonquin peoples also called Colorado home. Utes preferred the mountains from the Front Range west to Utah. Cheyenne, Arapaho, Comanche, Kiowa, Pawnee, Lakota, Blackfoot and Crow held largely to the Eastern Plains, following the great bison herds. The lives of Colorado's first inhabitants changed forever with the arrival of Europeans.

1598
Spain establishes settlements in northern New Mexico, heralding the advance of European interest in Colorado.

1706
Spanish explorer Juan de Ulibarri treks into southern Colorado and near present-day Pueblo, he claims the Arkansas River Valley for the Spanish crown.

1714 to1719
Spanish soldiers mount expeditions into Colorado, quelling raids by Ute and Comanche warriors.

1765
Spanish explorer Juan Maria de Rivera penetrates deep into Colorado exploring the San Juan Mountains and the Gunnison River Valley.

1776
Following the path of de Rivera, Franciscan friars Frailes Francisco Atanasio Dominguez and Silvestre Vélez de Escalante explore western Colorado in search of routes to California.

1779
Founder of San Francisco and Governor of New Mexico, Juan Bautista de Anza defeats Cuerno Verde (Green Horn) near present-day Walsenburg, temporarily pacifying the warlike Comanches. An adobe settlement is erected but soon abandoned.

1803
President Thomas Jefferson convinces Congress to acquire the Louisiana Territory from France, adding most of eastern and northern Colorado to the United States.

1806
Lt. Zebulon M. Pike, along with 15 companions, first glimpses the Rocky Mountain Front Range while tracing the headwaters of the Arkansas River. Wintering on the Conejos River, his party encounters Spanish dragoons and is escorted to Santa Fe.

1810
Adventurous fur trappers penetrate the Colorado mountains to search for beaver and other pelts desired by Eastern and European markets.

1820
Major Stephen Long leads a scientific expedition up the South Platte River. From his evaluation, northeastern Colorado is confirmed as the "Great American Desert."

1821
With Mexico's independence from Spain, New Mexico trade markets open to U.S. entrepreneurs. Missourian William Becknell treks between Missouri and Santa Fe, returning with a fortune in Mexican silver.

1830s
Intrepid frontiersmen John Gantt, William Bent, Ceran St. Vrain, Charles Bent, Louis Vasquez, Lancaster Lupton and others establish trading

left: A Ute couple: Red Dog and unidentified woman

Civil War veteran turned Colorado prospector

posts on the Arkansas and South Platte rivers.

1846
Commander Stephen W. Kearney rests his men at Bent's Fort in preparation to invade Santa Fe following the outbreak of the Mexican-American War. Later, the Treaty of Guadalupe Hildalgo transfers southern and western Colorado from Mexican sovereignty to that of the United States.

1851
The Treaty of Fort Laramie establishes the area between the Oregon and Santa Fe trails (effectively most of eastern Colorado) as being under the joint control of the Southern Cheyenne and Arapaho peoples.

After nearly two decades of failed attempts to settle the Rio Grande River Valley, Colorado's first permanent Hispanic settlement is established at San Luis.

1858
William Green Russell and other miners pan gold along the banks of Little Dry Creek near present-day Denver.

1859
Thousands of gold-hungry prospectors join the Pikes Peak or Bust Gold Rush, trekking to find their fortunes in newly discovered gold fields. John Gregory hits a good streak along the North Fork of Clear Creek, leading to rich finds around Idaho Springs and Central City.

1861
The secession of Texas from the United States spurs Congress into action to protect the West for the Union. President James Buchanan creates the Colorado Territory four days before the end of his term.

1862
John Slough, commanding the First Regiment of Colorado Infantry, marches to New Mexico and routes a small army of Texans near Glorieta Pass, thus protecting Colorado gold fields from Confederate interests.

1864
Colonel John Chivington, commanding the Third Regiment of Colorado Volunteer Cavalry, massacres Cheyenne and Arapaho people encamped along Sand Creek in southeastern Colorado. Responding to the attack, Native Americans raid freighting stations and homesteads. Sporadic warfare continues until 1867, when the Treaty of Medicine Lodge confines Arapahos and Cheyennes to Oklahoma reservations.

1867
After intense lobbying, Denver is designated the permanent territorial capital.

1868
Professor Nathaniel Hill of Brown University opens the Boston and Colorado smelting operation at Black Hawk, revolutionizing Colorado hardrock mining.

Bicyclists in Denver at the turn of the century

Major George Forsyth, along with 50 scouts, undergoes a nine-day siege by Northern Cheyenne and Sioux warriors at Beecher Island in northeastern Colorado.

1869
The last Indian battle on the Colorado Plains occurs between Southern Cheyenne Dog Soldiers and U.S. Forces at Summit Springs near present-day Atwood.

1870
Horace Greeley and Nathan Meeker, both of the New York *Tribune*, establish the agricultural town of Greeley as a Union Colony. Colonists pooled their resources for the common good, hoping to created a utopian society.

After fierce rivalry between competing railroad factions, Denver becomes a terminus for both the Union Pacific out of Cheyenne and Kansas Pacific out of Kansas City. General William Jackson Palmer organizes the Denver and Rio Grande Railroad, laying tracks south to Pueblo.

1871
General Palmer establishes the "Fountain Colony," later called Colorado Springs, as a new settlement for the wealthy. Immigration, particularly from Great Britain, gives Colorado Springs a continental demeanor, earning the city the nickname of "Little London."

1873
With the enactment of the Brunot Treaty, Utes cede southern Colorado, opening the San Juan Mountains to prospectors.

1874
Due to railroad expansion into the mountains west of Denver, silver finds at Georgetown and surrounding areas become economically accessible. For the first time in Colorado's mining history, the value of silver produced in Colorado exceeds that of gold.

1876
Colorado becomes the nation's centennial anniversary present, for on August 1, the territory is admitted as the 38th state.

1877
The arrival of smelting operations at Leadville unlocks the huge potential of silver trapped in deposits of carbonate ore. Soon, Leadville sports 31 restaurants, 120 saloons, 115 gambling houses and 35 brothels.

1879
Frustrated Utes rise against reform-minded Indian agent Nathan Meeker at the White River Agency, killing Meeker and others. Public opinion advocates the exile of the "Indian threat," banishing the Utes to reservations in Utah and southern Colorado.

1882
After two years under construction, Colorado Coal and Iron, located in Pueblo, begins to manufacture Bessemer-

processed steel. Drawing from vast coal deposits near Trinidad, the furnaces churn out pipes, spikes and rails in addition to supplying coke to Colorado's burgeoning smelting industry.

1888
Ranchers Richard Wetherill and Charlie Mason discover magnificent cliff dwellings in the mesas of southwestern Colorado. The Mesa Verde area soon achieves international attention from archaeologists and souvenir hunters.

1890
Cattleman Robert Womack finds gold southwest of Pikes Peak at Cripple Creek. Within months, the word is out and the rush is on. Over the next decade, Cripple Creek mines produce nearly $20 million in gold annually.

Passage of the Sherman Silver Purchase Act sparks silver prices to more than a $1.00 an ounce. Silver strikes in the San Juan Mountains herald the boom of communities such as Telluride and Ouray.

1893
The repeal of the Sherman Silver Purchase Act devastates Colorado's silver-mining industry, turning overnight millionaires into overnight paupers.

1894
After nearly four years in construction the State Capitol, modeled after the U.S. Capitol in Washington D.C., is completed at the then-considerable cost of $2.5 million.

1906
Due in large measure to the lobbying efforts of two Colorado women, Virginia McClung and Lucy Peabody, Mesa Verde National Park is created to preserve the cliff dwellings of Ancestral Puebloans.

Amache, Colorado; Japanese internment camp during WWII

1909
Completion of the Gunnison River Tunnel and the Uncompahgre Reclamation projects doubles the irrigated land on Colorado's Western Slope and opens the valve to agricultural expansion.

1914
A decade of tension between mine and smelter owners and organized workers erupts into tragedy when the National Guard attacks a tent colony of striking coal miners north of Trinidad. The battle results in the death of five strikers and 13 women and children. Termed the "Ludlow Massacre," the event sets off 10 days of civil unrest in Colorado's coal fields.

1915
Naturalist and innkeeper Enos Mills sees the fulfillment of a long campaign to create Rocky Mountain National Park outside Estes Park.

1922
Secretary of Commerce Herbert Hoover works out an agreement between seven states to share the water wealth of the Colorado River. Colorado is allocated only 25 percent of the river's flow, with the rest going to Wyoming, Utah, New Mexico, Nevada, Arizona and California.

1934
With the enactment of the Taylor Grazing Act, Colorado ranchers look forward to a stable permit system for using the Bureau of Land Management (BLM) public domain.

1942
Colorado becomes an industrial hotbed for the emerging Cold War as the Rocky Mountain Arsenal is established north of Denver for production and storage of chemical weapons.

Motorcyclists and skier face off at St. Mary's Glacier

1950s
The development of the ski industry transforms old mining towns such as Aspen into premier winter vacation destinations. A uranium boom begins in western Colorado as the Atomic Energy Commission encourages amateur prospectors to search for yellow carbonite ore.

1957
A granite mountain south of Colorado Springs is selected as the site for the ultra-secretive North American Air Defense Command (NORAD) headquarters, charged with the coordination of America's nuclear weapon defense program.

1958
Colorado Springs becomes the site of the prestigious Air Force Academy, further establishing Colorado as one the military's most beloved outposts for its growing operations.

1960
Colorado's love affair with sports begins as the Denver Broncos are placed with the American Football League's western division along with Dallas, Oakland and Los Angeles. The Broncos play their first home game in Bears Stadium against Oakland, defeating them 31 to 24.

1972
Richard Lamm leads a successful environmentalist movement to reject Colorado as the site for the 1976 Winter Olympics.

1994
The Colorado Rockies debut as the state's major league baseball franchise. Attendance records for a major league season hit the record books as 4.4 million fans converge on Mile High Stadium.

1995
After four years in construction and several embarrassing delays, the $4.3 billion Denver International Airport (DIA) finally opens.

1995
Formerly the Québec Nordiques, the Colorado Avalanche comes to Denver. The "Avs" snap a spot in the Stanley Cup Finals, taking the title from the Florida Panthers in a four-game sweep.

1997
Timothy McVeigh, the "Oklahoma City Bomber," is found guilty and sentenced to death during proceedings in Denver.

1997
Denver hosts presidents and prime ministers from the world's leading industrialized nations during the "Summit of Eight."

Recreation

A wrangler guides riders at a guest ranch

Here are some common sights in Colorado: Cars laden with bikes, skis or kayaks heading into the mountains; snowshoers and cross-country skiers making tracks through glistening meadows; crowded swimming pools; busy baseball diamonds; mountain trailheads full of hikers preparing for a trek; fisher-folks lining rivers and streams.

Coloradans are a busy lot. Many moved here by choice from less scenic and recreation-oriented regions. More often than not, the reason these immigrants came is because they wanted to experience the recreational opportunities the state offers. And Colorado offers active diversions of every imaginable kind.

The following guides provide brief introductions into the state's outdoor opportunities. Topics covered include hiking, scenic driving, rafting, biking, jeeping, fishing, accessible recreation, excursion trains, guest ranches, hot springs, golf, fall color drives, downhill skiing, snowboarding and a glimpse of off-slope winter activities.

Unfortunately, to list every fishing hole, every hike and every bike track would take several books. Where possible, the lists are complete—listing every ski area, for instance, and more than three dozen river outfitters. Areas with too much breadth, like hiking and golf, have been narrowed down; experts have assembled a "best-of" list.

The ideal way to find a fishing spot or hiking trail is simply to ask. Hotels provide brochures and booking counters, and nearly everyone in the state knows the locale of a scenic trail or a low-traffic bicycle route.

left: Whitewater kayaking

Colorado Scenic and Historic Byways

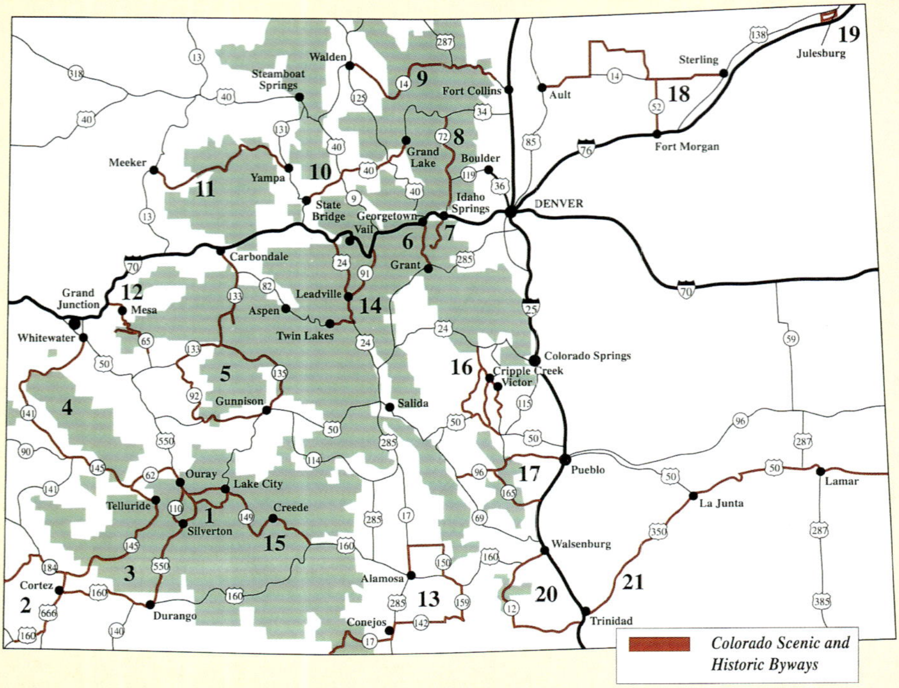

Map of the Scenic and Historic Byways

Many people ramble to Colorado every year for the sheer joy of hopping into their car, 4x4, or RV and ambling along the highway soaking up the scenery.

The Colorado Scenic and Historic Byways Commission has designated 21 routes in the state that are particularly beautiful and historic. Although many seem off the beaten path, each rewards the traveler with glimpses of the "real" Colorado.

Some are long on history. The tiny "South Platte River Trail" includes a stop at the only site of a Pony Express station in the state, the site where the legendary William F. Cody—"Buffalo Bill"—signed up to be a rider. "Top of the Rockies," "Silver Thread" and "Alpine Loop" traverse trails were charted by miners through the spectacular vistas of the ore-laden Rocky Mountains. The "Trail of the Ancients" reaches the furthest back in time, enlightening visitors as to the lifestyle of the Ancestral Puebloans of the Four Corners area.

Other routes focus more on scenery. The "West Elk Loop" surrounds two national forests, the Black Canyon of the Gunnison National Park, Curecanti National Recreational Area and two state parks. One of the shortest drives—"Guanella Pass"—drapes a drop-dead-splendid 22 miles across Guanella Pass, leading viewers through high-mountain alpine tundra.

The "San Juan Skyway," has also been designated a "National Scenic and Historic Byway" by the U.S. Department of Transportation. While this loop may be driven in a day, that wouldn't allow nearly enough time to enjoy its many attractions: the Durango and Silverton Narrow Gauge Railroad, energetic Ouray, festival-crazy Telluride, or the half-dozen hot springs that steam along this 236-mile-long trail.

Copies of "Discover Colorado," a colorful brochure outlining the byways, are available at many visitor centers in the state.

Colorado Scenic and Historic Byways

No.	Name	Length in miles	Minimum driving time in hours	Highlights	Comments
1	Alpine Loop	63	4–6	Wilderness, ghost towns, alpine passes	Stretches require 4-wheel-drive
2	Trail of the Ancients	114	3	Mesa Verde National Park, Hovenweep Natl. Monument, Anasazi Heritage Center, Ute Mountain, Ute Tribal Park	Some roads are gravel, may be muddy when wet
3	San Juan Skyway	236	6 (without stops)	Historic mining towns, Mesa Verde National Park, four wilderness areas	Extremely scenic, also recognized by the Dept. of Transportation as a national byway
4	Unaweep/ Tabeguache	133	3	San Miguel River Environmental Area, Unaweep Seep	Long distances between services
5	West Elk Loop	205	6–8	Black Canyon of the Gunnison, Mount Sopris	Kepler Pass is gravel for 30 miles
6	Guanella Pass	22	1	Historic Georgetown	A great-but-short fall color drive;
7	Mount Evans	28 Round trip	2 Round trip	Highest paved road in North America, wildlife	may be chilly year-round
8	Peak to Peak	55	1.5	Central City, Estes Park, Rocky Mountain National Park	Spectacular views, spectacular history
9	Cache la Poudre	101	3	Cache la Poudre River, wildlife, fishing	Watch for livestock on road
10	Colorado River Headwaters	80	2	Grand Lake, Colorado River, fishing, wildlife	Some gravel roads, limited visitor services
11	Flat Tops Trail	82	2	Flat Tops Wilderness Area,	Limited visitor services
12	Grand Mesa	63	2	Grand Mesa Natl. Forest	Limited visitor services
13	Los Caminos Antiguos	129	3 (without stops)	Great Sand Dunes National Monument, Cumbres & Toltec Scenic Railroad	Explores Colorado's earliest settled area, the San Luis Valley
14	Top of the Rockies	82	2	Leadville, Minturn, Tennessee and Fremont passes	Difficult driving during winter
15	Silver Thread	75	2	Historic Lake City, Collier State Wilderness Area	Limited services
16	Gold Belt Tour	131	5 (without stops)	Royal Gorge Bridge, Florissant Fossil Beds Natl. Monument, Cripple Creek	Long stretches of rough gravel road
17	Frontier Pathways	103	2	Wet Mountain Valley, Pueblo	Great views of the Sangre de Cristo mountains
18	Pawnee Pioneer Trails	125	2	Pawnee National Grassland, Pawnee Buttes, expansive vistas	Limited services, gravel roads
19	South Platte River Trail	19	30 minutes	Fort Sedgwick, Pony Express site	Numerous historic sites
20	Highway of Legends	82	2	Spanish Peaks, interesting geology	Quiet towns with interesting attractions
21	Santa Fe Trail	188	4 (without stops)	Bent's Old Fort, Comanche National Grassland, Trinidad	Region famous for its fruits and vegetables

Hiking the Hills

When Alex Danzberger arrived in Colorado in the early 1980s, the Colorado Mountain Club had already been leading hikers for 100 years. Danzberger had hiked the state before accepting a job offer to come here. Danzberger and his wife joined the Club, took some hikes and soon Alex was leading treks. Before long, he found himself scouting trails and heading up the club's safety and leadership committee.

So he knows what he's talking about when he discusses safety. "We see people in T-shirts, sandals and shorts all the time heading out on hiking trails," he says. "It kind of makes us worry."

Danzberger believes that all hikers should carry a pack containing the hiking essentials. According to the Colorado Mountain Club, those necessities are: fire-starting kits, pocket knife and wire saw, space blanket, large plastic bags, electrician's tape, headlamp and batteries, map and compass, extra clothing, metal cup for water, plenty of extra water, whistle and signal mirror, sunglasses and sunscreen, first aid kit, toilet paper and a small snow shovel if you are headed into a snowy area.

People should also know their physical and mental limits, Danzberger adds, as well as how to build a fire (practice with the starter kits), what to do about lightning (lay low) and how to stay warm and dry.

"Hiking, like sailing," says Danzberger, "is sexy, fun, sporty, and adventurous—as long as we're responsible and stay within our skill and conditioning limits."

Hiking the Hills

The very easiest of hikes is simply a gentle stroll. Some popular walks with little elevation gain, easy distances and spectacular scenery are Bear Lake in Rocky Mountain National Park, the Animas River Walk in Durango, Denver's Cherry Creek bike path, Glenwood Canyon recreation trail near Glenwood Springs and Maroon Lake at the Maroon Bells Wilderness Area near Aspen.

Here are eight medium-length hikes recommended by Alex Danzberger, longtime member and hike scout for the Colorado Mountain Club.

Name	Locale	Starting point	Elevation Gain (feet)	Length (miles)
Roxborough State Park	Southwest Denver	Parking lot in State Park	500	5
Mt. Falcon	Morrison	Morrison Cutoff parking lot	1,200	5
Mesa Trail	South of Boulder	Eldorado Springs	1,100	7
Murray Lake	Georgetown	Guanella Pass trail parking lot	1,200	8
Waterton Canyon	Southwest Denver	Kassler water plant parking lot in state park	500	6
Lake Isabelle	Rocky Mountain National Park	Long Lake Trailhead	500	5
Golden Gate Canyon	Near Golden	Golden Canyon State Park parking lot	1,000	6
St. Marys Glacier	Idaho Springs	St. Marys glacier parking lot	500	2

More Advanced Hikes

Here are eight advanced-skill hikes recommended by Alex Danzberger, a guide for the Colorado Mountain Club. These are for more advanced hikers. Take precautions; most of these include serious exposure to the elements. Before you go: know the season, the weather, your strength, your party's strength and the time you need to complete the trek before starting out. Tell someone where you're going and when you plan to return.

Name	Locale	Description	Elevation Gain/feet	Length/miles
Mt. Silverheels	Hoosier Pass	1.75 miles south of the pass, over Beaver Ridge	3,400	6
James Peak	St. Marys Glacier	St. Marys Glacier parking lot, around the lake, then over the glacier to alpine meadows	2,900	8
Lawn Lake	Rocky Mountain National Park	Follow Roaring Fork to lake in the Mummy Range	2,250	12
Longs Peak	Rocky Mountain National Park	Arduous trek, consult with park rangers	up to 5,000	16
Mt. Bierstadt	Guenella Pass	Advanced hiking, arduous	3,500	10
Mt. Audubon	Mitchell Lake Trailhead	Mitchell Lake trail, boulders and tundra to summit	2,743	8
Mt. Democrat	Kite Lake Campground	Steep climb above Kite Lake	2,100	6
Twin Sisters	Rocky Mountain National Park	Along timbered trail switchbacks to summit	2,340	8

Rafting the Rockies

From half-day excursions through whitewater to multi-day paddles through spectacular wilderness and national monuments, river-rafting trips are among the most popular vacation experiences for Colorado visitors.

But with more than a hundred operators offering packages that range from simple to simply fantastic, choosing the right one can be intimidating. The Colorado River Outfitters Association is made up of more than 50 outfitters, all of whom meet stringent training and experience requirements. They offer a broad range of trips on a multitude of rivers that bob rafters down their canyons.

These questions should help first-time "river rats" paddle in the right direction.

- How long is the trip? Half-day, full-day, multi-day?
- Where does the trip originate? Do they provide door-to-door transport or do you meet the guide on the river?
- What meals are provided? What is their quality?
- What "classes" of water does the trip have? The higher the number, the bigger the thrill—but the more dangerous the ride.
- Do you paddle too, or does the guide do all the work?
- How experienced are the guides? What kind of training have they had?
- What equipment is provided? Wet suits? Camping equipment? Safety gear? Is there a rental fee?
- What does the outfitter do for children? Is there a minimum age? Any extra safety precautions?
- How many years have they been in business? Do they meet the requirements of the Colorado River Outfitters Association? Are they members?
- Finally, what is included in the price? Does it seem reasonable for what you're getting?

Rafting and Kayaking

Name	City	Phone	Part/half day	One day	Multi day	Kayaking	Fishing	Rivers
Bill Dvorak Kayak and Rafting	Nathrop	800-824-3795 719-539-6851	•	•	•	•	•	Arkansas, Roaring Fork, Rio Grande, North Platte, Upper and Lower Colorado, Gunnison, San Miguel, Dolores, Green
A Wanderlust Adventure	Fort Collins	800-745-7238 303-484-1219	•		•			Cache la Poudre, Dolores
Peregrine River Oufitters	Durango	800-598-7600 970-385-7600	•	•	•			Piedra, Gunnison, Dolores, Animas, San Juan
Acquired Tastes Whitewater Rafting	Buena Vista	800-888-8582		•	•			Arkansas
Whitewater Voyageurs	Poncha Springs	800-255-2585	•	•	•			Arkansas
Arkansas River Tours	Cotopaxi	800-321-4352 719-942-4362	•	•	•		•	Arkansas
Four Corners Rafting	Buena Vista	800-332-7238	•	•	•		•	Arkansas, Dolores
Geo Tours	Denver	800-660-7238 303-756-6070		•	•	•		Arkansas, Upper Colorado, Clear Creek, South Platte
Canyon Marine Whitewater Expeditions	Salida	800-643-0707	•	•	•		•	Arkansas
Wilderness Aware Rafting	Buena Vista	800-462-7238 719-395-2112	•	•	•	•	•	Arkansas, North Platte, Upper Colorado, Gunnison, Dolores
Rocky Mountain Outdoor Center	Howard	800-255-5784 719-942-3214	•	•	•	•		Arkansas, Dolores
Raft Masters	Cañon City	800-568-7238	•	•	•			Arkansas
Buffalo Joe River Trips	Buena Vista	800-356-7984 719-395-8757	•	•	•			Arkansas, Dolores
Mountain Waters Rafting	Durango	800-748-2507 970-247-5514	•	•	•			Piedra, Animas
American Adventure Expeditions	Salida	800-288-0675	•	•	•	•		Arkansas, Piedra, Upper Colorado
Adventure Bound River Expeditions	Grand Junction	800-423-4668			•	•		Lower Colorado, Green, Yampa
A-1 Wildwater Inc.	Fort Collins	800-369-4165 970-224-3379	•	•	•	•		Arkansas, North Platte, Cache la Poudre, Upper Colorado, Dolores
Clear Creek Rafting	Idaho Springs	800-353-9901 303-277-9900	•	•	•			Arkansas, Clear Creek
Echo Canyon River Expeditions	Cañon City	800-748-2953 719-275-3154	•	•	•	•	•	Arkansas, Piedra, Upper Colorado, Gunnison, San Miguel, Lake Fork
River Runners,	Salida	800-525-2081	•	•	•			Arkansas
Rocky Mountain Adventures, Inc.	Ft. Collins	800-858-6808 970-493-4005	•	•	•	•	•	Arkansas, North Platte, Cache la Poudre, Upper Colorado, Dolores

Mountain Biking Meccas

With the advent of less expensive mountain bikes and easy-to-load bike racks, folks now pedal along trails in numbers approaching those of hikers.

But if you're from out of town, how can you get out on two wheels? The easiest way by far is to pull off the road into a ski resort. With few exceptions, ski areas rent bicycles and helmets. Riders simply put the bike on a ski lift, hop on themselves, ride to the top and cruise down the mountain, burning their brakes and admiring the wildflowers and summertime vistas. The state offers few finer experiences.

If you're not resort-minded, don't despair. Nearly every mountain town has a bike shop that rents equipment by the hour or the day. Make sure they include a helmet and a local map as well. Many Colorado cities, particularly Denver, Boulder, Vail, Breckenridge and Fort Collins, contain hundreds of miles of paved trail. Many trails wind through scenic areas, or right through town.

Some precautions: wear a helmet, take it easy (the altitude has more effect than you might think), drink plenty of water, be prepared as the weather can change suddenly, and take sunglasses and sunscreen.

If you brought your own bike, here are some short, relatively easy trails to pedal.

City	Brief directions	Approx. distance (miles)	Approx. time (hours)	Terrain/roads
Boulder	Boulder Creek to Baseline Resevoir, Marshall Lake and Broadway path back to downtown	16	Two	Flat/paved trail and road
Denver	Downtown Bike Path to Cherry Creek Reservoir	30	Three	Flat/continuous paved trail
Summit County	Trail from Copper Mtn. to Dillon Reservoir to Breckenridge	11	Two	Flat/paved trail, two lane
Glenwood Canyon	Path parallels I-70, Glenwood Springs to Dotsero	16	Three	600-foot elevation change/paved trail
Durango	Train Station to CO 203 to Trimble Hot Springs, back on CO 250	22	Three	Fairly flat/paved rural roads
Steamboat Springs	Bike trail from downtown to ski mountain	10	Two	Fairly flat/paved trail, dirt road
Denver Foothills/ Waterton Canyon State Park	Kassler Treatment Plant to Strontia Springs dam, return	13	Two	Slight elevation gain/smooth dirt road

Jumpin' Jeeping

With miles of old mining roads looping across Colorado's peaks, recreational four-wheeling—often called jeeping—has become enormously popular. Many Coloradans own four-wheel-drive vehicles and head to the high country on their own. Visitors may find it more economical—and safe—to sign on for an excursion with an outfitter.

Outfitters provide the vehicle (usually an open-top four-wheel-drive, re-fitted to carry passengers), a driver and plenty of up and down excitement on half- and full-day trips. The San Juan Mountains in the state's southwest corner are the hub of four-wheeling activity.

Plan to take sunscreen and layers of clothing; life at 12,000 feet can be both sunny and chilly.

Alpine Express 4-Wheel Drive Tours
Gunnison, Colorado
970-641-5074

Colorado West
Ouray, Colorado
970-325-4014

Crystal River 4x4 Tours
Marble, Colorado (near Aspen)
970-963-1991

Fun Time Jeep Tours
Salida, Colorado
800-833-7238

Mad Adventures
Winter Park, Colorado
970-726-5290

Nova Guides
Vail, Colorado
970-949-4231

River Runners
Salida, Colorado
719-539-2144

Switzerland of America
Ouray, Colorado
970-325-4484

Steamboat Lake Outfitters
Clark, Colorado
970-879-4404

Tiger Run Tours
Breckenridge, Colorado
970-453-2231

Fishing

Each year, the Colorado Division of Wildlife (CDW) stocks the state's rivers and lakes with millions of fish. Licenses cost about $20 per year for non-residents and are available at bait shops around the state along with copies of the many rules and regulations. For information about fishing, contact the Colorado Division of Wildlife, 6060 Broadway, Denver, CO, 80215; call 303-297-1192.

Here are 20 fishing holes which, according to the CDW, have produced an above average number of quality fish.

Location	Fish Types/Comments	General Directions
Aurora Reservoir	Rainbow trout, walleye, perch	One mile east of Gun Club Road on Quincy Ave.
South Platte River	Rainbow and brown trout	Below Cheesman Reservoir is world class
Bear Creek	10–12 inch rainbow trout	Evergreen to Bear Creek Reservoir
Arkansas River	Brown and rainbow trout	U.S. 50 from Parkdale to Salida
Spinney Mountain Reservoir	Large trout and Snake River cutthroats	South of Hartsel on County 59
Eleven Mile Reservoir	Cutthroat and brown trout, Kokanee salmon	Near Hartsel
High Mountain Lakes of Collegiate Peaks	Cutthroat trout;Most require hiking, be prepared for drastic weather	
North Park Streams	Among the state's best for brown, brook and rainbow trout	Around Walden
Delaney Butte Lakes	Brown, cutthroat	Around Walden
Cache la Poudre River	Rainbow stocked all summer, Mountain whitefish	From the South Platte to headwaters
Big Thompson River	Stocked rainbow and brown trout. Try eggs in spring, flies in summer	East of Estes Park on U.S. Highway 34
Rio Grande River	Rainbow and lunker brown trout	From the Highway 149 bridge at South Fork, up to 16 miles downstream
Blue Mesa Reservoir	Rainbow trout, Kokanee salmon	Near Gunnison
Gunnison River	Trophy rainbow	Between Crystal and the confluence of the North Fork
Stagecoach Reservoir	Two-pound rainbow trout common	South of Steamboat Springs
Fryingpan, Crystal, Roaring Fork rivers	Among the best for trout in the country	South of Glenwood Springs
Rifle Gap Reservoir	Best walleye in northwest Colorado	Flattops Wilderness Area
Dillon Reservoir	All species of Colorado trout, Kokanee salmon	I-70 at Frisco exit
Blue River	Fantastic rainbow and brown trout, flies and lures only	North of Dillon Reservoir

Tracks Through the Rockies

Durango and Silverton Narrow-guage Railroad skirts the Animas River

Diesel and coal-fired steam engines in Colorado pull both open-top and enclosed cars along the narrow- and standard-gauge track beds that thread through Colorado's scenic masterpieces.

The Royal Gorge Route
Canon City, Colorado
888-724-5748
Opened in 1999, The Royal Gorge Route runs passengers from Canyon City to Parkdale and back, 24 miles. The highlight? Riding the rails through the depths of the Royal Gorge itself.

Cripple Creek and Victor Narrow Gauge Railroad
Cripple Creek, Colorado
719-689-2640
Winding its way out of historic Cripple Creek, the open-air cars weave through the hills on their way toward Victor pulled by a steam locomotive on the 45-minute round trip. A recorded narration instructs riders about mining, wildlife and railroading as the train wends its way through glades of trees, over wooden trestles and past dozens of abandoned mines. It stops three times on the trip for picture-taking.

Leadville, Colorado & Southern
Leadville, Colorado
719-486-3936

This standard-gauge, diesel-powered train rolls out on 2.5 hour round trips from Leadville's Victorian station up to the water tower at Climax, Colorado, 25 miles away. Along one side, the headwaters of the Arkansas River flow down the glacial valley; on the other rise some of Colorado's most spectacular forested peaks. Watch for waterfalls. Near Climax, there's time for some exploring and a peek back across the valley at Colorado's highest crest—Mt. Elbert.

Cumbres & Toltec Scenic Railroad
Antonito, Colorado
719-376-5483

This is the longest and highest-elevation narrow-gauge steam railroad in the United States. Colorado and New Mexico saved it from the scrap heap and created this 64-mile line. The route wriggles through some of the West's grandest landscape.

Passengers hop aboard vintage cars at either Chama, New Mexico, or Antonito, Colorado. The railway actually operates two trains, one from each town. Both converge at Osier, Colorado for a hearty lunch. From there, travelers either return the way they came or proceed to the other end, where a van awaits to return riders to their original starting point.

Durango and Silverton Narrow Gauge Railroad
Durango, Colorado
970-247-2733

In its late 1800s heyday, the Durango and Silverton Railroad served prospectors and camp followers eager to cash in on the San Juan's mineral bounty. This vintage rolling stock is strung with a huffing and puffing antique locomotive and pumpkin-orange coaches. Now, several times each day and year-round, it still follows the curvacious 46-mile route between good-time Durango and old-time Silverton.

Daily excursions hug the wild Animas River through granite-faced canyons strewn with pine, aspen and wild rose. Guests arrive in Silverton with two hours to spend on lunch and an exploration of this classic Victorian mining camp before re-boarding.

Georgetown Loop Railroad
Georgetown, Colorado
303-569-2403

High-altitude vista-viewing awaits visitors on the eight-mile Georgetown Loop Railroad. The line's name stems from the engineering marvel enabling trains to tackle the nearly eight percent grade from Georgetown to Silver Plume. Designers conquered this steep ascent by installing a "loop" which takes the train on a corkscrew course around and across the narrow valley. Devil's Gate Viaduct, the spindly bridge, hangs 100 feet over Clear Creek. Old timers used to say that the bridge swayed under the locomotive's weight, but not to worry, there's a solid new trestle in place now.

Pikes Peak Cog Railway
Manitou Springs, Colorado
719-685-5401

Cheery red coaches take 90 minutes to climb this eight-mile route, gaining 1.5 miles in elevation to attain the top of Pikes Peak. To negotiate the 25 percent incline, gears under the locomotive grab a rack of teeth that is zippered between the rails. Boulder-clogged canyons give way to alpine meadows splashed with color.

The summit brings the reward—a 360-degree view of the Continental Divide and the Great Plains beyond. It's the very same view that inspired Katharine Lee Bates to write *America the Beautiful.*

Colorado for the Challenged

Recreational opportunities abound for physically challenged Colorado visitors. City and state parks throughout Colorado have adapted walks, trails and other sites to accommodate wheelchairs. Many ski areas offer skiing and other wintertime activities. Several reservoirs have wheelchair-accessible boat ramps or fishing piers.

Accessible Trails

- Chatfield State Park near Denver: ten miles of paved trail
- Glenwood Canyon: Glenwood Springs; 16 miles of paved trail
- Ridgeway State Park, Montrose: paved and gravel trails
- Rocky Mountain National Park: Beaver Ponds Boardwalk; Sprague Lake Trail; Lily Lake; Tundra Trail
- Winter Park Outdoor Center: over a mile-long trail

Resources:

Colorado Therapeutic Riding Center; Boulder, Colorado 303-665-1138

Wilderness on Wheels; Grant, Colorado; hiking, fishing, camping 303-751-3959

Denver Commission for People with Disabilities; publishes *Colorado on Wheels* guide 303-640-3056

Outdoor Buddies; 303-771-8216

Breckenridge Outdoor Education Center; river canoe adventures, rope courses, camping, backpacking 970-453-6422

National Sports Center for the Disabled; Winter Park, skiing, rafting, nature trails 970-726-1540

Aspen Camp School for the Deaf; 970-923-2511

Disability Information and Referral Service; 800-255-3477

Striking Colorado "Gold"

Colorado's aspen tend to start turning to "gold" in mid-September. The city of Aspen itself and Independence Pass are great places to view the splendor. Other popular aspen-spotting locales are Rabbit Ears Pass near Steamboat Springs; the west side of Rocky Mountain National Park; the Peak to Peak Scenic and Historic Byway from Rocky Mountain National Park to Central City; Kenosha Pass near Bailey; Guanella Pass south of Georgetown; Monarch Pass east of Gunnison; La Veta Pass in the Sangre de Cristos near Trinidad; Wolf Creek Pass east of Durango; and pretty much anywhere in the San Juans in the vicinity of Ouray, Telluride, or Silverton.

Some lesser-known "gold mines": Lake Isabel in the Sangre de Cristos above Trinidad; north of Cotopaxi on County Road 12; Chalk Creek Canyon along County Road 162 south of Buena Vista; out of Telluride to Lizard Head Pass on Colorado 145.

Many leaf-peepers head to Breckenridge for a special loop drive. Take Boreas Pass out of Breckenridge on Forest Road 223 over to Como. Drive south to Fairplay on Colorado 185 then onto Colorado 9 and across Hoosier Pass back into Breckenridge. The Boreas pass portion of the drive is a well-maintained gravel road.

Dude and Guest Ranches

Ranch between Durango and Silverton

Long before Billy Crystal and his buddies rounded up wayward strays in *City Slickers* (filmed in Colorado), dude and guest ranches were giving Wild West wannabes a chance to saddle up and hit the dusty trail.

Most ranches run three- or seven-day horse programs. Expect to have a horse assigned to you for your entire stay, to receive extensive instruction, and to take up to two rides each day (though most dudes take a day or two off). On most ranches, the amount of care you give your horse depends on you; some guests like to groom and tack their own horses. Others want to walk out from breakfast and find their horse saddled and ready to ride.

Meals are served family-style and range from gourmet herb-encrusted salmon to plain old spaghetti and meatballs. While the weekly price is a good indicator of the type of food that will be served, don't confuse food cost with quality.

Price runs from around $1,000 to $1,800 per adult per week. Average rates are in the $1,100 to $1,500 range and include lodging, meals, horseback riding, instruction and many activities.

Dress is decidedly casual. Cowboy boots and a cowboy hat are must-wears.

Colorado has more dude and guest ranches than any other state in the Union. Because there are more than a hundred—each with its own foibles—selecting one can be harder work than hauling hay. To figure out which ranch is right for you, the Colorado Dude and Guest Ranch Association (970-887-3128) suggests ordering their brochure, which contains listings for the 30 or so ranches in their group. Then, based on size, cost, locale and other factors, they recommend calling several, getting their brochures and chatting with the owners before making a decision.

Dude and Guest Ranches

Name	Telephone	Nearest city	Max. number of guests	Cost *
Aspen Canyon Ranch	970-725-3600	Winter Park	24	Moderate
Aspen Lodge Ranch Resort	970-586-8133	Estes Park	175	Moderate
Bar Lazy J Guest Ranch	970-725-3437	Winter Park	38	Moderate
C Lazy U Ranch	970-887-3344	Granby	115	Deluxe
Cherokee Park Ranch	970-493-6522	Livermore	35	Moderate
Colorado Trails Ranch	970-247-5055	Durango	60	Moderate
Coulter Lake Guest Ranch	970-625-1473	Rifle	30	Budget
Deer Valley Ranch	719-395-2353	Nathrop	130	Budget
Don K Ranch	719-784-6600	Pueblo	45	Moderate
Drowsy Water Ranch	970-725-3456	Granby	60	Moderate
Elk Mountain Ranch	719-539-4430	Buena Vista	35	Moderate
Focus Ranch	970-583-2410	Slater	30	Budget
Fryingpan River Ranch	970-927-3570	Meredith	30	Deluxe
Harmel's Ranch Resort	970-641-1740	Almont	150	Budget
The Historic Pines Ranch	719-783-9261	Westcliffe	40	Moderate
Lake Mancos Ranch	970-533-7900	Mancos	55	Moderate
Latigo Ranch	970-724-9008	Kremmling	40	Deluxe
Lazy H Guest Ranch	303-747-2532	Allenspark	50	Moderate
Lost Valley Ranch	303-647-2311	Sedalia	98	Deluxe
North Fork Ranch	303-838-9873	Shawnee	40	Moderate
Old Glendevey Ranch	970-435-5701	Glendevey	18	Moderate
Peaceful Valley Ranch	303-747-2881	Lyons	100	Deluxe
Powderhorn Guest Ranch	970-641-0220	Powderhorn	30	Moderate
Rainbow Trout Ranch	719-376-5659	Antonito	60	Moderate
Rawah Ranch	970-435-5715	Glendevey	32	Moderate
San Juan Guest Ranch	970-626-5360	Ridgway	32	Moderate
7 W Guest Ranch	970-524-9328	Gypsum	18	Moderate
Sky Corral Ranch	970-484-1362	Bellvue	30	Moderate
Skyline Ranch	970-728-3757	Telluride	38	Moderate
Sundance Trail Guest Ranch	970-224-1222	Red Feather Lakes	24	Budget
Sylvan Dale Guest Ranch	970-667-3915	Loveland	60	Moderate
Tarryall River Ranch	719-748-1214	Lake George	30	Moderate
Tumbling River Ranch	303-838-5981	Grant	55	Deluxe
Vista Verde Ranch	970-879-3858	Steamboat Springs	36	Deluxe
Waunita Hot Springs Ranch	970-641-1266	Gunnison	48	Moderate
Whistling Acres Guest Ranch	970-527-4560	Paonia	21	Moderate
White Pine Ranch	970-641-6410	Gunnison	14	Moderate
Wilderness Trails Ranch	970-247-0722	Durango	48	Deluxe

* Rates per week, per person: Budget = less than $1,000; Moderate = $1,000 to $1,400; Deluxe = over $1,400

Hot Springs

Colorado boasts dozens of hot springs—water warmed deep in the heart of Mother Earth, laden with minerals and bubbling out of the ground. They range from secluded, clothing-optional gurgles along the side of a remote road to the largest hot-springs pool in the world.

Most of the springs listed here are much like swimming pools—large man-made pools mixing swimming areas and warmer soaking pools for a bit of relaxation. Many offer massage and other spa amenities. While a soak nearly always improves one's mental attitude, be wary of outrageous health claims.

Expect to pay about $8 to $15 to enjoy a day of soaking. Pack a suit, towel, sunscreen and drink plenty of water—a good soak is surprisingly dehydrating.

Strawberry Hot Springs
44200 County Road 36, Steamboat Springs, Colorado 80477
970-879-0342
Four stone-walled, gravel-bottomed soaking pools with water combined from the 150-degree spring and the frigid water of Spa Creek, six miles north of Steamboat. The ambiance in this spectacular setting of aspen and fir is relaxing. Clothing optional after dark. Among the nicest soaking experiences in the state.

Steamboat Springs Health and Recreation Association
136 Lincoln Ave., Steamboat Springs, Colorado 80477
970-879-1828
This has soaking, play and lap pools, all at different temperatures, in a facility with workout and aerobics rooms.

Glenwood Springs Hot Springs and Pool

Family-oriented. A great swim in the heart of Steamboat.

Glenwood Springs Hot Springs Lodge and Pool
401 North River St., Glenwood Springs, Colorado 81602
970-945-7131
The largest hot springs pool in the world—two blocks long. One pool is for swimming-style activities and another smaller pool is for soaking.

Penny Hot Springs
Colorado 133 between Carbondale and Marble.
Look for the small "C.R.11" sign 15 miles south of Carbondale. These free springs simply bubble up at the edge of the Crystal River. Soakers arrange rocks to make a comfy pool and crawl in. Very informal, clothing optional. Beware the swirling water mid-stream if you venture into the river itself.

Indian Springs Spa
302 Soda Creek Road, Idaho Springs, Colorado, 80452
303-623-2050
A toasty warm swimming pool under a greenhouse roof. A favorite après-ski stop because they are right off Interstate 70. The "vapor" caves offer soaks of three different temperatures in pools located in rooms drilled out of solid rock.

Ouray Hot Springs Pool
1000 Main St., Ouray, Colorado 81427-0468
970-325-4638
This large pool with spectacular views of the San Juan Mountains is divided into seven areas, each with a different temperature. Nice, clean shower facilities.

Trimble Hot Springs
6473 County Road 203
Durango, Colorado 81301
970-247-0111
This modern, well-kept pool is centrally located for the many recreational activities in Durango.

Cottonwood Hot Springs
18999 Highway 306, Buena Vista, Colorado, 81211
719-395-6434
Located between Mt. Yale and Mt. Princeton, these remote, stone-walled pools provide relief for hikers, kayakers and scenery spotters.

Colorado's Best Links

With more than 12 percent of Coloradans golfing, the sport is becoming a favored way to enjoy mountain views, sunshine, fresh air—and that fabulous frustration only golf can arouse. Colorado has more than 200 courses, many in urban areas, as well as many in spectacular resort settings.

For more information on golfing the high country (your ball may fly up to 15 percent farther), contact: Colorado Golf Association, 5655 S. Yosemite, Englewood, Colorado, 80111, 303-779-GOLF (4653).

In October, 1996, *Colorado Golf magazine* conducted a poll among the state's P.G.A. golfers, course superintendents and members of the Rocky Mountain Golf Salesman Association. They were asked to rate their favorite public and resort courses. Note: use of some courses may require being a guest at the resort or, at public courses, calling ahead for tee times several days in advance.

Crested Butte Country Club

Public Courses

Fox Hollow Golf Club, 13410 W. Morrison Road, Lakewood, CO, 80228; call 303-986-7888

Riverdale Golf Course—Dunes Course, 13300 Riverdale Rd., Brighton, CO, 80601; call 303-659-6700

Legacy Ridge Golf Course, 10801 Legacy Ridge Parkway, Westminster, CO, 80030; call 303-438-8997

Walking Stick Golf Course, 4301 Walking Stick Blvd., Pueblo, CO, 81001; call 719-584-3400

Indian Peaks Golf Course, 2300 Indian Peaks Trail, Lafayette (near Denver), CO, 80026; call 303-666-4706

Mariana Butte, 701 Clubhouse Dr., Loveland, CO, 80537; call 970-667-8308

Pine Creek Golf Club, 9850 Divot Drive, Colorado Springs, CO 80920; call 719-594-9999

Plum Creek Golf Club, 331 Players Club Dr., Castle Rock, CO 80104; call 303-688-2611

Buffalo Run Golf Course, 15700 E. 112th Ave., Commerce City (near Denver), CO, 80022; call 303-289-1500

Battlement Mesa Golf Course, 3930 N. Battlement Parkway, Parachute, CO 81635; call 970-285-7274

Resort Courses

Broadmoor, One Pourtales, Colorado Springs, CO 80906; call 719-577-5790

Breckenridge Golf Club, 200 Clubhouse Drive, Breckenridge, CO 80424; call 970-453-9104

Sonnenalp Golf Club, 14 miles west of Vail off I-70, Edwards, CO; call 970-926-3533

Codillera Mountain Course, 650 Clubhouse Dr., Edwards, CO 81632; call 970-926-5100

Tamarron Hilton Resort - Cliffs Course, 40292 Hwy. 550 North, Durango, CO, 81301; call 970-259-2000

Pole Creek, 11 miles northwest of Winter Park on Highway 40, Winter Park, CO; call 970-726-8847

Beaver Creek Golf Club, 103 Offerson Rd, Beaver Creek, CO, 81620; call 970-845-5775

Keystone Ranch Golf Club, 1437 Summit County Road 150, Keystone, CO, 80435; call 970-468-4250

Grandote Peaks Golf Club, 5540 Highway 12, La Veta, CO, 81055; call 719-742-3391

Crested Butte Country Club (formerly Skyland), 385 Country Club Dr., Crested Butte, CO, 81224; call 970-349-6127

Skiing

Name & telephone	Skiable acreage	% of terrain beginner/ intermediate/ expert	Vertical drop (feet)	Adult full-day lift ticket price range *	Comments
Arapahoe Basin 970-496-7077	490	10/50/40	2,270	B	Stays open into spring
Aspen Highlands 970-925-1220	619	20/50/30	3,635	D	Aspen's intermediate mountain
Aspen Mountain 970-925-1220	675	0/35/36	3,267	D	For experts only
Beaver Creek Resort 970-949-5750	1,625	34/39/27	4,040	D	Fine skiing, carriage trade
Breckenridge Ski Resort 970-453-5000	2,031	14/26/55	3,398	M	Fine skiing, great mountain town
Buttermilk Mountain 970-925-1220	410	35/39/26	2,030	D	For Aspen's beginners
Copper Mountain Resort 970-968-2882	2,433	20/24/56	2,601	M	Runs nicely separated
Crested Butte Mountain Resort 970-349-2333	1,160	24/56/20	2,787	M	Expert mecca, extreme skiing
Cuchara Ski Valley 719-742-3163	195	40/40/20		B	Great value, good learn-to-ski area
Eldora Mountain Resort 303-440-8700	386	20/55/25	1,400	B	Easy to reach, affordable
Howelson Hill 970-879-4300	70	20/30/50	440	B	Colorado's oldest
Keystone Resort 800-258-9553	1,755	13/36/51	2,900	M	Fine destination resort
Loveland Ski Area 303-569–3203	1,365	22/55/23	2,410	M	Close to Denver
Monarch Ski & Snowboard Area 719-539-3573	670	21/37/42	1,110	B	Terrific value, good snocat skiing
Powderhorn Resort 970-268-5700	510	20/60/20	1,650	B	Mesa views, family oriented
Purgatory Resort 970-247-9000	1,200	23/51/26	2,029	B	Great terrain
Silver Creek Resort 970-887-3384	251	30/50/20	1,000	B	Excellent for learning, families
Ski Cooper 719-486-3684	365	30/40/30	1,200	B	Good value, families
Snowmass 970-925-1220	2,655	10/52/38	4,406	D	Immense, intermediate mecca
Steamboat 970-879-6111	2,939	14/56/30	3,668	M	Good tree skiing, great western town
Sunlight Mountain Resort 970-945-7491	460	20/55/25	2,010	B	Pools in Glenwood a plus
Telluride 970-728-4431	1,050	21/47/32	3,522	M	Great steeps, great mountain town
Vail 970-476-5601	4,644	28/32/40	3,330	D	World's largest, excellent amenities
Winter Park Resort 970-726-5514	2,581	19/38/43	3,060	B	Excellent skiing for Denver families
Wolf Creek Resort 970-264-5639	800	20/45/35	1,425	B	Nice local area

*Single adult, full-day lift ticket rates: B=budget (less than $40); M= moderate; between $41 and $50; D= deluxe; more than $50.

In Colorado, the term skiing summons snowy superlatives. The state boasts more than 250 lifts whisking beginners and aficionados to nearly 30,000 skiable acres. Colorado's 25 resorts (see chart, opposite page) are a mere 5 percent of the nation's total, yet the Centennial State pitches in fully 20 percent of all ski visits. Vail is the largest ski area in the world. With an average of 25 feet of snow a year, much of it champagne dry, Colorado claims the finest powder skiing anywhere.

The range of options may seem overwhelming. Large resorts offer bewildering arrays of terrain and activities, while smaller areas may concentrate on developing certain kinds of runs—beginner, intermediate, or advanced. Some can provide everything from tobogganing and ballooning to dogsledding and night skiing, but all are working on perfecting their basics—snowy slopes for absolutely everyone.

A Snowboarding Primer

Nearly two million people have taken up snowboarding worldwide. The sport that began as "Snurfing" in the 1960s has gained so much respectability that middle-aged ex-skiers are as likely to be found freestyling across the halfpipe as are jester-hatted kids.

One of snowboarding's greatest attributes is that attaining an easy elegance on the board requires much less time than does skiing. Many vacationers dedicate themselves to learning these skills quickly and find themselves well pleased at the end of a week's practice.

As with any sport, it is best to invest in lessons before heading up the slope. Many visitors sign up for a cost-efficient group lesson, enjoying the camaraderie of fellow falling souls, but a one-on-one with an expert may provide the inspiration needed to get up after each fall. Beginners do fall—many times.

Most beginners prefer to rent equipment rather than invest in it. This allows first-timers to discover the equipment that's best for them. All the resorts and ski rental stores rent a variety of board and boot types.

Boards are a trickier matter. There are four basic types: freeride, freestyle, race boards, and freecarve boards. The freecarve boards are generally recommended for beginners.

It took a few years, but now only one Colorado ski area—Aspen Mountain—bans boarders. All the others not only allow "boardheads," but welcome them. Special areas are devoted to halfpipes, tabletops, kickers and terrain gardens.

Many resorts now offer beginner packages as well. Expect to get a lift ticket, group lesson for a couple of hours and equipment rental for $50 to $100 per day. Ask about special multi-day programs for kids or women. The Kevin Delaney Adult Snowboard Camp in Aspen is worth looking into, as is his brother's similar camp in Beaver Creek. Winter Park also has an excellent boarding school.

Breckenridge was one of the first areas to court boarders. In fact, Front Range residents think of Summit County's four resorts as being "Board Central." In the "Summit," boarding is not an activity, it's a lifestyle intertwined with nightlife. Extreme boarders head for Crested Butte, particularly during the U.S. Extreme Snowboarding Championships held in late March.

Boarder Lingo

Ride—to snowboard
Halfpipe—tube-shaped run
Phat—big (example: "phat air" means huge jump)
Eat it—to fall face forward
Gnarly—difficult, awesome
Awesome—incredible
Betty—female boarder
Poser—a wanna-be
Sick—great, in a crazy way
Rag Doll—to bounce uncontrollably down a steep slop after a fall
Label Babies—brand-name gear junkies
Stoked—elated, happy
Sweet—anything wonderful
Crud—difficult-to-ride snow

The Front Range

Roxborough Park

Explorer Lt. Zebulon Montgomery Pike first made mention of Colorado's massive Front Range of Rocky Mountains in November, 1806. " At two o'clock in the afternoon I thought I could distinguish a mountain to our right, which appeared like a small blue cloud." That "small blue cloud" turned out to be a 14,110-foot peak west of present-day Colorado Springs: Pikes Peak. What Pike didn't see on that November afternoon was that this was only the first hint of a series of mountain ranges that stretch westward 100 miles and for some 170 miles north to south along Colorado's midsection.

The Front Range acted as a wall to Colorado's pioneers. Early immigrants invariably gathered along the valleys and canyons that spill out from the foothills. Here, they rested and re-supplied themselves before tackling the high passes into the mountains. Many never bothered to forge into the hills at all, preferring to settle down right then and there. Communities soon sprouted, growing over time into towns and cities. Today, the principal metropolitan areas that comprise the Front Range—Denver, Boulder, Colorado Springs, Pueblo, Greeley and Fort Collins—comprise over 80 percent of the state's total population.

Enough is enough, cry some Coloradans as

SuperAmerica Guide's Front Range Recommendations

- Devote at least two days to exploring the natural wonders of Rocky Mountain National Park.
- Take a day to stroll through the galleries and enjoy a leisurely lunch in Denver's historic LoDo and Larimer Square areas.
- Spend an afternoon or evening on Boulder's Pearl Street Mall to shop and enjoy the street entertainers.
- Hop aboard the Manitou and Pikes Peak Cog Railway.
- Motor through spectacular routes such as Peak to Peak or Highway of Legends Scenic and Historic Byways.
- Pay a visit to Colorado's historic mining towns of Central City, Black Hawk and Cripple Creek, all gussied up now with low-stakes gambling casinos.

left: View of Denver including Elitch Gardens Amusement Park

Dale
287
25
Rockport
85
Pawnee National Grassland
Paw
125
MEDICINE BOW MOUNTAINS
Walden
14
Rustic
Poudre Park
Wellington
Fort Collins
Ted's Place
Briggsdale
Ault
Eaton
Roosevelt National Forest
125
Windsor
Greeley
Kersey
Riverside Reservoir
South
Rocky Mountain National Park
Rand
Divide
34
Estes Park
Loveland
Evans
Gilcrest
Masters
Longs Pk 14,256 ft
7
36
Lyons
66
Longmont
Platteville
Grand Lake
Hot Sulphur Springs
Granby
FRONT RANGE
72
Ft. Lupton
76
Keenesburg
Hudson
Prospect Valley
40
Kremmling
Silver Creek
Tabernash
Fraser
Eldora
Boulder
Lafayette
Louisville
Brighton
119
Nederland
Winter Park
Winter Park
72
Westminster
79
Central City
Idaho Springs
Golden
Aurora
Bennett
9
Empire
Georgetown
Lakewood
DENVER
Byers
Vail
Silverthorne
Loveland
Arapahoe Basin
6
Keystone
Frisco
Vail
Mt Evans 14,264 ft
Conifer
470
Littleton
Parker
85
Copper Mtn.
Breckenridge
Breckenridge
Cooper
285
Grant
Sedalia
Bailey
Elizabeth
Kiowa
Jefferson
Castle Rock
91
9
Como
Deckers
86
Leadville
Fairplay
Pike National Forest
Westcreek
25
24
Lake George
Woodland Park
Peyton
24
Hartsel
Divide
Colorado Springs
Buena Vista
Florissant Fossil Beds Natl. Mon.
Mt Harvard 14,420 ft
9
67
Pikes Pk 14,110 ft
94
Security-Widefield
Fountain
Cripple Creek
Mt Antero 14,269 ft
Fort Carson Military Res.
Salida
Cañon City
Monarch
Poncha Springs
Texas Creek
Parkdale
Royal Gorge Bridge
Penrose
Pueblo West
50
Cotopaxi
Florence
Bonanza
285
Villa Grove
67
96
Wetmore
Pueblo
Avondale
Mineral Hot Springs
Westcliffe
78

Downtown Denver

development along the Front Range continues to expand. Some people say that it won't be long before the Front Range is one continuous city stretching 200 miles from Fort Collins in the north to Pueblo in the south. City planners feel the threat of increased commercial and housing growth, and consequently have formulated long-range plans for additional greenways and parks.

To be sure, the Front Range has become a more crowded place, but also more sophisticated. Denver has become the cultural and business capital to an area similar in size to Western Europe. Boulder is home to the University of Colorado, and a host of high-technology businesses. Colorado Springs is a military mecca and training facility for several U.S. Olympic teams. Farther south, Pueblo holds a chapter of Colorado's early Hispanic and pioneering heritage. Greeley and Fort Collins, both college towns and agricultural centers, bridge the gap between the rural Eastern Plains and the urban Front Range.

SuperAmerica Guide's Denver Recommendations

- Experience Denver's many museums, especially the Denver Art Museum, the Denver Museum of Natural History, the Colorado History Museum, the Black American West Museum and Heritage Center and Buffalo Bill's Grave and Museum.
- Drive through Denver's Mountain Park System.
- See the wildlife at the Denver Zoo, in particular "Primate Panorama" and "Northern Shores," a polar bear habitat.
- Book a performance at the Denver Performing Arts Complex.
- Spend an afternoon and evening strolling through LoDo and Larimer Square.
- Take in a Colorado Rockies baseball game at Coors Field.

Denver

It's probably a safe bet to assume that the gold-hungry miners who founded what would later become Denver would be amazed to see her now. The city that started as a rag-tag collection of tents in a raw mining camp now encompasses 40 communities and more than two million people. Denver is the cosmopolitan epicenter for shopping, dining and entertainment within a six hundred mile radius, clearly earning her the title of "Queen City of the Plains."

History

In July, 1858, a sharp-eyed prospector from the state of Georgia, William Green Russell, churned up gold flakes along the banks of Little Dry Creek, near the confluence of Cherry Creek and the South Platte River. Word of the find spread like a prairie wildfire. The gold rush was on with thousands of get-rich-quickers heralding "Pikes Peak or Bust." By November, two mining camps straddled the banks of the South Platte River: Auraria

left: Colorado's Front Range

38TH AVE
37th Ave
36th Ave
35th Ave
34th Ave
33rd Ave
32ND AVE
31st Ave
30th Ave
29th Ave
28th Ave
27th Ave
26th Ave
25th Ave
24th Ave
23rd Ave
22nd Ave
21st Ave
20th Ave
17th Ave
COLFAX AVE
14th Ave
13th Ave
12th Ave
11th Ave
10th Ave
9th Ave
8TH AVE
7th Ave
6TH AVE
5th Ave
4th Ave
3rd Ave
2nd Ave
1st Ave
Irvington Pl
Irvington Rd
Ellsworth Ave
Archer Pl
BAYAUD AVE
Maple Ave
Cedar Ave
Byers Pl
W. ALAMEDA AVE
E. ALAMEDA AVE
W. Nevada Pl
W. Dakota Ave
W. Alaska Pl
W. Virginia Ave
W. Custer Pl
W. Center Ave
W. Gill Ave
W. EXPOSITION AVE
E. EXPOSITION AVE
E. Ohio Ave
Denver Pl
ZUNI ST
PECOS ST
OSAGE ST
SPEER BLVD
AURARIA PKWY
BROADWAY
LINCOLN ST
DOWNING ST
KALAMATH ST
SANTA FE DR
S. LIPAN ST
BLAKE ST
WALNUT ST
MARKET ST
14TH ST
20TH ST
22ND ST
23RD ST
CHAMPA ST
STOUT ST
PARK AVE
14TH AVE
17TH AVE
Rockmont Dr
South Platte River
Cherry Creek
Viking Pk
Residence Inn by Marriott
Super 8 Motel Downtown
Forney Museum
Confluence Park
Elitch Gardens Amusement Park
Children's Museum
Ramada Inn Mile High Stadium
Mile High Stadium
McNichols Arena
Union Station
Oxford Hotel
RTD Market St Bus Terminal
Coors Field
Sakura Square
Tabor Center
Writer Square
Westin Hotel
Embassy Suites Hotel
Holtze Executive Place
Marriott
Hyatt Regency Denver
Executive Tower Inn
16th Street Mall
Denver Performing Arts Complex
Currigan Hall
Colorado Convention Center
Paramount Theatre
Holiday Inn Downtown
Brown Palace
Adam's Mark Hotel
RTD Civic Center Bus Terminal
Visitor Information
Comfort Inn
Warwick Hotel
Queen Anne Inn
Black American West Museum & Heritage Center
Light Rail Transit
Tivoli Denver
University of Colorado–Denver
Auraria Campus
Metro St. College
Denver Community College
9th Street Historic District
US Mint
City & Country Building
State Capitol
Denver Art Museum
Byers-Evans House
Library
Colorado History Museum
Molly Brown House
Cambridge
Broadway Plaza Hotel
Burnsley Hotel
Capitol Hill Mansion (B&B)
Lincoln Park
Rude Park
Suriken Gardens Park
Museo de las Americas
Governor's Mansion
Turner Museum
Denver General Hospital
Children's Hospital
Washington Park
25
40
287
6
26
33

Sports

One of the quickest ways to start up a conversation with a Denverite is to mention one of these words: Broncos, Rockies, Avalanche or Nuggets. Denver's enthusiasm for its sports teams is nothing short of exceptional.

Denver Broncos Football Club
It took nearly 40 years, five AFC championships and four previous shots at a Super Bowl title for the Denver Broncos (303-649-9000) to finally score top honors at Super Bowl XXXII, besting the Green Bay Packers 31 to 24. Long-suffering fans went wild, heaping adulation on their favorite underdog team. The timing for a big win couldn't have been better; a vote on a new taxpayer-supported football stadium initiative was pending.

Colorado Rockies Baseball Club
Denver waited years to snag a baseball franchise. And when the Colorado Rockies (303-762-5437) debuted in 1994, Denverites proved their worthiness. Attendance records for a major league single season soared as 4.4 million fans converged on Mile High Stadium. The next year, the Rockies moved into the newly built 50,000-seat Coors Field. The Rockies responded by playing their way into the National League Championship Series.

Colorado Avalanche
Formerly the Quebec Nordiques, the Colorado Avalanche (303-893-6700) skated into the rink—and into hearts of Denver hockey hounds in—1995. That same year, they snapped up a spot in the Stanley Cup Finals, taking the title from the Florida Panthers in a four-game sweep. It was Denver's first ever major sports championship, and consequently, the city fell in love with the "Avs."

Denver Nuggets
Denver has hoop dreams for the Nuggets (303-893-6700). While the team has only reached the NBA playoffs twice, in 1993-94 and again in 1994-95, fans follow the team's progress diligently. The planned $150 million Pepsi Center, an ultra-modern sports arena located near LoDo, signifies Denver's commitment to seeing the Nuggets through to a title.

Colorado Rapids
While soccer doesn't quite attract Denver's devotion the same way that football, baseball, hockey and basketball do, the city has a place in its heart for the game and for its winning team. The Colorado Rapids (800-844-7777) have captured the American Professional Soccer League Championship three times.

on the west, St. Charles on the east. The name Denver wasn't adopted for the combined communities until 1859.

The gold-seeking pioneers that flowed into Denver during 1859 became known as the "59ers," and there were legions of them. It is estimated that as many as 100,000 people heeded the siren's call to Colorado's gold fields. No more than 40,000 actually made it to Denver, and of them, only about 2,000 stayed. Many of those hardy souls went bust. Denver's gold reserves were meager at best, and soon petered out.

When noted journalist and editor Horace Greeley visited the struggling newborn town in July, 1859, he described Denver as a "log city of 150 dwellings, not three-fourths completed nor one-third fit to be." Fate, however, had already begun to intervene for the fledgling metropolis. In May of 1859, prospector John Gregory hit the jackpot near present-day Idaho Springs, located in the foothills 40 miles west of Denver. Soon, other claims along Clear Creek and its forks were showing "color," turning dirt-poor miners into overnight millionaires. Denver's location on the high-rolling plains east of the mountains, coupled with its mild climate, made it a natural staging ground and supply terminus for Colorado's mountain mineral fields. The coming of the railroad in 1870 set the track to Denver's future as a thriving trade center.

The mineral wealth that streamed down from the mountains transformed Denver into a Western boomtown.

left: map of Denver

Gold and silver barons erected elaborate Victorian mansions. City projects created parks, outlined boulevards studded with fountains and statues, planted thousands of trees and built impressive neoclassical-style civic buildings. Private money spawned newspapers, theaters and the best hotels between Kansas City and San Francisco.

While it was mining that made Denver an important trade and transportation hub in the late 19th century, it was cattle that helped the city get through the lean times after the gold rush. Thanks in large part to the Monfort family and their innovation of "feedlot ranching," Denver became a stockyard terminus second only to Chicago. In short, Denver willingly and wholeheartedly became a "cow town."

With the coming of the world wars, the character of Denver changed again. The U.S. military brass claimed wide-open spaces that were perfect for installations such as Lowry Air Force Base, Fitzsimmons Army Hospital, the controversial Rocky Mountain

Denver International Airport

Few civic projects in Denver's history have caused as much flap as the $4.3 billion Denver International Airport (DIA). Rarely did a day go by over its four-year construction period when the local media didn't surface some new scandal from shoddy workmanship to the infamous suitcase-shattering baggage system. Disappointing delays followed much-hyped opening announcements. Little wonder that wags quipped that DIA was "DOA" on more than one occasion.

The controversy ebbed from memory as the gleaming white peaks of the airport's Teflon-covered, tent-like superstructure—designed to mimic the jagged peaks of the Front Range—finally greeted passengers in late February of 1995. You could almost hear the sighs of relief from politicians, contractors and bond holders. Since then, DIA has been hailed as one of the nation's most efficient airports. It ranks among the best for on-time arrivals and there are few air-traffic control delays.

In truth, the DIA debacle had a perversely positive effect. Many people believe the airport's notoriety finally placed Denver squarely on travelers' mental

maps. And visitors have been coming. DIA welcomes over 85,000 passengers a day.

To be sure, a good deal of DIA's gargantuan budget went into high-tech gadgetry, radar controllers, weather sensors and the like. It's the kind of stuff that would surely warm the heart of a NASA scientist, but it's hardly entertaining to folks cooling their heels waiting for flights. So, for the arriving and departing masses, DIA ensured that people would have a few *objets d' art* to stave off boredom while pleasing the eye.

The result: Thirty-nine artists created original works centered around a "journey" theme. Together, the pieces comprise an impressive airport art program. Whimsical kinetic propellers rotate in the terminal's train tunnels; soothing projections light up ceilings; fiberglass mustangs grace entrances. Many people's favorite seems to be the wonderfully sardonic "Notre Denver" by Terry Allen. These unobtrusive bronze sculptures, tucked into the baggage pick-up area, depict gargoyles (à la Parisian Notre Dame) mischievously peeking out from opened suitcases.

At last, an explanation for battered baggage.

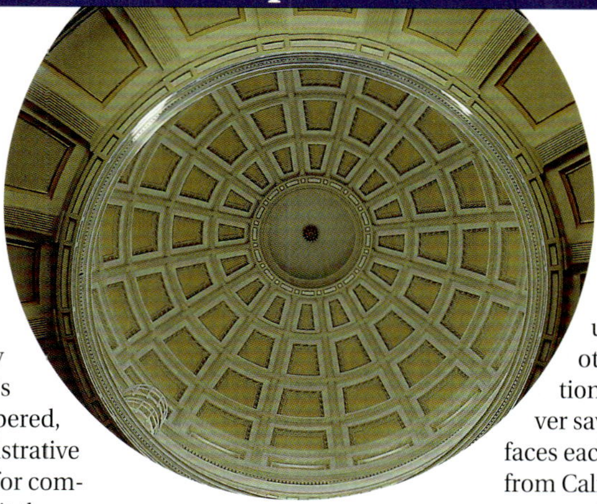

State Capitol Dome

Arsenal where chemical weapons were produced, and the still more notorious Rocky Flats, a top-secret facility for making nuclear device triggers.

During the energy crises of the late 1970s and 80s Denver prospered, serving as the administrative and financial center for companies eager to exploit the region's vast deposits of coal, natural gas and oil shale. Denver's skyscrapers rose as fast as oil prices, fashioning the skyline we see today.

Contemporary Aspects

Denver is once again in the midst of a boom. Owing to the city's strategic location halfway between Europe and Asia, Canada and Mexico, Denver is emerging as a 21st-century international distribution and trade center. Several multinational corporations have their headquarters in Denver, including defense giant Lockheed Martin, cable TV titan TCI and communications king US WEST. Moreover, the city's relaxed ambiance, relatively low crime rate, favorable four-season climate and a spate of civic improvement projects have made Denver a prime destination for urban escapees from other parts of the nation. Until recently, Denver saw some 2,000 new faces each week, transplants from California, Texas, Arizona and Florida. The population spurt is now slowing to more moderate growth levels.

Over the past few years, business concerns, along with the city, have been investing in an array of resident- and visitor-pleasing amenities: $7.7 million for "Prehistoric Journey," an elaborate paleontology exhibit at the Denver

The "Unsinkable" Molly Brown

Leadville was a rough-and-ready mining outpost drunk on silver lust when Margaret (Molly) Tobin of Missouri arrived in town. A hard-working Irish Catholic lass filled with spunk, she took odd jobs until she married James Brown, who had a one-eighth share in the Little Johnny mine. The mine's wealth proved to be immense, making the Browns' fractional holding worth millions.

In time, the couple moved to Denver and bought a lavish home at 1340 Pennsylvania Street in the heart of city's most stylish neighborhood. Soon, Molly set her sights on breaking into Denver's fussy high society, at that time lorded over by a close-knit few known as the "Sacred 36." The upper crust saw Molly, despite her wealth, as being too lowly for their attention and rebuked her social advances.

In a twist of fate, Molly was a passenger on the *Titanic*'s ill-fated maiden voyage, but survived the ordeal by escaping in one of the lifeboats. Under the dire circumstances, Molly's pluck emerged in full force as she browbeat the helmsman into action, rallied the scared survivors and shared her $60,000 chinchilla coat with her mates. Newspapers of the day lauded her as a heroine. After that, Molly's celebrity status helped open the doors of Denver's begrudging élite.

Sadly, Molly's fortunes took a dive after the death of her husband and a bitter suit over his will. Her riches dwindled, but not her style. She was forever outspoken, crusading on behalf of women's suffrage rights and giving generously to worthy causes.

Molly died in New York in 1932, but her former home is one of Denver's finest house museums; call 303-832-4092.

Denver Museums

Black American West Museum and Heritage Center, 3091 California Street; 303-292-2566. Comprehensive collection of historical materials and exhibits on African-Americans in the West. Open Monday-Friday, 10 a.m.-5 p.m.; Saturday 12 noon-5 p.m. Admission is charged.

Buffalo Bill's Grave and Museum , Top of Lookout Mountain, I-70 Exit 256, Golden; 303-526-0747. Honors the exploits of the frontier scout and showman. Panoramic view of Denver from Buffalo Bill's grave. Open Monday-Sunday, 9 a.m.-5 p.m.; winter hours: Tuesday-Sunday, 9 a.m.-4 p.m. Admission is charged.

Byers-Evans House Museum, 1310 Bannock Street; 303-620-4933. Elaborate Victorian house restored to 1912–1924 period, reflecting the character of two prominent Colorado families. Open daily 11 a.m.-4 p.m. Admission is charged.

Children's Museum of Denver, 2121 Children's Museum Drive; 303-433-7444. Participatory experience with touch, try and explore exhibits. Open Tuesday-Sunday 10 a.m. to 5 p.m. Admission is charged.

Colorado History Museum, 13th and Broadway; 303-866-3682. Filled with Colorado-themed exhibits, detailed dioramas, historical photographs and artifacts. Open Monday-Saturday 10 a.m.-4:30 p.m.; Sunday noon-4:30 p.m. Admission is charged.

Colorado Railroad Museum, 17155 W. 44th Avenue, Golden; 303-279-4591. More than 50 historic locomotives and cars on exhibit. Open daily 9 a.m.-5 p.m. Admission is charged.

Children's Museum of Denver

Denver Art Museum, 14th Avenue and Bannock Street; 303-640-4433. With more than 36,000 works of art, the DAM is the largest art collection between Kansas City and Los Angeles. Includes Native American art, Spanish Colonial / Pre-Columbian, plus modern and contemporary collections. Open Tuesday-Saturday 10 a.m.-5 p.m.; Sunday noon-5 p.m. Admission is charged; free on Saturday.

Denver Museum of Natural History, 2001 Colorado Blvd.; 303-322-7009. Features wildlife exhibits, gems, minerals, dinosaurs, IMAX Theater and a planetarium. Open Saturday-Thursday 9 a.m.-5 p.m.; Friday 9 a.m.-9 p.m. Admission is charged.

Denver Museum of Miniatures, Dolls and Toys, 1880 Gaylord Street; 303-322-1053. Collections of miniatures, doll houses, dolls and toys displayed in a historic home. Open Tuesday-Saturday 10 a.m.-4 p.m. Admission is charged.

Golda Meir House, 1146 9th Street Park (Auraria Campus); 303-556-2259. Original Denver home of Golda Meir with historic photographs. Open Thursday and Friday, 10 a.m. to 2 p.m. Free.

Denver Museum of Natural History

Mizel Museum of Judaica, 560 S. Monaco Parkway; 303-333-4156. Changing exhibits on the history, culture and art of Jewish people around the world. Open Monday-Friday 10 a.m.-4 p.m.; Sunday noon-4 p.m. Free.

Molly Brown House Museum, 1340 Pennsylvania; 303-832-4092. Home of "Unsinkable" Molly Brown restored to its Victorian splendor. Guided tours by costumed guides. Open Tuesday-Saturday 10 a.m.-4 p.m.; Sunday noon-4 p.m. Admission is charged.

Museo de las Americas, 861 Santa Fe Drive; 303-571-4401. Collections of art and artifacts focus on Latino heritage. Open Tuesday-Saturday 10 a.m.-5 p.m. Admission is charged.

Museum of Natural History; $14 million for "Primate Panorama" at the Denver Zoo; $9 million for the renovation of the Denver Art Museum's installations, including its renowned Pre-Columbian and Spanish Colonial collections; $64 million for the new Denver Public Library; $35 million for the 2,800-seat, Broadway-show-style Temple Buell Theater; and to top it off, the new $4.3 billion Denver International Airport.

Then there's sports. In 1995, Denver, with the acquisition of the Colorado Avalanche hockey team, joined the ranks of New York, Philadelphia, Chicago, Dallas and San Francisco as one of the few cities in the nation to host a quartet of major league franchises. Denverites proved to be adoring fans when the "Avs" skated away with the 1996 Stanley Cup in the National Hockey League championships. A quarter of the city's population, 500,000 people, crowded downtown streets to welcome the team home after their victory.

Attractions

Denver's largest attraction is a actually a shopping mall, the Cherry Creek Shopping Center (303-388-3900), which dominates the upscale Cherry Creek area. With its sculpture-and-activity-filled atrium, visitors to its 160 stores find themselves slowing down to a more "western" pace as they dawdle away an afternoon or evening. So too with the Denver Pavilions (303-260-6000). Astride the 16th Mall downtown it offers lively restaurants and retailing.

As a cultural capital, Denver houses some of the West's best museums. Within the city limits are more than a dozen museums (see Denver's Museums box), which display everything from vintage locomotives to priceless Ming vases.

Not surprisingly, the best of Denver's art and artifact collections center around the region's tie to the West. The Denver Museum of Natural History (303-322-7009) is the fourth largest museum of its kind in the U.S. with fantastic life-sized dioramas of Colorado wildlife and exhibition halls devoted to unearthing the West's dinosaur era. The museum's newest permanent installation, "Prehistoric Journey," chronicles 3.5 billion years of the history of life on earth.

The Denver Art Museum (DAM) (303-640-2793), which looks something like a glass-tiled, high-tech version of a medieval fortress, houses more than 36,000 pieces. It is the largest art collection between Kansas City and Los Angeles.

The DAM also contains one of the country's most superb assemblages of Native American art. The American Indian Hall contains utilitarian and ceremonial objects from across North

ver Public ibrary

America, and the second floor houses a noteworthy totem pole collection. Other curatorial departments focus on architecture, design and Graphics, Asia, and the New World (pre-Columbian and Spanish colonial), in addition to contemporary and classical painting and sculpture.

A different side of the West is illuminated at the Black American West Museum and Heritage Center (303-292-2566), located two miles east of downtown. Here, in the former home of Dr. Justina Ford, Denver's first African-American physician, artifacts and exhibits tell the often-overlooked story of how African-American cowboys helped win the Wild West.

Southwest of downtown, along Santa Fe Boulevard, is the commercial and cultural center of Denver's Hispanic community and the site of the Museo de las Americas (303-571-4401). Founded in 1991, the museum celebrates the diversity of 21 Latin American countries and the U.S. It's the only museum in the Rocky Mountain region dedicated exclusively to displaying the art of Latino cultures. Permanent collections and changing exhibitions "rediscover the New World" through historic artifacts and cutting-edge contributions from contemporary artists.

The West's most famous frontiersman has a spot all to himself. At the crest of Lookout Mountain near the foothills suburb of Golden resides Buffalo Bill's Grave and Museum (303-526-0747). Inside, memorabilia chronicle the life and death of William Frederick Cody, a.k.a. Buffalo Bill, the frontier scout, Pony Express rider, bison hunter and celebrated showman. The museum's displays hold vintage Wild West show costumes and posters, and family photographs tell of Cody's life. The principal attraction, however, is his quartz-rock-encrusted grave.

When Cody died in Denver on January 10, 1917, the "old scout's" passing raised a ruckus over where to bury his body. As the story goes, Cody had specified Cedar Mountain outside Cody, Wyoming, as his preferred spot to spend eternity. With a little negotiating, Denver officials hung onto the remains, finally entombing them atop Lookout Mountain under several tons of steel-reinforced concrete.

Constructing a fortified final resting place for Buffalo Bill seemed necessary to Denverites since Cody, Wyoming townsfolk had vowed to send a militia to reclaim the body. They never did, but for a time

Colorado's Beer Bust

"Move over Milwaukee, Denver is the King of Beers" is the Mile High City's beer boast as Denver takes the crown for brewing more beer than any other American city.

After all, Golden, 12 miles from downtown Denver, is the home of the Coors Brewery, which is the world's largest single brewery. The giant kegger churns out some 17 million barrels a year of the foamy libation. But the tap doesn't dry up there. Denver also has the world's largest brew pub, the Wynkoop Brewing Company in historic LoDo. Also, Denver has the highest number of home brewers of any major city. Topping off the sudsy superlatives, Denver plays host to the annual Great American Beer Festival, the brewing industry's most prestigious event. In a city fond of sports analogies, it's likened to the "SuperBowl" of beer.

Denver isn't alone in its brewing fame. Throughout Colorado, there are more than 50 brew pubs, 18 microbreweries and two major breweries (Coors and Anheuser-Busch), making the state a "Napa Valley" of beer, as promoters like to say. On any given day, there are more than 80 different types of beer, from Railyard Ale to Mountain Wheat to Stout Street Stout, made and poured in Colorado.

Why Colorado? As any beer connoisseur will attest, water is crucial to a fine-tasting lager, ale, bitter, porter or stout. So, just as the water that flows across the Scottish moors adds that indelibly special flavor to Scotch whisky, Colorado's crystal clear Rocky Mountain waters mark the key ingredient for a memorable brewsky.

the Cody American Legion Post offered a $10,000 reward for it.

More of Colorado's colorful characters are encountered at the Colorado History Museum (303-866-3682). Filled with exhibits and dioramas depicting the Centennial State's Native American, mining, cowboy and pioneer past, a favorite stop is the Colorado Scrapbook. Covering the years between 1880 and 1949, the collection of family photos, treasured possessions and mementos presents the story of the state's booms and busts through her most important asset: her people.

If the Colorado History Museum holds the heart of Colorado's past generations, the State Capitol Building (303-866-2604) across the street rings with the voice of the present populace. Modeled after the U.S. Capitol in Washington D.C., this more modest-sized Greek Revival legislative temple is nonetheless crowned with 24 karat gold, 200 ounces in all. Step 15 of the western staircase indicates Denver's elevation above sea level—5,280 feet—but the 18th step is the true mile-high marker.

Guided weekday tours introduce the curious to this and other facts. For instance, that the building's most precious element is the rose onyx used in its interior wainscoting. Quarried near Beulah, Colorado, the onyx proved to be the world's entire supply of the richly colored rock.

Copper is the primary material evident at the nearby U.S. Mint (303-844-3582), one of only three in the country. Each year, more than eight billion coins, mostly pennies, roll off the stampers. It's also the second largest storehouse of gold bullion in the U.S. after Fort Knox. Free guided tours occur Monday through Friday.

Another kind of gold—cool, amber beer—awaits at the Coors Brewery (303-277-BEER) located in Golden. Founded by Adolf Coors in 1873, Coors now brews 17 million barrels of the foamy libation annually. Free tours of the brewery are conducted daily. The tour covers the brewing process from barley germination to bottling, and ends at the much-loved tasting room. For people interested in sampling sake, Hakushika Sake U.S.A. Corporation (303-279-SAKE) conducts a tour of their beverage facility on Golden's Table Mesa Drive.

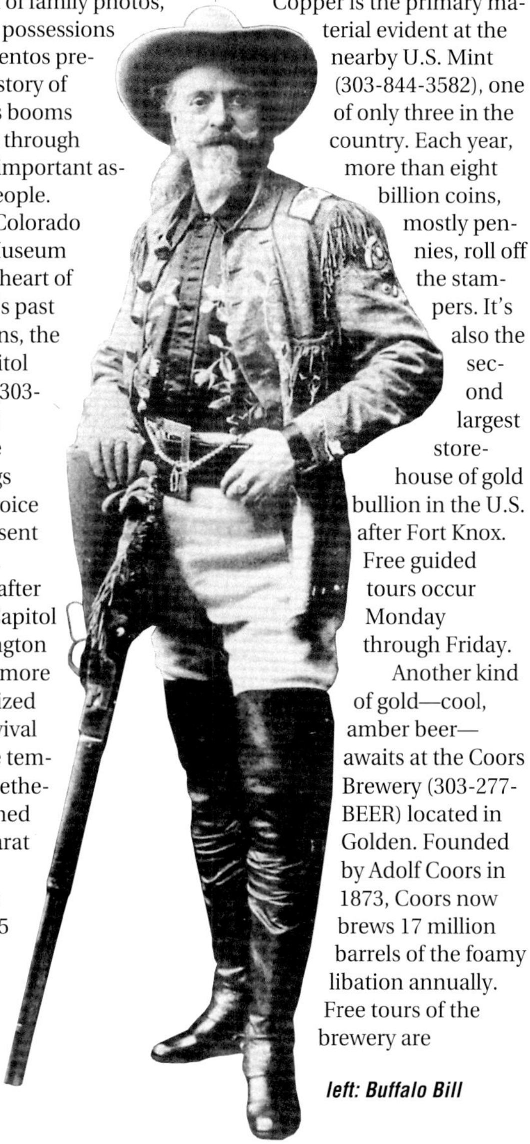

left: Buffalo Bill

Nature

With more than 300 days of sunshine a year, Denver is an outdoor lover's dream come true. City parks and recreation sites abound, giving the city one of the highest open-space ratios per capita in the nation. While any of the 206 parks offers some solitude in the hubbub of a big city, Denverites seem to love the active side of leisure time. City Park, comprised of 314 acres and two lakes, offers space for soccer, football, tennis, and a modicum of peace and quiet. For jogging, cycling and rollerblading there's the Platte River Greenway, stretching 20 miles along Cherry Creek and the South Platte River. In total, the city has more than 450 miles of off-street trails.

Hiking means heading to the hills, to places such as Red Rocks Park and Amphitheater (12 miles west of downtown Denver) to scramble atop 70-million-year-old sandstone spires. The amphitheater holds a 9,000-seat natural outdoor performing venue, where summer concerts keep the walls echoing with the sound of big-name acts. Past performers and personalities here have included the Beatles and Pope John Paul II.

Red Rocks' distinctive formations were once beachfront

Denver Art Museum

property, and formed the shores of an ancient inland sea that covered eastern Colorado and Kansas. Less than a mile away at Dinosaur Ridge, interpretive signs along a trail describe the unique features of the stone and point out the fossilized remains of dinosaurs. The world's first *Stegosaurus armatus* was discovered here in 1877, as were *Allosaurus* and *Brontosaurus* in later years. The finds helped inaugurate the great turn-of-the-century "Dinosaur Rush" as dozens of scientists descended on the West in search of their own Jurassic Parks.

Farther west in the foothills spreads the Denver Mountain Park System, 51 parks scattered over 14,000 acres of evergreen forest and grassy meadow. Some of the parks have names, and some don't. They range in size from diminutive Colorow Park at barely over one acre to Genesse Park at 2,341 acres. The parks are a great escape from Denver's hyperactivity, offering sylvan bastions where even buffalo roam. Two of the parks, Genesse and Daniels, are pastoral homes to small herds of bison transplanted here from Yellowstone National Park in 1914. The best

Rocky Mountain Arsenal National Wildlife Refuge

It's hard to believe that a state such as Colorado, which prides itself on its pristine beauty, would also contain one of the most toxic places on earth. Yet, 12 miles from Denver's city center is the Rocky Mountain Arsenal.

The Arsenal came into being during World War II when the U.S. was in the midst of stretching its muscle and gearing up to wage a decades-long cold war with the "evil empire." The U.S. military needed a site to produce chemical weapons, hence the Rocky Mountain Arsenal.

Along with the military's output of nasty gases, Shell Oil also leased part of the facility for manufacturing agricultural pesticides. In short, a portion of the 17,000-acre site became an environmental nightmare littered with lethal leftovers. Superfund clean-up dollars are making progress on the most contaminated areas, but much work remains to be done.

It seems a wonder that any place this poisonous could support life, let alone be considered a wildlife refuge. Yet, Mother Nature has her ways and the Arsenal's acreage supports a wide diversity of prairie critters. Weekend bus tours provide an overview of the Refuge's history, wildlife, and the environmental cleanup efforts underway. Visitors regularly see hawks and owls in addition to mule deer, coyotes and the swift-footed pronghorn. During the winter, the Refuge is a roosting site for bald eagles, and guests can watch the national bird on closed-circuit TV from an eagle watch area.

As reservations are required for the Saturday-only bus tour, contact the U.S. Fish and Wildlife Service at 303-289-0232.

left: Colorado State Capitol building in Denver

left: Pronghorn antelope

The Front Range from Denver's City Park

place to spot the magnificent creatures is along U.S. Interstate 70, just past exit 254.

Near downtown, the world's wildlife comes to the city at the Denver Zoo (303-331-4110), which houses more than 3,500 animals from all seven continents. In 1996, the zoo celebrated its 100th anniversary with the opening of "Primate Panorama," a $10 million home for 25 species of primates from squirrel monkeys to mountain gorillas. Fauna awaits at the Denver Botanic Gardens (303-331-4000), where conservatories and outdoor gardens display native Colorado flora as well as exotic plants from across the globe. The popular, new Ocean Journey (303-561-4450) recreates the ecosystems of two great rivers; the Colorado River and the Kampar River as each flows from mountain to sea. Ocean Journey houses some 300 animal species and 1,000 live plants — along with a 1,000,000 gallon aquarium.

Nightlife

These days, ground zero for an evening on the town is summed up in two syllables: LoDo; lower downtown.

Not many years ago, this northern portion of the urban center seemed destined for demolition. Tracts of turn-of-the-century warehouses and storefronts spoke of Denver's bustling beginnings, but sadly, many looked ready for the wrecking ball. Slowly, far-sighted (or at least nostalgic) business people began to reclaim the classic Victorian-era structures. Eventually, a 25-block section was designated an historic preservation area.

Ride 'em, Cowboy

While it's certainly true that Denver is a sports town zealously dedicated to her Broncos, Nuggets, Rockies and Avalanche, the city also revels in another sport: Rodeo.

Each January, Denver takes on a cow-town look as thousands of cowpokes and guests from around the world mosey on in for the National Western Stock Show and Rodeo (303-297-1166). For almost 100 years, Denver has hosted the affair, which is now considered to be the world's largest breeding cattle show and one of the top five rodeos in the country.

The event calls many a Denverite to forsake Reeboks or Sorrels for a scruffy pair of Tony Lamas, warm up the pickup truck and head to the stock show arena. Afternoon and evening performances feature rodeo's favorite matches, from bull riding to calf roping to steer wrestling. Yeeee hah!

Larimer Square

Then came the Colorado Rockies. When the team announced that their new $120 million baseball-only stadium, Coors Field, would be located in LoDo, the area became prime real estate. Developers thundered in like a cattle stampede hell-bent for green pastures. Today, this one-time skid row district sports more than 40 art galleries and some 80 bars, restaurants and brew pubs.

Next to the LoDo lies Larimer Square, the

Denver Annual Festivals and Events

January
The National Western Stock Show and Rodeo—World's largest livestock exhibition and fourth largest PRCA-sanctioned rodeo. Denver Coliseum; call 303-297-1166.

March
St. Patrick's Day Parade—One of the nation's largest tributes to the "wearin' of the green." Downtown Denver; call 303-645-3446.

May
Cinco de Mayo—More than 200,000 people come to celebrate Denver's Hispanic heritage. Civic Center Park; call 303-534-8342.

Capitol Hill People's Fair—This city festival draws over 100,000 people for food, music and lots of browsing at over 500 shopping booths. Civic Center Park; call 303-830-1651.

June
Juneteenth—African-American celebration recalls June 19, 1865, when Texas slaves finally received word of their freedom. Five Points Area; call 303-645-3446.

Cinco de Mayo Festival

July
Cherry Blossom Festival—Tea ceremony demonstrations, bonsai displays, music and dance display the rich traditions of Denver's Japanese community. Sakura Square; call 303-295-0305.

Cherry Creek Arts Festival—Some 200 artists and craftspeople display their work in one of the country's best outdoor juried art shows. North Cherry Creek; call 303-355-2787.

September
Festival of Mountain and Plain/Taste of Colorado—A major food festival interspersed with live entertainment and dozens of arts and crafts booths. Civic Center Park; call 303-295-7900.

December
World's Largest Christmas Display—Over 40,000 colored lights illuminate the City and County Building. Civic Center Park, call 303-645-3446.

Red Rocks Amphitheater

Urban Pioneer

Call John Hickenlooper an urban pioneer. Like all intrepid settlers, he has gone into uncertain territory to set down roots and, along the way, to create a dream.

Back in 1986, Hickenlooper, a geologist by training and a house renovator by passion, found himself searching for a new career. He hit upon the concept of the microbrewery, at that time only a fledgling industry. He then chose an old warehouse in lower downtown to house his bubbly operation.

The scars from decades of neglect lay around the site he planned to use for his brewery. Once the area's bustling trade center, lined with warehouses and the rumbling clang of horse-drawn wagons, lower downtown languished over time and degenerated into an historically rich, but commercially poor, urban orphan. A few developers had dabbled in the area's revitalization,

but successes were meager.

Hickenlooper knew he faced stiff odds to transform his concept into reality. Although even his own mother had respectfully declined to invest in her son's scheme, he nonetheless attracted enough investors to open the Wynkoop Brewing Company (cum restaurant and pool hall) in 1988. In 1992, Hickenlooper opened several loft residences cleaved from his converted warehouse. Shortly thereafter, he purchased four other nearby warehouses with the help of business partner Joyce Meskis, owner of the successful Tattered Cover Bookstore. Apartments and another Tattered Cover location were on their agenda. Lower Downtown was becoming LoDo, a place with things to do and places to go.

In time, other dreamers and developers eyed Denver's historic warehouse area as worthy of investment. The decision to choose LoDo as the site for Coors Field sealed the area's fate, confirming it as the city's hottest new urban darling.

Today, Wynkoop Brewing Company (303-297-2700) is one of the nation's largest microbreweries, home to finely crafted brews such as Railyard Ale and Stout Street Stout. And Hickenlooper lives with his dream daily; his loft's address above the pool hall at 18th and Wynkoop reads, "Above Table 11."

progenitor of Denver's historic revitalization. Real estate developer Dana Crawford got the idea in the late 1960s that Denver shouldn't lose the best of its Victorian-era storefronts along Denver's oldest street, so she set out to renovate the block. The result is 18 elegant buildings filled with trendy eateries and even trendier shops. For a peek into the area's past, stop by the information kiosk at the tiny Noel Park for a walking-tour map that covers 10 historic sites.

Of particular note is the Gallup-Stanbury Building, at one time the Antlers Hotel and Tambien Saloon. Today, it houses The Market, a popular gathering place and coffee shop. Their sidewalk tables offer the city's best people-watching perches—a perfect floor show to go along with one of Denver's best cups of coffee. It's also a good place to pick up a copy of *Westword,* Denver's largest circulation alternative newspaper. *Westword* regularly carries a complete review of Denver's current entertainment options and favorite-of-the-month restaurants.

A block to the south of Larimer Square is the Denver Performing Arts Complex (PLEX) (303-893-4000), the second largest performing venue in the nation after New York City's Lincoln Center. With nine theaters, including the 2,800-seat state-of-the-art Temple Hoyne Buell Theater and the 2,600-seat Boettcher Concert Hall, PLEX is a regular stop for Broadway productions and top-flight entertainment shows. It is also the home for the Colorado Symphony Orchestra, Opera Colorado, the Denver Center Theater Company and the Colorado Ballet.

Across Cherry Creek (where one of Denver's first tent communities once stood) now sits Six Flags Elitch Gardens Amusement Park (303-595-4386). For more than 100 years, this amusement park entertained thrill-seekers with carnival rides in northwest Denver. In 1996, it was transplanted to this new $125 million, 58-acre extravaganza along the South Platte River. Denverites call the place "Wheee-Elitchs," for it's the ideal place to squeal away a few hours atop the Ferris Wheel, the antique carousel, and especially aboard the wooden rollercoaster called "Twister."

The Denver Metro Convention & Visitors Bureau is located in the Tabor Center, downtown, at 1668 Larimer St.; call 800-645-3446.

below: Brown Palace Hotel

Denver Mountain Parks

Shortly after the turn of the century, the Denver Chamber of Commerce heard a proposal to create a series of mountain parks within a day's drive of the city. The idea caught the attention of Denver Mayor Robert Speer and soon gained the support of voters. After its initial purchase of 7,000 acres, the system has grown to encompass 51 parks and nearly 14,000 acres. The 150-mile "Denver Mountain Parks Circle Drive" takes in a good sampling of the Mile High City's high-altitude real estate.

Greeley and Fort Collins

Situated on Colorado's Eastern Plains but with a western horizon cut by the Rocky Mountains, Greeley and nearby Fort Collins are the northern anchors of the state's line of Front Range cities. With their orderly and soothingly small-town atmospheres, both cities maintain distinct identities. However, they have much in common as agricultural and ranching centers, in addition to having major educational institutions.

Established in 1870 by teetotaling farmers, Greeley's namesake was Horace Greeley, editor of the influential New York *Tribune*. Greeley saw a future in Colorado's soil, and along with his agricultural editor, Nathan Meeker, he formed the Union Colony Association. The two men gathered together like-minded folks for a combined agrarian assault on the "great American desert." For a membership fee of $155, homesteaders received a town lot and farm plot, and pooled left over money for establishing public services and cleaving irrigation canals to water their crops. Twelve thousand acres were purchased at the confluence of the South Platte and Cache la Poudre rivers, with Meeker designated as the colony's leader. Within months, Greeley had 3,000 families all pulling together to create their collective American Dream.

Fort Collins' founding mirrors that of Greeley. In this case, private investors purchased an abandoned military post, Camp Collins, and subdivided it, selling memberships which included both a town and farming site, as well as a canal infrastructure.

Fond remembrances of the area's early days are found at Greeley's Centennial Village (970-350-9224), where numerous restored buildings from 1860 to 1920 portray the prairie life—from a Cheyenne teepee to a Swedish Stuga home to a Queen Anne-style mansion. The nearby Meeker Home Museum (970-350-9221) preserves the adobe dwelling of Nathan Meeker. Family artifacts and memorabilia outline the life of this

Cache la Poudre

Colorado's last remaining stretch of wild river flows in the Cache la Poudre, a straight shot west of Fort Collins along Colorado Highway 14 tracking through the Front Range to the town of Walden. The route follows the river up Poudre Canyon, climbing into the Laramie and Medicine Bow Mountains, and ending at North Park. The National Wild and Scenic Rivers Act preserves 75 miles of the Cache la Poudre from dams and water diversion.

Spectacular scenery and outdoor recreation are the twin temptations for traveling this designated state scenic byway, which covers 101 miles. At an elevation ranging between 6,200 and 8,600 feet, the landscape represents the transition zone between the prairie grasslands and the Rocky Mountains. Douglas fir, lodgepole and ponderosa pine cloak the shoulders of the rocky ravines, which are gnashed by the Cache la Poudre and its south fork. Reaching Walden, the terrain spills into North Park, a huge intermountain basin.

Respectable numbers of outdoor enthusiasts come to the region, but not in crowding masses. Anglers cast lines for trout and hardy backpackers trek into the 160,000 acres of Comanche Peak, Rawah, Neota and Cache la Poudre wilderness areas. Rafters put into the Class III and IV (difficult or very difficult) river along a 45-mile expanse, where recreational use is allowed.

Birdwatchers, too, find a special treat. The Arapaho National Wildlife Refuge outside Walden is the stage for the showy nesting rituals of the sage grouse occurring during late spring. Contact the North Park Chamber of Commerce in Walden (970-723-4600) for more information.

SuperAmerica Guide's Greeley & Fort Collins Recommendations

- Pay a visit to Greeley Centennial Village, one of the best representations of pioneer prairie life in Colorado.
- Stroll down the streets of Fort Collins Historic Old Town.
- Stop by Fort Vasquez near Platteville to explore a onetime fur trading post.
- Catch a scrimmage or two at the Denver Broncos training camp on the University of Northern Colorado campus.

Pawnee National Grassland

Pawnee Buttes

At more than 250 feet tall, the Pawnee Buttes towering over the prairie 55 miles northeast of Greeley rank as one of the Eastern Plains most impressive natural wonders. These ancient sandstone guideposts are remnants of eroded rock that have a commanding presence, serving as sentinels to countless generations of Native Americans and early Colorado pioneers.

The buttes are but one draw of the Pawnee National Grassland, a 193,000-acre hodgepodge of U.S. Forest Service (USFS) land tracts scattered across northeastern Colorado. The seemingly endless, parched expanses recall the time when this type of terrain blanketed the horizon. To early explorers, it was a monotonous and sterile environment, "tiresome to the eye and fatiguing to the spirit."

Industrious farmers saw it differently, and soon, windmills and irrigation canals nurtured the land into fields of wheat and corn. The Pawnee National Grassland was spared plows' furrows by the U.S. government, which purchased it in the 1930s. Today, they are islands of refuge for symphonies of songbirds, keen-eyed hawks and falcons, gatherings of always-wary pronghorn, and many a wily coyote.

Generally speaking, the grassland is divided into two large districts: the Crow Valley Area in the west near Briggsdale, and the Pawnee area to the east, accessible via the town of New Raymer. The 125-mile Pawnee Pioneer Trails, a Colorado Scenic and Historic Byway, connects the acreage, taking in the unspoiled high points of the low-lying terrain. Not on the designated route but near the abandoned town of Keota is one of humankind's unfortunate contributions to the grassland: a Minuteman III Intercontinental Ballistic Missile (ICBM) silo. During the Cold War, the U.S. Air Force pockmarked the region with 200 such sites.

For additional information, contact the USFS Pawnee National Grassland Ranger Station (970-353-5004), located north of Greeley on Colorado Highway 85 and "O" Street.

idealistic man, who ironically established the thriving community of Greeley and then later precipitated the expulsion of Utes from their homeland on the Western Slope.

Greeley recalls the wild west late each June at the Greeley Stampede (800-982-BULL).

Fort Collins recalls its past at Historic Old Town, a triangular-shaped section of city center with buildings dating from the 1870s. Hop aboard the Fort Collins Municipal Railway (970-224-5372) for a short ride on Sherman Street in a restored 1919 Birney streetcar. The Fort Collins Museum (970-221-6738) in the onetime Carnegie Library delves into the region's ancient past with an excellent collection of arrowheads, including points and scrapers used by Paleo-Indians who once camped 25 miles north of Fort Collins.

Fort Vasquez (970-785-2832), 17 miles south of Greeley near Platteville, presents a peek into northern Colorado's frontier days. The year was 1835 when mountain men Louis Vasquez and Andrew Sublette established the post, hoping to capitalize on the emerging trade route along the South Platte River. The expected fur trade never materialized, and eventually the fort's 12-foot-high adobe walls crumbled.

The Greeley and Fort Collins of today present a vibrant face as some 40 percent of the population is under age 44. Greeley's University of Northern Colorado (UNC) and Aims Community College, plus the Colorado State

Boulder and surrounding area

University (CSU) in Fort Collins account for this. The area's demographics are slanted ethnically toward white and young. Hispanics form the principal minority, accounting for nearly 20 percent of the total population.

Agriculture and livestock rearing dominate the economy with ConAgra, Western Sugar and National Hog Farms as major employers. In addition, there are many self-employed farmers and ranchers. Weld County, which contains Greeley, has the nation's fifth highest agricultural economy. It's said that there are four times as many cows, twice as many sheep and pigs and 20 times more chickens than people. That said, high-tech industry has a place as well with an Eastman Kodak photo processing center and a Hewlett Packard storage device facility.

Beer and football seem to go together for the two towns, with Fort Collins supplying the suds and Greeley, the gridiron. Downtown Fort Collins sports three microbreweries, notably Coopersmith's Pub and Brewing (970-498-0483), and just outside town, the massive Anheuser-Busch brewing complex (970-490-4691). Free daily tours cover the brewing process and include a look at the magnificent Budweiser Clydesdale horses.

Greeley's sports claim is the Denver Broncos, as this is where the team holds their training camp. In the six weeks

Boulder Flatirons

from July to mid-August, the four-time AFC champions strut their stuff at UNC's Nottingham Stadium. The public is welcome to watch, free of charge. Call UNC's Athletic Department at 970-351-2007 for more information.

The Greeley Convention & Visitors Bureau is located at 1407 8th Avenue; call 970-352-3566 or 800-449-3866. The Fort Collins Convention & Visitors Bureau is located at 420 S. Howes, Suite 101; call 800-274-FORT or 970-482-5821.

Boulder

Few cities enjoy a more magnificent backdrop than Boulder. The city of 96,000 rests against the first upward folds of the Rocky Mountain foothills 30 miles northwest of Denver. In Boulder's foreground rise the Flatirons, a spectacular series of sandstone outcroppings. The upthrusted formations of red rock look like the exposed, spiny backplates of a long-buried dinosaur. Indeed, the stony conglomerates were forced into their current angles around 65 million years ago, about the same time that dinosaurs became extinct.

History

Prospector, Thomas Aikins, a Missouri farmer, came here in 1858, looked at the Boulder Valley and deemed it "the loveliest of all the valleys, a landscape exceedingly beautiful." Aikins and his band were looking for gold, and in January of 1859, they found it along a narrow creek between Sunshine and Four Mile canyons. Within a month, merchants and other miners moved in and the local Arapaho found themselves with 2,000 new neighbors.

The area's gold proved to be scarce. However, rich strikes in the mountains west of the struggling town rescued Boulder from obscurity. Silver at Caribou and gold at Gold Hill kept the economy going. Later, other mineral finds, tungsten around Nederland and coal at Louisville, along with the discovery of oil and gas deposits kept the city growing through the turn of the century.

Boulder's reputation as a center for higher education started with the founding of Colorado's first school in 1860. By the time Colorado achieved statehood in 1876, the University of Colorado was already under construction. In September of 1877, a mere 44 students comprised the entire student body, all under the tutelage of one instructor. Two decades later, a group of professors from Texas chose Boulder as a Chautauqua site, and introduced the community to this organization's varied learning programs and appreciation for nature.

The first half of the 20th century left Boulder a

SuperAmerica Guide's Boulder Recommendations

- Spend an afternoon or evening on the Pearl Street Mall to shop and enjoy the street entertainers.
- Check out the heavens at both the National Center for Atmospheric Research and Fiske Planetarium and Science Center.
- Take in a radio broadcast taping of E-TOWN, held at the historic Boulder Theater.
- Drop in at Celestial Seasonings for an aromatic tour of the famed tea producer's facilities.
- Go mountain biking as Boulderites do along the Boulder Creek Path.
- Take a rock climbing lesson to see the heights of Eldorado Canyon or the famous Flatirons.

relatively quiet place, home to the university and not much more. High-technology government agencies and industries discovered the area in the 1950s and 60s. The Atomic Energy Commission opened its secret weapons plant, Rocky Flats, just south of Boulder. The National Center for Atmospheric Research (NCAR), the Environmental Science Services Administration (ESSA) and the National Oceanic and Atmospheric Administration (NOAA) set up shop as well. Private concerns like IBM and Storage Technology moved in too. Boulder's cerebral identity is well deserved.

Boulder is also worthy of its reputation as a "New Age" center. In the 1960s, Boulder was Colorado's hippie capital, a town filled with counter-culture thinkers. More than a few flower children stayed on to follow their dreams. Mo Siegel founded Celestial Seasonings and brewed up an herbal tea empire. Tibetan Buddhist Chögyam Trungpa Rinpoche started the Naropa Institute in 1974. Two years later, the Boulder School of Massage Therapy opened, and is now ranked among the country's most prestigious bodywork institutes.

Contemporary Aspects

Boulder is one of Colorado's most livable cities, mixing cosmopolitan amenities with a good dose of Mother Nature. Boulderites know they have a good thing going and want to keep it that way. Residential growth is limited to two percent annually. On more than one occasion, big business with big growth plans have been given a firm "no thank you" by city planners.

While the economy is supported by a number of computer, aerospace, scientific and research firms, it is CU, the University of Colorado, that sets Boulder's

Rock Climbing: Learning the Ropes

Boulder is aptly named. Only minutes from downtown, thick slabs of pink sandstone thrust skyward like hands saluting the Rocky Mountains. Says Casey Newman, director of the Boulder Rock School, "For a climber this is heaven—there's great climbing right in the city. Increase the radius a bit and some 20 to 25 different cliffs and peaks offer miles of routes."

Little wonder that Boulder supports an estimated population of 5,000 "adrenaline addicts." As one resident puts it, "there are more climbers per square foot here than anywhere else on earth."

The city also pulls in thousands of "wanna-know-the-ropes" visitors from all over the world. Rock climbing as a sport is hitting the mainstream; women and children are the fastest growing segment of new entrants.

This isn't a sport to be taken lightly—lessons are a must. And while there are many qualified climbing guides in Boulder, the long-standing choice for training is the Boulder Rock School. Programs offered throughout the year cover everything from beginner climbing safety techniques to advanced anchor and lead clinics. There are also classes geared exclusively to women and children. For more information, call the Boulder Rock School at 303-447-2804.

pace. Each year, more than 25,000 students enroll in classes that cover more than 150 fields of study, including 51 different graduate schools. CU is known academically for its science programs, followed by psychology, engineering and law, but its highest marks go to the stunning campus of red-tile-roofed buildings. Like any university town, Boulder has an ample dose of well-educated youth. Nearly 60 percent of the city is under age 40. More than 25 percent of the population holds a graduate degree. Consequently, to say that Boulder has a certain vitality is an understatement at best.

Attractions

People-watching may be Boulder's prize attraction. And the place to do it is the Pearl Street Mall. Considered one of the nation's most successful open-air pedestrian malls, this byway between 11th and 15th streets is set with sculptures, fountains and cozy sitting areas. It never fails to deliver an eyeful of zany diversions. In fact, at times it seems more like a circus parade than a shopping district. Jugglers, mimes and street musicians treat the brick-lined street as their stage.

A slightly more down-to-earth side of Boulder is revealed at the National Center for Atmospheric Research (NCAR) (303-497-1000) located atop Table Mesa. Self-guided tours and interactive exhibits introduce visitors to the inner workings of the world's weather. The great blue yonder gets additional attention at the Fiske Planetarium and Science Center (303-492-5001) on the campus of the University of Colorado. Regularly scheduled star-gazing seminars and laser light shows probe the mysteries of the celestial dome.

Celestial in Boulder, however, means Celestial Seasonings. The corporate headquarters of the renowned herbal tea producer is located just north of town. Free daily tours cover the tea-packaging

Celestial Seasonings

Boulder's cure for a stuffy nose is Celestial Seasonings. One whiff of the 5,000 or so bales of peppermint stored in a special isolation room here clears any clogged sinus passages.

The "Mint Room" is one of several stops on a factory tour of the world famous herbal tea company headquartered northeast of Boulder on Sleepytime Drive. The 45-minute stroll takes visitors—some 50,000 annually—through the plant to see how herbs and spices are processed and packaged. An art gallery displays the original paintings for those fanciful illustrations used on Celestial Seasonings' boxes. An interesting teapot collection rounds out the tour.

Mo Siegel, the founder of Celestial Seasonings, started gathering wild herbs for natural teas in 1969 while he was living near Aspen. By 1970, he was in Boulder, where he discovered a rich harvest of herbs and started packaging his finds in hand-sewn muslin bags for local health food stores. His burgeoning herbal tea business attracted the interest of food conglomerate Kraft, Inc., which purchased the company in 1984. The arrangement lasted a mere four years before Kraft sold the company back to its current management. Ever since, they've been brewing up the sweet smell of success.

Tours of Celestial Seasonings are on a first come basis, Monday through Saturday, every hour starting at 10 a.m. with the last tour of the day at 3 p.m. Sunday hours are from 11 a.m. to 3 p.m. Free admission. For more information, call 303-581-1202.

process amidst the rich aromas of dozens of spices and herbs. It's the finest olfactory factory in the nation.

For visual stimulation, BMoCA, the Boulder Museum of Contemporary Art (303-443-2122), exhibits works by local artists in addition to live performances of music, dance and poetry. The Leanin' Tree Museum of Western Art (303-530-1442), located northeast toward Longmont, holds a fine collection of contemporary western artwork including pieces from the National Academy of Western Art and Cowboy Artists of America. Historic western memorabilia and artifacts are displayed at several sites around Boulder including CU's Heritage Center (303-492-6329) and the University of Colorado Museum (303-492-6892) in the Henderson Building. Add to this the Boulder Museum of History (303-449-3464), which features an excellent clothing collection, particularly fancy-beaded dresses from the 1920s.

Pearl Street Mall, Boulder

Nature

Clearly, one of the reasons that people choose to live in Boulder is its accessibility to nature. All told, the city, along with Boulder County, contains approximately 80,000 acres of open space as well as nearly 7,000 acres of park and 150 miles of hiking trails.

The most beloved swath of Mother Nature is the Boulder Creek Path, which runs for 16 miles right through town. Starting at Boulder Canyon, the trail skirts along Canyon Boulevard, then runs near Arapahoe Road before heading out into the Eastern Plains. Many Boulderites use the trail

Boulder Annual Festivals and Events

February

Chocolate Lover's Fling
All-you-can eat chocolate binge on amateur and professional creations. Boulder; call 303-449-8623.

May

Kinetic Conveyance Challenge
Contestants race zany human-powered contraptions across mud flats and water at Boulder Reservoir. Boulder Reservoir; call 303-694-6300.

Boulder Creek Festival
Parade, carnival and dance with lots of activities for kids. Boulder Creek; call 303-441-4420

Bolder Boulder 10K
Prestigious run that attracts more than 40,000 participants. Folsom Stadium, University of Colorado; call 303-444-RACE.

June to August

Colorado Music Festival
Classical music concerts held in the lovely 1898 Chautauqua Auditorium; call 303-449-1397.

Colorado Shakespeare Festival
Company members and well-known guest performers present Shakespeare plays in an outdoor garden setting. Mary Rippon Outdoor Theater; call 303-492-0554.

August

Rocky Mountain Bluegrass Festival
Musicians from across the globe strum and fiddle in a meadow next to the St. Vrain River. Rocky Grass Hollow, Lyons; call 303-449-6007.

September

Boulder Blues Festival
Local and internationally known musicians sing the blues. Boulder Courthouse Area; call 303-443-5858.

as their commuter expressway, foregoing cars for mountain bikes, in-line skates or simply a good pair of walking shoes.

Hiking is not so much a pastime in Boulder as it is a passion. And for good reason; the hills above the city are stitched with trails. The most accessible trailheads begin at Chautauqua Park, Flagstaff Mountain and at Table Mesa near the National Center for Atmospheric Research, then track up toward Green Mountain, Devils Thumb and Bear Peak. The Boulder Chamber of Commerce sells a good trail map of the mountain parks that outlines the length and difficulty of the various trails.

E-TOWN

"Direct from the foothills of the Rocky Mountains, this is **E-TOWN."**

It's Sunday evening at the historic Boulder Theater and co-producer Helen Forster has just announced another edition of Boulder's voice to the world: E-TOWN, an environmentally minded radio variety show taped live before a studio audience. The show is regularly carried by National Public Radio to more than 150 cities across the U.S. Call it Boulder's version of *The Prairie Home Companion*.

Husband-and-wife team Nick and Helen Forster co-produce the show. He's a skillful and imaginative musician and former member of the Grammy-nominated bluegrass band, Hot Rize. She's an actress, writer, singer and former co-producer/owner of the Telluride Bluegrass Festival. In 1991, they harmonized their considerable talents to launch E-TOWN.

The 90-minute taping sessions follow an easy-going format mixing top-flight entertainment with discussions on the environment. Nick Forster, along with the house band, the E-Tones, warms up the audience before the appearance of the night's guest stars. Performers have included the likes of Joan Baez, Lyle Lovett and James Taylor. After a couple of sets, Helen presents this week's "E-Chievement Award," which recognizes individuals and organizations around the country who have implemented positive solutions to environmental and social problems. More music follows, generally from a well-known local talent. Then, Nick introduces the speaker for the evening, who could be anyone from former president Jimmy Carter to consumer advocate Ralph Nader.

By any measure, it's a lot of work and a lot of fun to put together a radio broadcast. The audience gets to clap and hoot and holler, while sound technicians and stage assistants scurry around flipping dials and queuing performers for their takes. As sometimes happens, a set gets flubbed and then it's time for a re-tape. Out-takes are part of the E-TOWN experience, and besides, nobody minds hearing an instant replay from these entertainers.

For information, call 303-443-8698, or check out their Website at http://www.etown.org.

Many Boulderites prefer to leave the path and head straight up the sandstone canyon walls that line many of the trails. Boulder is internationally famous as a rock-climbing nirvana. Several climbing and mountaineering schools are based here, offering short training courses that show novices the ropes. In the course of a day's training, almost anyone in relatively good condition can sample the thrill of tackling the crags of the Flatirons or a wall in Eldorado Canyon.

When the snow starts flying, Boulderites have their own winter playground only 21 miles way. Eldora Mountain Resort (303-440-8700) will never compete with the likes of Vail or Aspen, but it is convenient and sports a nice vertical drop of 1,400 feet that is served by nine lifts. Eldora is perhaps better known for its Nordic Center with 28 miles of groomed trails and access to several trails that run through the Roosevelt National Forest.

Nightlife

As might be expected in a university town, there are plenty of nighttime diversions. Topping the list of favorite places to wile away a few hours is the Pearl Street Mall. Warm summer evenings bring out plenty of street performers and the sidewalk cafes are packed to overflowing. Nearby taverns and brew pubs—the Oasis Brewery & Restaurant (303-449-0363), the Marquee Club (303-447-1803), the James Pub and Grille (303-449-1922) and a half-dozen others—make downtown Boulder the place to see and be seen.

Boulder also has its share of

high-brow entertainment. Chautauqua Park Auditorium (303-442-3282) hosts a regular summer concert series drawing professional musicians as part of the Colorado Music Festival. The Mary Rippon Theater on the University of Colorado campus is the setting for the annual Colorado Shakespeare Festival (303-492-0554). For something distinctly Boulder, the Naropa Institute Performing Arts Center (303-546-3574) carries a varied schedule of talent from poetry readings to dance performances. The Boulder Convention & Visitors Bureau is located at 2440 Pearl Street; call 303-442-2911 or 800-444-0447.

The Peak to Peak Highway

Colorado's oldest picturesque driving excursion is the Peak to Peak Scenic and Historic Byway, established in 1918. Like folks from the turn of the century, today's Front Range urban escapists like the fact that this 55-mile route is easily accessible from both Denver and Boulder. While it is close to major cities, it offers a splendid view of Colorado's natural beauty.

The road follows Colorado Highways 72 and 7 north from Central City to Estes Park (or vice versa), delivering a windshield full of wooded valleys and breathtaking vistas of the Continental Divide. Golden Gate Canyon State Park, Arapaho and Roosevelt National Forests, the Indian Peaks Wilderness Area and Rocky Mountain National Park all lie within the road's reach.

Civilization isn't far away, however, as small towns like Ward, Nederland and Allenspark serve as good places to stop and browse high-country galleries and shops. Gold Lake Mountain Resort (800-450-3544), 12 miles northwest from Nederland off Colorado Highway 72, tempts outdoor enthusiasts with a full range of seasonal activities: hiking, canoeing, rock climbing, fly-fishing and horseback riding in

Central City Name-dropping

Central City's mineral wealth and subsequent mass immigration made it Colorado's largest and most vibrant city in the 1860s. Celebrities like Mark Twain, Walt Whitman, Oscar Wilde and the Baron de Rothschild made it a "must stop" on their meanderings through the West. When President Ulysses S. Grant rode into town in 1873, the sidewalk to his hotel was sheathed in silver ingots.

Celebrity also followed a few of Central City's onetime residents:

- George Mortimer Pullman, of Pullman railroad car fame, conjured up the idea of a luxurious hotel room on wheels while toiling as a miner here.
- Henry Stanley reported the news for the *Central City Register* before trading the Colorado mountains for the African savanna to search for Dr. Livingston.
- John Stetson sold his first wide-brimmed "Boss of the Plains" hat in Central City, creating a cowboy fashion statement which still endures.

The Face on the Barroom Floor

The portrait of a young woman with wispy brown curls, full red lips and smiling eyes is perhaps the most beguiling face in Colorado. Her place of honor, however, is on the floor of an old saloon at the Teller House, considered during Central City's boom years as the best hotel between Kansas City and San Francisco.

As the legend goes, the image was drawn by an itinerant artist in exchange for a drink. The truth is that a *Denver Post* artist, Herndon Davis, painted it on the floor in 1936 on a lark.

The hoax, however, has had a lasting effect. H. Antoine D'Arcy penned a poem about the painting, *The Face on the Barroom Floor*, which later inspired the creation of a piece to commemorate the 1978 centennial of the Central City Opera. Since its premiere, it has gained enormous acclaim, becoming the most performed one-act opera in the nation.

Chapel on the Peak to Peak Highway

the summer, and cross-country skiing, snowshoeing and ice skating in the winter.

Colorado history is amply evident as well, particularly at Black Hawk and Central City. Indeed, the two towns mark the blast off point of the state's mining era. Magnificently rich mines helped spawn the area's designation as the "Richest Square Mile on Earth," firmly establishing Colorado as a prospector's dream come true.

John H. Gregory, a mule-skinner turned miner, produced the first evidence of "Gregory Gulch"'s incredible wealth in May of 1859. Other prospectors eyed his diggings along North Clear Creek, dug in themselves and soon saw the glimmer of gold. Camps sprang up virtually overnight—Mountain City, Nevadaville, Gregory Point, Dogtown, Missouri City, Hoosier City and Central City, the latter of which was named for its center-of-the-gulch locale. Over time, the area produced in excess of $500 million in mineral treasure.

By the turn of the century, the scarred hills around the towns had yielded the best of their fabulous fortunes. The area's population, which crested at 40,000, dwindled to a mere 400 by 1925. Central City and Black Hawk, surviving on summer tourists' curiosity about the towns' faded Victorian splendor, eked out an existence until 1990. That year, Colorado voters amended the state constitution to permit low-stakes gambling ($5 maximum bet), instantly revitalizing the timeworn towns. Some 30 casinos now line the narrow streets of Central City and Black Hawk. Historic storefronts and newly created look-alikes ring with the sound of 8,600 slot machines, while inside, the flutter of poker cards whiz across the tables.

When the gambling glitz wears thin, a number of historical sites recall past glory days. Gilpin County Historical Society (303-582-5283), located in the old high school, displays mining equipment and vintage clothing. For a walk down memory lane, sign up for one of the society's regularly scheduled events to explore the "Little Kingdom of Gilpin"—mines, mills, cemeteries and even a few ghosts.

Friendly spirits in the guise of knowledgeable docents await at restored historic homes such as Black Hawk's Lace House (303-582-5221), named for its delicate Carpenter Gothic filigreed facade, and Central City's Thomas-Billings House (303-582-5283), a respectable middle-class abode of the 1890s.

The Central City Opera House (303-292-6700), built in 1878 by Welsh and Cornish miners, is a Victorian gem. Its sturdy stone exterior speaks of the fortitude that miners possessed in order to pursue their

SuperAmerica Guide's Rocky Mountain National Park Recommendations

- Plan a morning's hike along one of the park's many easy or moderate trails in the Moraine Park, Bear Lake or Glacier Basin areas.
- Drive Old Fall River Road up to the Alpine Visitor Center, then take Trail Ridge Road back down to either Estes Park or Grand Lake.
- Participate in one of the many ranger-led hikes or campfire chats.
- Check out the interesting displays at the Park Visitor Center / Headquarters, Alpine Visitor Center and Moraine Park Museum.

ROOSEVELT NATIONAL FOREST
COMANCHE PEAK WILDERNESS
NEOTA WILDERNESS
Comanche Pk (12,702)
Stormy Pks (12,135)
Cameron Pass (10,276)
Long Draw
La Poudre Pass (10,194)
Long Draw Reservoir
COLORADO STATE FOREST
RANGE
Hagues Pk (13,560)
Mummy Mtn. (13,425)
Mt Ypsilon (13,514)
MUMMY
Mt Richthofen (12,940)
Crystal L.
Lawn L.
Specimen Mountain (12,489)
Medicine Bow Curve
Alpine Visitor Center
Mt Chiquita (13,069)
Ypsilon L
Fall River Pass
Black Canyon Creek
Continental Divide
Poudre Lake
Mt Chapin (12,454)
Gore Range
Lava Cliffs
Milner Pass (10,758)
Highest Point on Road (12,183)
Fall River Road ← one way - closed in winter
Big horn Mountain (11,463)
The Needles (10,068)
Fall River
Red Mountain (11,605)
Iceberg Pass (11,827)
Trail Ridge Road
Sundance Mountain (12,466)
Fall River Entrance Station
Rock Cut
Rainbow Curve
Beaver Ponds
Mt Nimbus (12,705)
Colorado River Trailhead
Road closed from here east to Many Parks Curve mid-October to June
Farview Curve
Forest Canyon
34
Aspenglen
Deer Ridge Junction Trailhead
Hidden Valley
Many Parks Curve
Road closed from here west to Colorado River Trailhead mid-October to June
Gorge Lakes
Timber Creek
Never Summer Ranch
Mt Ida (12,700)
36
Big Thompson River
Estes Park
Moraine Park
Visitor Center Park Headquarters
ROCKY
Stones Pk (12,922)
Parking for Bear Lake Shuttle Bus
Nakai Pk (12,216)
Mt Flattop (12,324)
Hallet Pk (12,713)
Bear Lake Road
Glacier Basin
Tonahutu Creek
Glacier Creek
ARAPAHO NATIONAL FOREST
34
Lily Lake Visitor Center
Mt Patterson (11,424)
MOUNTAIN
Estes Cone (11,006)
N. Fork of the Colorado
Andrews Glacier
N. Inlet
Twin Sisters (11,428)
Longs Peak
Grand Lake Entrance
Kawuneeche Visitor Center
Taylor Pk (13,153)
Taylor Glacier
Grand Lake
NATIONAL
Longs Pk (14,255)
Grand Lake
Andrews Pk (12,566)
Chiefs Head (13,579)
Mt Meeker (13,911)
Meeker Park
Shadow Mtn Lake
East Inlet Trailhead
East Inlet
Mt Craig (12,007)
7
Wild Basin Trailhead
Shadow Mtn
Olive Ridge
Green Ridge
Mt Bryant (11,034)
PARK
Isolation Pk (13,118)
N. St. Vrain Cr
Allenspark
Mt Adams (12,121)
Mt Copeland (13,176)
Mt Meadow (11,632)
Lake Granby
Twin Peaks (11,957)
Mt Watanga (12,375)
Ogalalla Pk (13,138)
Mt St. Vrain (12,162)
ROOSEVELT NATIONAL FOREST
INDIAN PEAKS WILDERNESS
72
ARAPAHO NATIONAL FOREST
Arapaho National Recreation Area
14

The Front Range from Trail Ridge Road

precarious profession. The opera house's original hickory wood chairs testify to the fortitude of the miners' backsides, too. The simple seats encourage a sit-up-straight-and-take-notice posture, though that's hardly necessary as the opera company attracts top talent for its summer schedule of two operas and one operetta, all sung in English.

Artists appreciate the theater's cozy feeling, for the hall holds less than 800 people. Its production quality rivals that of far grander houses. It's also a place of time-honored tradition, not only as a training ground for operatic stars, but also as a venue to re-stage classics like *Camille* and *The Merry Widow*. Past performers have featured the voices of such greats as Lillian Gish and Beverly Sills.

Less respectable ladies had their own voice in raucous Central City, and the town remembers them during the annual late-June Lou Bunch Day. Main Street takes on the rowdy feel of a bygone era as residents pay tribute to its last and most famous "soiled dove" with brass bed races followed by the Madams and Miners Ball.

Longs Peak Scottish Fair

The sound of bagpipes rings through the Estes Park valley come mid-September with the annual Longs Peak Scottish Fair (800-44-ESTES). More than 20,000 people join a long-weekend Celtic gathering of the clans to watch hammer throws and caber (tree trunk) tosses, listen to drumming competitions, do a highland jig and marvel at traditional tattoos filled with pomp and pageantry.

Rocky Mountain National Park

At only 415 square miles (one-tenth the acreage of Yellowstone National Park), Rocky Mountain National Park nonetheless delivers big on superb scenery. Draped across the Continental Divide northwest of Boulder, the park unfurls high mountain terrain from alpine glacial valleys to lush pine forests meadowed with wildflowers. Peaks, 78 of them over 12,000 feet, crumple the earth with vertical vistas. Indeed, a third of the park is above timberline.

The Colorado River, in addition to both the Cache la Poudre and the Big Thompson rivers, has its headwaters in the park. Within this protected sanctuary reside dozens of animal, bird and fish species—bighorn sheep, elk, moose, mountain lions, bald eagles, hawks, greenback trout—sheltered by a diverse environment. Stunted tundra, forests of Englemann spruce,

left: Rocky Mountain National Park

Estes Park

An overview of Estes Park

Each year, some three million visitors vacation at Rocky Mountain National Park. A good many of them pass through Estes Park, the eastern gateway to the preserve. During the height of the summer season, the otherwise quiet community teems with a diverse cross-section of guests, everyone from hearty backcountry backpackers to leisure-minded tourists. Comfortable accommodations are plentiful, as are good restaurants. There are scores of nature pursuits perfect for day trips or multiday adventures.

The Estes Park area has been a favorite montane sanctuary for generations. Both Ute and Arapaho peoples summered amid its pristine and picturesque glacial valleys. Joel Estes homesteaded the land between the Big Thompson and Fall rivers in 1860. Estes, his wife and 13 children took in William Byers, the editor of the *Rocky Mountain News*, when he came in 1864 to climb 14,255-foot Longs Peak. Byers failed to reach the mountain's summit, but he wrote glowing reports of the spectacular scenery and named the place after his host: Estes Park.

By the time an adventurous and acquisitive Irish aristocrat, Lord Dunraven, came to Estes Park in the 1870s, tourists in the form of hunters and mountaineers were already extolling the virtues of the territory. Dunraven proceeded to acquire 15,000 acres for his sole noble pleasure. The fact that he was a foreigner, and therefore restricted from homesteading, didn't dissuade him. He simply skirted the law, having others (not always alive) front for him on 160-acre parcels, which he then quietly purchased and transferred to his Britain-based "English company." In time, legitimate homesteaders discovered his scheme and forced him into leasing arrangements. Dunraven eventually grew tired of the squabbles, selling most of his holdings to a partnership headed by Freelan O. Stanley.

Stanley, a wealthy inventor, had come to Colorado to ease his tuberculosis. The clear, alpine air inspired him, and soon he envisioned Estes Park as the ideal place for overworked Victorian socialites to come and let off steam. In 1909, he opened the posh Stanley Hotel (970-586-3371), ferrying guests to the mountain retreat from Lyons, Colorado via the jaunty Stanley Steamer Mountain Wagons. Tourists came by the thousands. With the establishment of Rocky Mountain National Park in 1915, Estes Park's position as Colorado's premier nature destination was firmly secured.

The Greek Revival-style Stanley Hotel is still one of Estes Park's most popular accommodations, partly due to its historic presence and partly because it was the inspiration for Stephen King's psycho-thriller,

Estes Park

The Shining. Daily tours take guests through ornate public rooms, with stops for a few ghost stories.

The story at the MacGregor Ranch (970-586-3749) is that of Alexander Q. MacGregor, an early rancher and staunch opponent to Lord Dunraven's real estate dealings. Photographic exhibits, documents, paintings and household items chronicle ranch life from the late 1800s to the mid 20th century. At the Estes Park Historical Museum (970-586-6256) the valley's heritage is rounded out with pioneer artifacts.

Elkhorn Avenue is the commercial heartline of Estes Park and shopping central for the nature weary. Sweet aromas of taffy and caramel corn scent the byway, which is lined with a good many of the town's boutiques, galleries and gift shops. Fine establishments such as Artisans of Colorado, the Ricker-Bartlett Casting Studios, or the Charles Eagle Plume Gallery and Museum of Native American Arts shouldn't be overlooked.

Nature, though, can't be overlooked in Estes Park. It's all around. On any given day from June to September, one can sample any number of treats from this high-country smorgasbord of recreational pastimes. The Aerial Tram (970-586-3675) spreads out the landscape from atop Prospect Mountain, while at ground level the Lake Estes Hike & Bike Trail circumnavigates Lake Estes. More rigorous cycling outings into nearby Roosevelt National Forest can be arranged through Colorado Bicycling Adventures (970-586-3440).

For people who prefer four wheels, several four-wheel drive routes, such as Johnny Park Road off Colorado Highway 7 and Pole Hill Road off U.S. Highway 36, take in the scenic highlights of roads less traveled. American Wilderness Tours (970-586-4237) takes over the steering wheel on guided backcountry drive outings guaranteed to visit the spots most people miss.

River rafters head down the Cache la Poudre River with outfits like Estes Park Mountain Shop (970-586-6548) or Estes Park Adventures (970-586-2303). Adventure seekers will find that the Colorado Mountain School (970-586-5758) offers several rock-climbing courses from introductory classes to guided technical ascents. Hikers might want to lace up boots for trails such as the 1.5-mile Lily Mountain Trail offering grand views of the Front Range, or the 2.5-mile Lion Gulch Trail to Homestead Meadows. More challenging is the Crosier Mountain Trail, 8 miles and 2,000 feet up into sprightly aspen groves. Hikers not fond of carrying their own packs might want to sign on with Keno's Llama & Guest Ranch (970-586-2827) for an escorted walk to the top of Teddy's Teeth.

The Estes Park Visitor Center is located at the intersection of U.S. Highways 34 and 36; call 970-586-4431 or 800-44-ESTES.

swatches of red-barked ponderosa pine, slopes of aspen and rivers edged with willows sweep across the land.

Credit goes to Enos Mills, naturalist and ardent conservationist, for establishing the movement that promoted this area as a national park. It was so designated in 1915, and America's tenth national park quickly became a top tourist destination. By 1920, Old Fall River was cut to lead guests high into the park's panoramas. Soon, superintendent Roger Toll was laying out additional routes, Trail Ridge Road and Bear Lake Road, to accommodate a growing number of automobile adventurers.

Indeed, park personnel estimate that 80 to 85 percent of visitors experience the park from cars. Three spectacular scenic drives encourage auto excursions, delivering, despite the occasional traffic jam, peeks at vistas and valleys easily worth a moment or two of behind-the-wheel frustration. It's a good idea to ensure that your car is up to the challenging altitude, and to check road conditions at 970-586-1333 before heading out. Park visitor centers sell auto tapes and books with information about historic spots, geological sites and wildlife.

Trail Ridge Road

The 48-mile stretch of U.S. Highway 34, by far the most popular route, takes about three hours one-way (with stops) to snake across the Continental Divide to Grand Lake from Estes Park. Generations of Native Americans followed roughly the same trail as a way into Middle Park, or vice versa, into the Great

Plains. In fact, evidence exists of prehistoric peoples who once hunted in the alpine tundra here 11,000 years ago.

Deer Junction is the eastern terminus at 8,940 feet elevation and from there, the asphalt threads to a summit at 12,183 feet before descending into the Kawuneeche Valley. Trail Ridge Road is the highest continuous paved road in the U.S. At the higher elevations, the landscape opens into alpine tundra, not unlike the terrain of the Arctic. The Alpine Visitor Center located atop Fall River Pass contains excellent exhibits on this extraordinary ecosystem. Pullouts along the route such as "Many Parks Curve" and "Rock Cut" offer incredible views of the Front Range and opportunities to watch herds of elk or the antics of yellow-bellied marmots and tiny pikas. Trail Ridge Road is open from late May until mid-October, depending on the weather.

Old Fall River Road

Completed in 1920, this is the

Rocky Mountain National Park Facilities

Rocky Mountain National Park has three principal entrances: on the east via U.S. Highway 34 and 36 or Colorado Highway 7 through Estes Park, and on the western side of the Continental Divide at Grand Lake via U.S. Highway 34. The park has an extensive array of ranger-led hikes and campfire chats, which focus on topics ranging from bird behavior to beaver dam building. Children from ages four to twelve might want to ask for a Rocky's Junior Ranger activity book filled with games and fun nature facts. The park entrance fee is $10 per vehicle for a week's stay, and $5 per hiker, motorcyclist or bicyclist.

Five visitor centers welcome guests to Rocky Mountain National Park. National Park Service (NPS) rangers are on duty to answer questions and give advice, while interpretive centers outline the park's ecosystem, terrain and wildlife.

Park Visitor Center/ Headquarters near Estes Park is open daily from 8 a.m. to 9 p.m. in the summer, and 8 a.m. to 5 p.m. the rest of the year; it is closed on Christmas day. An orientation film and relief model put the park in perspective. Call 970-586-1206.

Kawuneeche Visitor Center is located on the western side of the Continental Divide near Grand Lake. The center is open daily 7 a.m. to 7 p.m. in the summer, and 8 a.m. to 5 p.m. the rest of the year; it is closed Christmas day. Multimedia displays give an excellent park overview. Call 970-627-3471.

Moraine Park Museum is 2.5 miles southwest of the park headquarters and is only open from mid-May to mid-October. Exhibits designed by the Denver Museum of Natural History showcase the history, flora and fauna of the park.

Alpine Visitor Center, atop Fall River Pass, is open during the summer and features extensive information about the park's tundra region. A concessionaire operates the park's most complete gift shop and bookstore and the only food/beverage spot within the park.

Lily Lake Visitor Center is located eight miles south of Estes Park on Colorado Highway 7 and is only open during the peak summer season. Park literature and exhibits cover the history, flora and fauna of the park. Information regarding Roosevelt National Forest is also available here.

Numerous hotels, motels, cabins and RV sites are available in both Estes Park and Grand Lake. In addition, within the park itself are five roadside campgrounds and one site, Sprague Lake Handicamp, for people with disabilities.

Campground	Tent/RV Sites	Cost	Open / Day Limitation	Reservations
Aspenglen	54	$12/night	Open year-round; 7 day max stay	First-come, first served
Glacier Basin	150	$14/night	Open June to September	Reservation required Memorial Day to September; 800-365-2267
Longs Peak	26 tents; no RVs	$12/night	Open year-round; 3 day max stay	First-come, first served
Moraine Park	247	$12 non-reserved; $14 reserved	Open year-round; 7 day max stay	Reservation required Memorial Day to September; 800-365-2267
Sprague Lake Handicamp	One site, for 12 people	$15	Open year-round; 3 day max stay	Reservation required; 970-586-1242
Timber Creek	100	$12/night	Open year-round; 7 day max stay	First-come; first served

left: Longs Peak from Rock Cut on Trail Ridge Road

original road through the park. It follows an old Arapaho pass through the mountains, which they called the "Dog's Trail" since dogs were used to pull the heavy travois laden with their supplies. Today, it's an adventurous alternative to Trail Ridge Road. Leaving from Endovalley, the one-way-only gravel road covers nearly 10 miles, climbing Mount Chapin and negotiating 15 tight switchbacks to reach the Alpine Visitor Center. Expect to mosey along at about 10 MPH, a pace that provides ample opportunity to enjoy the view of Fall River Canyon. Trailers and RVs more than 25 feet long are restricted from taking the route.

Bear Lake Road

Beginning at Moraine Park, this paved, 10-mile drive is a favorite for hikers as it leads past several trailheads on its way up to Bear Lake. Consequently, the parking lot at Bear Lake is generally full during the summer months. An alternative is to park at the Glacier Basin parking lot, then take the free shuttle bus four miles to Bear Lake. The bus runs frequently and stops at several trailheads along the way, making it ideal transportation for day hikers wishing to take in the easy and moderate trails to Nymph Lake, Bierstadt Lake, Emerald Lake or Alberta Falls. It's the best way to capture the essence of what Enos Mills once wrote:

> *This is a beautiful world, and all who go out under the open sky will feel the gentle, kindly influence of nature and hear her good tidings.*

Downtown Colorado Springs

SuperAmerica Guide's Colorado Springs Recommendations

- Hop aboard the Manitou and Pikes Peak Cog Railway for an ascent of Pikes Peak.
- Time a visit to the Air Force Academy to see the cadets march in formation on their way to lunch.
- Spend a few hours with champions at the ProRodeo Hall of Fame & Museum and also at the U.S. Olympic Complex.
- Drive through Garden of the Gods to see the whimsical rock formations of this National Natural Landmark.
- Explore the shops and attractions of quaint Manitou Springs.
- Drive the Gold Belt Tour Scenic and Historic Byway leading to Cripple Creek. Pay a visit to the Royal Gorge Bridge, the world's highest suspension bridge.

Bighorn Sheep

The introduction of domesticated sheep (and their diseases), along with the encroachment of man, nearly decimated the bighorn sheep population in Rocky Mountain National Park. However, strict U.S. Forest Service conservation efforts have saved the animals.

One of the best viewing spots is at Sheep Lakes in Horseshoe Park, where during the May to June lambing season, ewes are fond of the natural mineral licks. The rock-walkers are also often seen on the stony escarpments along Lumpy Ridge north of Estes Park and on Sheep Mountain, just south of the Continental Divide turn-out on the park's western side.

Recreation

Hiking

More than 350 miles of trails wind through Rocky Mountain National Park, making this the most popular activity of the park. Detailed trail maps are available at the park visitor centers and outline the options, which range from easy nature trails with little vertical elevation gain to strenuous ascents of the park's alpine peaks. Be sure to wear comfortable shoes, take clean drinking water along (even for a short stroll) and pay heed to lightning storms that usually develop in the late afternoon. Early morning hikes ensure the best weather and chances to observe wildlife.

Fishing

A Colorado State Fishing license is required to fish the streams and lakes in the park. In some areas, such as Bear Lake, fishing is forbidden. Size limits and catch-and-release requirements are also imposed, so check at park headquarters for the latest fishing brochure. The high altitude and cold waters don't promise large fish, but instead, plenty of feisty rainbow, brook, German brown and cutthroat trout.

Horseback Riding

Approximately 260 miles of the park's trail system are open to equestrians and pack animals. Deer Mountain, Horseshoe Park, Moraine Park, Glacier Basin and Emerald Mountain are the primary zones open to horses, and in these areas nearly 80 percent of the trails are equipped with hitch racks. In addition, park concessionaires offer several scenic half-day and day-long saddle trips, guiding visitors to Beaver Meadows, Mill Creek, or along the Old Ute Trail. Call Glacier Creek Stables at 970-586-3244 for the Glacier Creek area, and Moraine Park Stables at 970-586-2327 for the Moraine Park area.

Backcountry Backpacking

Permits are required to spend the night in any backcountry areas within the park. Permits may be obtained at the park headquarters, Kawuneeche Visitor Center and during the summer at the Longs Peak and Wild Basin ranger stations. Reservations are required for May to mid-August and cost $10; call 970-586-1242.

Climbing

Rock climbing is a treat in Rocky Mountain National Park, offering great bouldering and challenging technical ascents. No permit is required unless there is an overnight stay. The best place to see climbers practicing belays is at Lumpy Ridge in the MacGregor Park area north of Estes Park. For climbing information and lessons, contact the Colorado Mountain School in Estes Park at 970-586-5758.

Cycling

All hiking trails are off limits to bicycles. Therefore, the only cycling routes follow the principal roads in the park: Bear Lake Road, Trail Ridge

left: Chapel at the Air Force Academy

Colorado Springs and surrounding area

Road and a loop in Horseshoe Park. No fee is required other than the standard park entrance charge for cyclists. Heavy vehicle traffic is common, and bikers should prepare for unpredictable weather and high altitude.

Swimming

In a word: don't. Mountain water is exceedingly cold and quickly induces hypothermia, the condition that results when the body is too chilled to warm itself adequately. Further, *giardia lamblia*, tiny protozoa, thrive in the streams and lakes. Diarrhea, cramps and bloating are the nasty effects that accompany giardiasis. Don't drink the water.

Cross-country Skiing/Snowshoeing/Snowmobiling

During the winter, ranger-led cross-country ski tours depart on Saturdays at the Kawuneeche Visitor Center. Numerous self-guided trails originate at Moraine Park, Longs Peak, Timber Creek and Glacier Basin campgrounds as well. Ranger-led snowshoe hikes leave from Bear Lake on

Saturdays and Sundays.

Trail Ridge Road from the Kawuneeche Visitor Center to Poudre Lake is a designated snowmobile route, and snowmobilers are required to register at the visitor center before entering. Snowmobiling is prohibited on the east side of the park. Both Grand Lake and Estes Park have rental shops. Call 970-586-1333 for park road and weather information, and 970-586-9561 for additional weather information.

Colorado Springs

People couldn't help but frequent, and settle, the high plateau that is now the site of present-day Colorado Springs. Swept with scenic rolling hills and ravines, all in the shadow of majestic Pikes Peak, it's easy to understand why Colorado Springs has become the state's second largest city and the gateway to a visitor-friendly locale called the Pikes Peak Region.

History

Native Americans from both the mountains and the Great Plains hunted and camped in the foothills that fan out from the omnipresent profile of the "Long One," later known as Pikes Peak. By 1859, prospectors founded the town of El Dorado at the base of Ute Pass Trail. The settlement became Colorado City, and briefly served as the territorial capital before Denver jumped the claim to that honor.

Colorado Springs itself owes its existence to a Civil War veteran, General William Jackson Palmer. After the war, Palmer traveled west as a construction surveyor for the Kansas Pacific Railroad to Denver. He favored the idea of a route up the Arkansas River to the Front Range and from there, north to Denver. Produce from the abundant fields of the Arkansas Valley and the mounting industrial output of Pueblo would fill the boxcars. His bosses saw things differently, and chose a more direct line to skirt across the northern plains.

Palmer didn't forsake his plan, and in 1871 he launched the Denver and Rio Grande Railroad. Not a man of limited vision, Palmer concurrently formed the Colorado Springs Company with the idea of founding a resort enclave with

Wild Blue Yonder

U.S. Air Force cadets

As one of America's top-flight four-year institutions of higher learning, the United States Air Force Academy offers 25 degrees from astronautical engineering to humanities. Extracurricular activities range from playing on one of the varsity sports teams (all called "Falcons") to actually participating in the genteel sport of falconry.

The first graduating class of 1959 chose the falcon, a member of the hawk family, as the cadet mascot. They liked the fact that the noble bird symbolizes courage and grace, two attributes to which any young man or woman might wish to aspire.

Today, 12 to 15 falcons (largely prairie falcons native to Colorado) call the academy home. Housed in enclosures called "mews," the raptors are cared for by 12 cadet falconers who share the duties of training the magnificent birds.

While instruction classes for the "feathered" cadets are strictly off-limits to visitors, the mascots regularly take flight at outdoor sporting events held at Falcon Stadium. The birds' speed and aeronautic adeptness never fail to inspire spectators.

Oh, I have slipped the surly
bonds of earth
And danced the skies on
laughter-silvered wings
High Flight
-John Gillespie Magee, Jr.

following page: Pikes Peak from the Garden of the Gods

Pikes Peaks as the postcard backdrop. Within a year, tracks ran 76 miles south from Denver to the newly formed town envisioned as a "model of taste and refinement."

Owing to a good deal of shrewd public relations and a growing interest in exploring the Wild West, Colorado Springs soon became an adventurous and health-inducing escape for the well-heeled from the East Coast and Europe. Before long, the town was tagged as the "Newport of the Rockies" and many English visitors spoke of it as "Little London."

In 1891, huge gold strikes at Cripple Creek, 20 miles due west of Colorado Springs, added luster to the peaceful resort. Overnight, mining millionaires lavished new wealth on castles and mansions while merchant princes set up shop, making Colorado Springs the richest city per capita in the country. Katharine Lee Bates engendered the association of the area with *America the Beautiful* when, after an excursion up Pikes Peak in 1895 she penned the poem that would become one of the nation's most beloved anthems.

Manitou and Pikes Peak Cog Railway

With the coming of World War II, other military generals took the high ground in the development of Colorado Springs. Camp Carson, named after frontiersman Kit Carson, became the Fort Carson Army Installation. Peterson Air Force Base followed in 1952, and in

Singing America's Praises

On July 22, 1893, Katharine Lee Bates, a Massachusetts English teacher, boarded a covered wagon for a sightseeing trip up Pikes Peak. She came back with two lines of poetry: "Oh beautiful for spacious skies, For amber waves of grain." It's a Colorado souvenir the entire nation now enjoys.

Born in 1859, Bates was the daughter of a Congregationalist minister. Her love of language urged her to pursue an English degree at Wellesley College. After graduation, she taught in only two schools before returning to her alma mater. Eventually, she would oversee their English department.

Her other love, travel, brought her to Colorado Springs. She joined other noted professors—including future president Woodrow Wilson—to teach the summer quarter at Colorado College. Bates and several companions celebrated the session's end with an expedition up Pikes Peak.

The visit lasted only a moment. Two of the party sickened with the altitude; the driver insisted that they descend. Miss Bates later wrote, "The Peak remains in memory hardly more than one ecstatic gaze."

That night, in her room at the Antlers Hotel, she completed her thought:

For purple mountain
majesties
Above the fruited plain!
America! America!
God shed His grace on
thee
And crown thy good with
brotherhood
From sea to shining sea!

On July 4,1895, her lines first appeared in *The Congregationalist* magazine. On the fifth, Katharine was a celebrity. Her mailbox brimmed with fan mail. One admirer requested ten copies for his grandchildren; Miss Bates carefully wrote out ten duplicates.

Sixty composers volunteered tunes to match her meter. Bates dutifully sang out each, but none quite fit. Searching hymnals she discovered S. A. Ward's *O Mother Dear, Jerusalem*. It harmonized perfectly. Together, words and melody seemed to express the abundance and lofty sentiments of the burgeoning nation.

Florissant Fossil Beds

1954, Colorado Springs became the home of the Falcons with the opening of the prestigious U.S. Air Force Academy. Three years later, the North American Aerospace Defense Command (NORAD) chiseled out Cheyenne Mountain as the headquarters for the nuclear missile strike early-warning system of the United States and Canada.

Colorado Springs continues to be a high-flying candidate for military maneuvers. Having recently become the new center for the U.S. Space Command, its mission is to oversee emerging space-oriented defense activities.

Contemporary Aspects

While the quip that Colorado Springs houses as many generals as the Pentagon may be an exaggeration, it underscores the prominence of the military to the area. Nearly 50 percent of the economy is directly tied

Pikes Peak Area Annual Festivals and Events

January

Great Fruitcake Toss—Individual competitions feature the fruitcake launch, fruitcake toss and the official fruitcake hurl. Manitou Springs Memorial Park; call 719-685-5089.

May

Territory Days Celebration—Street festival commemorating the days when Colorado City served as the territorial capital. Old Colorado City; call 719-577-4112.

June to July

Colorado Renaissance Festival—Country celebration steps back in time to Old Europe with costumed kings, queens, ladies in waiting, knights and wizards. Larkspur at I-25, exit 172; call 303-688-6010.

June

Clayfest and Mud Ball—Pottery-making competition for artists and amateurs. Manitou Springs, Soda Springs Park; call 719-685-5795.

Spring Spree—Annual city festival with parades, music, races and concession stands. Downtown Colorado Springs, Monument Valley Park; call 719-596-4002.

Donkey Derby Days—Annual street festival with donkey races, contests, food and music. Cripple Creek; call 719-689-2169.

July

Pikes Peak Auto Hill Climb—International "Race to the Clouds" up Pikes Peak. Pikes Peak Highway; call 719-685-4400.

Gold Rush Days—Parades, arts and crafts bazaar, music and children's carnival. Victor; call 719-689-2392.

July to August

Colorado Springs Opera—Annual festival to celebrate opera. Pikes Peak Center, Colorado Springs; call 719-520-7469.

August

Pikes Peak or Bust Rodeo—PRCA sanctioned rodeo. Penrose Stadium, Colorado Springs; call 719-635-3548.

Fiddlers on the Gorge—Annual fiddlers competition held at Royal Gorge. Royal Gorge Bridge; call 719-275-7507.

Great Pikes Peak Cowboy Poetry Gathering—Cowboy poets, artists and musicians. Pikes Peak Center, Colorado Springs; call 719-531-6333.

August to September

Colorado Springs Balloon Classic—Pancake breakfasts, balloon races and tethered balloon glows. Memorial Park, Colorado Springs; call 719-471-4833.

December

Fireworks From The Summit of Pikes Peak—Annual Adaman Club's trek to the summit of Pikes Peak for a New Year's Eve fireworks display.

Exploring the Pikes Peak Region

Great scenery, fossil beds, historic mining and gambling towns, and manmade wonders draw visitors to explore the western side of Pikes Peak. While all attractions are accessible via good highways, the more adventurous can drive the Gold Belt Tour, one of Colorado's Scenic and Historic Byways. The 131-mile circuit begins at Florissant, 40 miles west of Colorado Springs, and branches off south into three routes that eventually terminate near Cañon City. Be forewarned, the Gold Belt Tour follows gravel roads that are often rough.

Florissant Fossil Beds

In the Oligocene era some 36 million years ago, palm trees and giant redwoods spread across Colorado's landscape. Then a violent volcano spewed tons of ash atop the broad basin, and the remnants of that age were trapped in the Florissant Fossil Beds (719-748-3253). A self-guided, one-mile walking tour covers the geological phenomenon, including the huge trunks of petrified sequoia which once stood 250 feet tall.

Cripple Creek and Victor

In the 1890s, Cripple Creek (719-689-2169) and the neighboring town of Victor (719-689-2169) were the centers of Colorado's last gold boom. Saloons and brothels lined the bustling streets, entertaining miners by night who toiled in the mines by day. The area became the world's greatest mining camp, producing more than $600 million in gold—the largest amount for any single geological deposit on earth.

The heyday ended after the turn of the century, and for the next 80 years the towns welcomed tourists interested in seeing vintage Victorian buildings and houses. In 1990, low-stakes gambling was approved for Cripple Creek and a new boom began. Formerly timeworn hotels and storefronts have been refurbished into busy casinos.

The Royal Gorge Bridge

Non-gamblers also find numerous diversions. At the Mollie Kathleen Gold Mine (719-689-2465), guides lead guests 1,000 feet underground to experience the mining process. A trip aboard the Cripple Creek & Victor Narrow Gauge Railroad (719-689-2640) delivers a four-mile narrated history of the "Bowl of Gold." At Victor, the Lowell Thomas Museum (719-689-3307) tells the story of a famous broadcast journalist who got his start as a paper boy with the *Victor Record*. During the summer, Cripple Creek's Gold Bar Room Theater (719-689-7777) in the Imperial Hotel and Casino presents afternoon and evening performances of classic Victorian melodrama. Critics hail it as "high drama" at its best.

Buckskin Joe Frontier Town & Railway

Part Old West theme park and part movie set, Buckskin Joe's (719-275-5149) is a surefire hit with kids. A recreated Old West town made up of historic buildings around the state, it's been used as the backdrop for many movies. Today, gunfights erupt along Main Street 11 times a day, and there is usually a "hangin'" as costumed actors aim to please audiences with remembrances of the wild side of the Wild West.

The Royal Gorge

Lt. Zebulon Pike and his party camped near the eastern portal of the "Grand Canyon of the Arkansas," but dismissed the idea of traversing the narrow gorge with walls 1,000 feet high. Seven decades later, the Denver and Rio Grande Railroad fought a bitter dispute with the Santa Fe Railroad over the right-of-way through the canyon leading to silver-rich Leadville. The Denver and Rio Grande won, opening the chasm to the "Iron Horse." In 1929, the Royal Gorge Bridge (719-275-7507), the world's highest suspension bridge, was spanned over the canyon eight miles west of Cañon City. Ever since, people have come to marvel at the engineering feat and the spectacular vistas.

Miramont Castle

to defending and supporting the "Stars and Stripes." A hundred or so high-technology company subsidiaries, including those of MCI, Digital Equipment, Hewlett Packard and Atmel also call Colorado Springs home. One of the city's biggest employers, Current Inc., manufactures greeting cards and stationery.

Demographically, the city is overwhelmingly white—less than 20 percent of the population is from minority groups. From a sociological perspective, conservatism is the watchword. Some 58 Christian organizations, in particular "Focus on the Family," are headquartered in Colorado Springs.

Zebulon Pike–Secret Agent?

Lt. Zebulon Montgomery Pike has been called the "Lost Pathfinder," for on his expedition to trace the flow of the Red River, he wandered far and wide, completely missing the waterway he sought. Now some historians hold to a different story. They believe that Pike was really a secret agent on a mission to reconnoiter the Spanish-held lands which lay beyond the recently acquired Louisiana Purchase.

As the story goes, Pike's benefactor was General James Wilkinson, America's highest ranking general and the newly appointed governor of the Louisiana Territory. Along with the traitorous Aaron Burr, Wilkinson nurtured a plan to create a southwestern empire which they would rule together. Direct knowledge of the land was crucial, and Pike was their eyes and ears.

In this light, it is understandable why Pike spent most of his days following the banks of the Arkansas River and then the Rio Grande River far into New Spain. When Spanish soldiers finally encountered Pike's party wintering on the Conejos River in the San Luis Valley, they took them into custody.

The Spanish authorities proved to be hospitable, and Pike's poorly supplied band spent the rest of the winter comfortably in Santa Fe, New Mexico. Finally, in the spring of 1807, they were escorted to Chihuahua, Mexico, and from there, back to U.S. soil.

Although Pike's maps and notes were seized by the Spanish, his reports from memory were invaluable. Nonetheless, the alleged scheme of Burr and Wilkinson never came to fruition. As for Pike, he was promoted to brigadier general and was killed at the Battle of York, Ontario, during the War of 1812.

Attractions

The Pikes Peak area has no shortage of diversions, running the gamut from simply superlative to seriously silly. Truly, this is a place that has something for everyone.

Look to the west to see the area's highest superlative, Pikes Peak. At 14,110 feet, the mountain falls short of claiming any height records—30 other Colorado peaks stand taller. That said, the massive mound's presence so close to the flat plains makes it the grandest mountain for miles around.

Botanist Dr. Edwin James is credited as the first white man to conquer Pikes Peak, cresting the summit in 1820. When comfort-minded Zalmon Simmons, of Simmons Mattress fame and fortune, scaled the peak atop a mule in the late 1800s, he proclaimed the scenery stunning but the journey too strenuous. He remedied the situation by installing a Swiss-style cog railway to negotiate the perilous 25 percent grade inclines to the top of Pikes Peak. Although it's possible nowadays to drive to the summit via a well-maintained 19-mile gravel toll road, the historic Manitou and Pikes

Kissing Camels at Garden of the Gods

Peak Cog Railway (719-685-5401), is still the easiest way to ascend the mountain.

As its name implies, the railway departs from the town of Manitou Springs, situated in the foothills below Pikes Peak. Three-hour round trips ratchet up and down the mountain slopes at a leisurely 10 MPH, delivering vistas by the score. Atop the summit, a chilly landscape awaits, and a warm visitor's center welcomes those people who forgot to bring a jacket. The temperature on the pinnacle can be 30 degrees Fahrenheit cooler than that of the low-lying plains. On a clear day, the view is incredible, taking in hundreds of miles of spacious skies, amber waves of grain and purple mountains majesty.

Manitou Springs is the perfect place for a pre- or post-peak experience. Founded in the late 1800s as a retreat at which to "take the waters," the town's bubbling mineral springs and health-inducing climate garnered it the title of "Saratoga of the West." Now, it's known more as a countercultural bastion in otherwise conservative-minded Colorado Springs. Artists and craftspeople live here and their Victorian storefront shops offer a wide variety of hand-made creations.

For an entertaining

Hard Luck Mining

Poor luck has always been a miner's unwelcome companion, and Bob Womack had more than his share of bad acquaintances.

For years, Womack, a cowpoke with the Broken Box Ranch near Cripple Creek, had picked through the extinct volcano crater on the south side of Pikes Peak searching for gold. Everyone thought he was crazy; the terrain of rumpled hills doesn't look like gold country. Still, Womack persisted, having occasionally come across rocks and pebbles that showed color. In 1891, he staked a claim called the "El Paso Load" at Poverty Gulch.

A Colorado Springs carpenter, Winfield Scott Stratton, heard of Womack's claim and decided to stake one for himself on July 4, 1891, calling it "The Independence." The name was a good choice, and soon he became Cripple Creek's first millionaire, footloose and fancy free.

Womack, however, hadn't hit paydirt and parted with his claim, selling it for $500. He gave up too soon. Poverty Gulch was anything but poor, in time the El Paso load producing more than $5 million of gold.

Bob Womack still lives on in Cripple Creek

Broadmoor Hotel

introduction to the history of Manitou Springs, sign up for a free hour-long walking tour hosted by a member of the Mineral Springs Foundation. Stops along the way sample the waters of the town's 26 active springs. Miramont Castle (719-685-1011), off Ruxton Avenue invites guests to examine the former home of a wealthy French Catholic priest, Father Francolon. Nine distinct architectural styles collaborate to make the 46-room, 14,000-square-foot house the town's most exotic property.

Families visiting the area will find numerous activities for children. Arcade Amusements (719-685-9815), located in the center of town, is one of the West's oldest amusement complexes with some 250 spare-change-hungry contraptions—everything from old-time penny pinball machines to state-of-the-art video games.

Old West heros and desperados share the exhibits at the Buffalo Bill Wax Museum (719-685-5900), while the White House Living History Site (719-578-6777) presents a more genuine picture of western life. Interpreters in period attire depict and explain the ways of 19th-century Colorado homesteaders. At the Manitou Cliff Dwelling Museum (719-685-5242), Native Americans regularly perform dances in front of "authentic Indian" ruins. The distinctive stone houses tucked into the overhangs of Phantom Cliff Canyon were relocated here in the early 1900s by archaeologists who feared that their original southwestern sites were too susceptible to plundering.

Cave of the Winds (719-685-5444), situated above Manitou Springs in Williams Canyon, has had its share of souvenir vandalism over the years. Early visitors to this system of underground caverns often helped themselves to the sparkling odd-shaped stalactites and stalagmites that pierce the cave's hollows. Still, plenty of stone formations remain, and today the Cave of Winds is one of the area's most visited attractions. Forty-minute "Discovery Trail" tours regularly depart to lead visitors along well-lighted, paved paths to examine the cave's interior. Plan to take along a jacket as the caverns are always cool. Athletic spelunkers can sign up for a two-hour "Explorer's Trip" where participants scramble and wiggle into the darker fissures of the cave. Old clothes and a flashlight are essential.

For something completely different, the North Pole / Santa's Workshop (719-684-9432) lies not in the Arctic, but merely six miles west of Manitou Springs on U.S. Highway 24. Reindeer, gaily dressed elves and old St. Nick himself keep the little ones mesmerized at this ride-filled amusement park.

As a pilot, Santa has few equals, but in Colorado Springs he has numerous competitors. North of the city center, nearly 4,500 of America's best and brightest fill the cadet roster at the U.S. Air Force Academy (AFA).

The campus was established in 1954, surpassing 580 other proposed sites around the nation. Set against the backdrop of the Rampart Range, the 18,000-acre facility ranks as Colorado's third most popular tourist destination. Annually, more than a million guests pull into the Barry Goldwater Visitor Center (719-472-2025). From here, a self-guided "Follow the Falcon" walking tour takes in the highlights of the grounds, in particular the 17-spire Cadet Chapel. As much sculpture as architecture, the masterwork was five years in design and four years in construction. On weekdays throughout the academic year, cadets stage an impressive noontime show of teamwork and discipline. On their way to lunch, they parade in formation in the expansive square next to the chapel. The AFA band keeps the meter as the students march into the dining hall. Inside, 500 wait-staff dish up meals in 20 minutes.

Military discipline is highly evident at Colorado Springs' most exclusive tour, a visit into the impregnable fortress of the North American Aerospace Defense Command (NORAD). Constructed within a hollowed-out chamber of the hard granite Cheyenne Mountain, the installation south of Colorado Springs was built to withstand nuclear attack. Twenty-five-foot-thick steel doors seal the entrance and the entire command rests on 1,319 half-ton, shock-absorbing springs. Twenty times a month, the Air Force allows escorted visits into the top secret complex. Reservations are required and should be made

The Wet Mountain Valley

Although it is well known to serious backpackers, the Wet Mountain Valley west of Pueblo doesn't receive many visitors. Consequently, the area retains a remote, undiscovered feel, though it's easily accessible via a Colorado Scenic and Historic Byway called Frontier Pathways.

The 103-mile drive heads west on Colorado Highway 96 from Pueblo, passes through Wetmore into Westcliffe, then backtracks to Colorado Highway 165 into Colorado City before tying into U.S. Interstate Highway 25. The roadside panoramas are nothing short of superb. Vintage ranches and farms huddle in grassy meadows, framed by the jagged Sangre de Cristo Mountains on the west and the pine-ladened Wet Mountains to the east.

The towns of Westcliffe and Silver Cliff sport a combined population of around 700, making them the area's urban center. Silver Cliff was once Colorado's third largest metropolis during its brief silver boom in the 1870s. The town recalls its glory days at the Silver Cliff Museum, located in the old Town Hall & Fire Station. The train tracks of the Denver and Rio Grande stopped a mile short of Silver Cliff in 1881, as the railroad preferred to foster its own town of Westcliffe. The towns quickly became rivals. Silver Cliff's silver eventually ran out, and the railroad pulled out of Westcliffe. Now, the two towns share a number of public services.

Bishop's Castle

The character of the valley's residents is innovative and unique, qualities that are evident in Jim Bishop. Twenty-seven miles southeast of Westcliffe, Bishop is single-handedly building the "Bishop Castle" (719-564-4366). It's claimed to be the nation's largest one-person construction project, and so far, its stone walls reach to three stories, supported by flying buttresses and graced with a 130-foot-high tower. Guests are welcome to stop by and see the progress.

six months in advance. Call 719-554-2241, extension 2239 for tape recorded instructions.

Reservations are also required on the other side of Cheyenne Mountain, site of the Mobile five-star, AAA five-diamond rated Broadmoor Hotel. Reconstructed in 1918 by mining magnate Spencer Penrose, the lavish Broadmoor sports three championship golf courses, 16 tennis courts, a complete water spa, three spring-fed swimming pools, a skeet-shooting range, excellent restaurants and a veritable "Rodeo Drive" of high-end shops. A world-class ice-skating arena once graced the grounds too, but it was abandoned to make way for an addition.

The Broadmoor's ice rink had a place in skating history as it was a favorite training ground for Olympic Gold medalist Peggy Fleming. Her accomplishments are remembered at the World Figure Skating Museum and Hall of Fame (719-635-5200) located near the resort. The only facility of its kind, collections include displays of historic ice skates, including some made of bone, skating-themed paintings by Winslow Homer and Andy Warhol, and skating costumes, medals and other memorabilia.

World-class athletes aren't strangers to Colorado Springs. The U.S. Olympic Committee is headquartered here at the U.S. Olympic Complex (719-578-4644) situated near downtown. The 37-acre administration and training facility hosts thousands of athletes and is home to 23 national governing bodies for amateur athletics. Free daily tours escort visitors around the site, stopping to see the gymnasiums, swimming pools, shooting centers and weight training rooms where physical grace and talent are honed to "go for the gold."

Champions of America's most indigenous sport—rodeo—are honored at the ProRodeo Hall of Fame & Museum of the American Cowboy (719-593-8847) just north of downtown off U.S. Interstate 25. Two multimedia shows introduce guests to the Old West and the role of the cowboy. After the presentations, the Heritage Hall exhibits the development of cowboy gear, while the Hall of Champions commemorates the greats of the rough-and-tumble sport.

SuperAmerica Guide's Pueblo & Vicinity Recommendations

- Devote a morning for visits to El Pueblo Museum and the Rosemount Victorian House Museum, both in Pueblo.
- Plan an evening cruise aboard the *Prairie Princess II* paddlewheeler at Lake Pueblo State Park.
- Take the time to drive the Frontier Pathways Scenic and Historic Byway. Be sure to stop at the "Bishop's Castle."
- Spend an afternoon driving the Highway of Legends Scenic and Historic Byway to Trinidad.
- Stroll the Corazon de Trinidad National Historic District and stop at the Baca House, Bloom House and Pioneer Museum.

Nature

Colorado Springs' close proximity to the mountains makes hiking one of the best nature activities here. It's also one of the easiest places to bag a "14er" by scrambling to the summit of the 14,110-foot Pikes Peak. Barr Trail, 13 miles one way from its start in Manitou Springs, is the trek that most hikers use. The path can take two days (round trip) with an overnight at Barr Camp, though some experienced hikers go up and down in one day.

For people who prefer to confine their mountain climbing to descents only, Challenge Unlimited (719-633-6399) offers bike tours whereby participants are driven to the summit, then cycle back to the base. The views are spectacular.

Great vistas are the hallmark of the Garden of the Gods (719-578-6939), a 1,400-acre National Natural Landmark situated within the foothills of Pikes Peak. Pink and red sandstone formations twisted by eons of weather into fantastic shapes protrude throughout the park. Free driving and hiking maps from the visitor center point out where to find configurations dubbed with whimsical names such as "Kissing Camels," "Weeping Indian" and "Rocking Chair." A little imagination goes a long way here. Twice a day during the summer, park naturalists conduct 45-minute walks into the park.

Seven Falls (719-632-0741) has its share of oddly shaped rocks too, but the primary reason why 300,000 people come here each year is to see the majestic cascades hurtling down 300 feet of black granite. Located in South Cheyenne Canyon, two trails lead to vantage points to enjoy the waterfalls. To avoid the crowds, some people head to North Cheyenne Canyon and hike two miles up the Mt. Cutler Trail to watch the tumbling waters.

The scenic setting of Cheyenne Mountain Zoo (719-475-9555), perched hillside at an elevation of 6,800 feet, is the country's highest-elevation controlled animal habitat. More than 100 endangered species have homes here, including snow leopards and Asian lions, in addition to a diverse collection of birds of prey. The Will Rogers Shrine of the Sun is located above the zoo grounds, paying tribute to the famous and much beloved American humorist. Arthropods, that is bugs, are the focus for the May Natural History Museum (719-576-0450) located south of Colorado Springs on Rock Creek Canyon Road. An oversized replica of a giant Hercules beetle greets visitors to this unique "insectorama," which houses over 8,000 specimens collected by James May over 63 years.

Nightlife

Colorado Springs retains a small-town feel when it comes to its nightlife. Certainly, there are numerous good restaurants and fine performances by the renowned Colorado Springs Chorale (719-634-3737), the Colorado Springs Symphony (719-633-4611) and the Colorado Springs Dance Theater (719-630-7434), but it's telling that "cruising" is still a popular pastime. Most Friday and Saturday evenings, a 10-block stretch of downtown Nevada Avenue turns into a movable car show. Souped-up Chevys and "cherry" Mustangs crawl along, vying for attention with the latest flashy sports cars.

Nostalgia has a stage at the Iron Springs Chateau (719-685-5104) in Manitou Springs. An all-you-can-eat dinner precedes some of the best "ham" in the state. This over-the-top melodrama stresses "boo-and-hiss" audience participation, interspersed with lively sing-alongs. Dinner theater takes on an Old West flavor at the Flying W Ranch (719-598-4000), which is north of the Garden of the Gods. It's a working ranch with a Western village comprised of restored buildings and a healthy helping of cowboy comedy and ballads. After a chuckwagon barbecue dinner, a campfire show begins and no one leaves without a belly laugh or two.

Laughter and singing ring out from the Golden Bee (719-577-5776), located in the Broadmoor Hotel. It's an authentic English pub that once had a London address, but was relocated piece by piece to the Broadmoor's International Center. A lively place by nature, ragtime sing-alongs (plus a few pints of ale) reward patrons with a merry taste of "Little London."

The Colorado Springs Convention and Visitors Center is located at 104. S. Cascade, Suite 104; call 719-635-7506 or 800-DO-VISIT.

Pueblo

Even many Coloradans don't hold Pueblo in high regard as a destination worth visiting. The city's long-standing reputation as "Pittsburgh of the West," earned with the belching smokestacks of CF&I Steel, easily obscured its charms. A new image is emerging as citizens have undertaken a revitalization effort, creating greenways and refurbishing its numerous historic sites.

History

Due to Pueblo's favorable location at the confluence of the Arkansas River and Fountain Creek, it has long been a gathering place and crossroads. Utes, Arapahos, Cheyennes, Comanches, Kiowas and even Spanish explorers have all camped here. Lt. Zebulon Pike passed through in 1806, staying long enough to construct a temporary fort. Freed slave and intrepid mountain man Jim Beckwourth is credited with establishing "El Pueblo" in 1842 as a trading post for dry goods and powerful "Taos Lightning" whiskey.

The arrival of the Denver

The Colorado State Fair

For 17 days from mid-August to Labor Day, Pueblo pulls out all the stops, hosting the annual Colorado State Fair. It's been doing so since 1872, and it's only gotten bigger and better over time. It features stock shows, lots of carnival rides, fiestas, championship rodeo and top-flight entertainment by well-known national acts. For ticket information, call 800-444-FAIR.

Rosemount Victorian House Museum in Pueblo

and Rio Grande Railroad (D&RG) in 1872 signaled Pueblo's emergence as Colorado's industrial workshop. With access to the mineral riches of Aspen and Leadville, in addition to vast deposits of coal near Trinidad and Walsenburg, Pueblo soon became a smelting center. Iron and steel production came on line too, supplying railroads with spikes and rails. By the turn of the century, Pueblo was a bona fide steel town with CF&I (originally Colorado Coal and Iron) as the city's lifeblood. Immigrant workers—Italians, Germans, Czechs, Slovaks, Croatians, Serbs and Russians—joined Pueblo's already substantial Hispanic population to create a diverse community.

Blast furnaces continued to spark Pueblo's growth into the 20th century, making it Colorado's second largest city for a time. The steel market cooled after WWII, and with it, Pueblo's prospects. Increased competition from foreign markets over the next four decades delivered additional dents to Pueblo's steel trade. By 1982, CF&I Steel was forced to lay off 4,000 workers, virtually melting down the local economy.

Contemporary Aspects

Despite the steel industry's ups and downs, CF&I Steel remains a mainstay of Pueblo's financial health, employing 1,400 people at its 640-acre site. Acquired by Oregon Steel in 1993, a $200 million investment modernized the plant that manufactures seamless tubing, wire, rods, bars and rails. Other major employers include Matrixx Marketing, an inbound telemarketing service bureau, and several health-related organizations such as QualMed, Inc. and the Colorado Institute of Mental Health.

Demographically, the city reflects its immigrant heritage, with a significant proportion of Hispanics owing to its onetime importance as a riverside outpost on the fringe of New Spain. An ambitious program called the Historic Arkansas River Project (HARP) will revitalize Pueblo's link to its famous waterway. A downtown stretch of the river will become a distinctive urban waterfront with plazas, leafy pedestrian paths, a recreational lake and historic/interpretive parks.

Attractions

Western history buffs will find plenty to occupy their interests, starting with the Union Avenue Historic District. This six-block area features some 40 buildings dating from the

1840s to 1890s. A self-guided walking tour map is available at the Pueblo Visitor Center.

To examine Pueblo's beginnings, the El Pueblo Museum (719-583-0453) is located at the site where Beckwourth constructed his trading post. Artifacts and exhibits tell the story of Pueblo's founding and the importance of the Arkansas River to both Native Americans and early frontiersmen. Don't miss the handiwork of saddlemaker Samuel Gallup, who made the "Pueblo" saddle a cowpoke favorite. Additional displays at the Pueblo County Historical Museum (719-543-6772), located at the vintage Vail Hotel, round out the city's history.

Refinement and elegance imbue the Rosemount Victorian House Museum (719-545-5290), completed in 1893 at a cost of more than $60,000. When banker John Thatcher and his wife Margaret moved into the pink rhyolite stone palace, it was described as one of the finest residences in the West. Certainly, it was one of the region's largest homes at 37 rooms, 24,000 square feet in all. Rosemount retains many of its original elegant furnishings and accessories, but an added collection is that of Andrew McClelland. On the third floor is displayed the memorabilia garnered by the Pueblo philanthropist during his 1904 whirlwind odyssey through 67 countries.

Pueblo's refined contemporary side is evident at the Sangre de Cristo Arts & Conference Center (719-543-0130). A permanent western art display,

Highway of Legends

Spanish Peaks outside La Veta

Tales of Native Americans, Spanish explorers and Hispanic settlers distinguish the 82-mile Highway of Legends Scenic and Historic Byway that runs along U.S. Highway 160 and then Colorado Highway 12 from Walsenburg to Trinidad. However, the area's history is only part of the allure for this trip, which skirts the magnificent Spanish Peaks and trails into historic towns.

Walsenburg, 37 miles south of Pueblo, is the northern gateway to the route. Named for Fred Walsen, who opened a trading post in 1870 on La Plaza de los Liones, the town bestrides an old Ute trail following the Cucharas River. For local history, check out the Walsenburg Mining Museum (no phone), which covers the area's coal mining past.

In Spanish, the words *la veta* mean "the vein," which is an apt name for the town that lies 15 miles southwest of Walsenburg. The term refers to "lava dikes," the now-ancient stone fins fanning out from the once-volcanic Spanish Peaks. Vestiges of La Veta's pioneer days are at the Fort Francisco Museum (no phone). Within the adobe-walled compound reside eclectic and fascinating collections of historic buildings and locally donated artifacts. Look for the 1850 letter from Springfield, Illinois, attorney Abraham Lincoln to a fellow lawyer in La Veta.

Roughly 15 miles south of La Veta, Colorado Highway 12 crests Cucharas Pass at 9,994 feet. From the summit, Cordova Pass (sometimes rutted and bumpy) branches off to the northeast and winds down into tiny Aguilar, while the Highway of Legends continues southeast into Trinidad.

Trinidad was the last stop on the Santa Fe Trail before it shot south to Raton Pass. Consequently, the town thrived as a trading post and later, as a station for cowboys herding longhorns from Texas along the Goodnight-Loving Trail. A self-guided walking tour map, available at the Colorado Welcome Center (719-846-9512), covers the highlights of the downtown Corazon de Trinidad, a National Historic District. Reserve time to explore the Baca House, Bloom House and Pioneer Museum (719-846-7217), an excellent complex of gardens and historic houses chronicling the 1870s.

four changing exhibit galleries and a performing arts theater make this the city's best creative diversion. A participatory Children's Museum, also located here, ensures that there is something to do regardless of your age.

Nature

At first glance, Pueblo may not seem to have many natural enticements. Yet, the Lake Pueblo State Park (719-561-9320) seven miles west of the city is one of Colorado's most visited areas. Sixty miles of shoreline tempt anglers to cast lines for walleye and small mouth bass, while the reservoir's open water is perfect for waterskiing, sailing and windsurfing. At the Northshore Marina, the *Prairie Princess II* (719-547-1126) paddlewheeler takes guests out for two-hour cruises.

Swimming is not allowed at the lake, but is permitted below the dam at the Rock Canyon Swim Area (719-564-0065). A small beach and picnic area makes this an ideal spot to cool off on hot summer days. Shady escapes and exercise draw bicyclists to paved recreational paths, which connect 16 miles of trails in Pueblo Lake State Park to tracks along the Arkansas River into downtown.

Near the bicycle path and accessible by car on Nature Center Road is the Greenway & Nature Center of Pueblo (719-549-2414). It's the city's best picnic area, offering a serene respite in which to explore the riverfront ecosystem. Nearby is the Raptor Center of Pueblo (719-545-7117) where injured birds of prey receive rehabilitation before being released back into the wild. More animals await at the Pueblo Zoo in City Park (719-561-9664), located east of Rock Canyon. "Ecocenter" encounters include a tropical rainforest and a black-footed penguin habitat, in addition to 300 other animal exhibits. Don't miss the wooden carousel across from the zoo's entrance. Built in 1911, it's a rare example of a Country Fair carousel. Its portability allowed it to grace special events in rural locations.

Nightlife

The place to be on a summer Friday evening is on the outdoor steps of the Sangre de Cristo Arts & Conference Center. The stairway has become an impromptu stage for live music concerts. Combine the entertainment with snacks from nearby food vendors and a nice sunset, and you couldn't ask for a better way to begin a weekend.

Good meals are easy to come by as the city's ethnic diversity promises a range of restaurants where tried-and-true homestyle recipes top the menu. The Grand Prix (719-542-9825), despite its French-sounding name, specializes in Mexican dishes prepared from scratch. The Irish Pub & Grill (719-542-9974) is Pueblo's new microbrewery, with a distinctive "nouvelle pub" fare. For the best pizza, the Do-Drop-Inn (719-542-0818) takes the prize at its downscale, downtown digs.

The Pueblo Visitor Information Center is located at the southwest corner intersection of I-25 and Highway 50; call 719-542-1704.

The Ludlow Massacre

Twelve miles northwest of Trinidad stands a monument to one of Colorado's worst tragedies: the Ludlow Massacre.

The date was April 20, 1914. Hundreds of striking mine workers and their families were settled here on the bleak prairie, having abandoned their company-owned housing for a makeshift camp. Six months had passed, and still they held steadfast to their struggle for better working conditions, higher wages and collective bargaining rights.

Tempers reached the flash point when heavily armed Colorado National Guard troops, peppered with coal-company toughs, moved in for a raid. A warning shot erupted into a pitched battle, leaving one militiaman and five strikers dead. Two women and 11 children also perished, suffocating from smoke while trapped in a cellar beneath a blazing tent.

For 10 days afterward, coal camps waged civil war on the Colorado militia. Finally, President Woodrow Wilson dispatched 1,600 federal troops, disarming the warring factions to end the killing. With the army firmly in control negotiations began, and by December of 1914, a settlement was reached.

The Rocky Mountains

Big Thompson River

Colorado's Rocky Mountains wriggle from the chilly-cool Wyoming border to the chili-hot New Mexico state line. Along the way, great stretches of these gnashing jawbones take on different titles, each more majestic than the last: Elkheads, Medicine Bows, Rabbit Ears, Gores, Never Summers, Front Range, Sawatch, Collegiate Peaks, Tenmiles, Mosquitos, West Elks, Elks, Ramparts, the San Juans and, perhaps most elegantly, the Sangre De Cristos. Together, Colorado's defining feature is simply called "The Rockies."

The term "rocky" certainly describes their makeup. Sheer stone masses of granite, gneiss, and schist reach for the wedgewood-blue sky. Along the eastern Front Range and Western Slope, layer upon layer of limestone and red-as-terra-cotta sandstone flank the stony central spine.

Lt. Zebulon Pike, exploring the region for President Thomas Jefferson, first spotted the Rockies in 1806. Fur trappers followed, traipsing the ranges for decades and swapping pots and pans for pelts with the Utes before a mountain man, George Jackson, found his way into Clear Creek Canyon. In 1859, Jackson pulled $1,500 worth of gold out of "them thar hills" and suddenly Colorado was a hot spot on the Kansas Territory map.

SuperAmerica Guide's Rocky Mountain Recommendations

- Dip weary bones into the hot springs at Strawberry Park near Steamboat Springs.
- Search for Rocky Mountain Bighorn Sheep at the Georgetown Wildlife Viewing Area.
- Shop for an afternoon along Breckenridge's Main Street.
- Pick any Summit County ski resort for a downhill fling.
- Savor the Betty Ford Alpine Gardens early one morning.
- Ski Vail's astonishing back bowls.
- Sigh at the beauty of Maroon Bells Wilderness Area.
- Play beach bum on the extensive sand dunes at Great Sand Dunes National Monument.
- Drive the 236-mile San Juan Skyway; take a train ride and a four-wheel-drive tour.

left: Waterfalls in Rocky Mountain National Park

The northern section of Colorado's Rockies, sometimes called the North Forty

SuperAmerica Guide's North Forty Recommendations

- Whisk down Winter Park's Alpine Slide, which includes 26 turns, 3,030 feet of track and a 630-foot drop.
- Drive the gravel road between Kremmling and State Bridge. Tracing the course of the Colorado River, this drive often rewards visitors with views of pronghorn and deer.
- Take the short hike from the East Inlet parking lot on the east end of Grand Lake to Adams Falls.
- Ski the powder with Olympic medalist Billy Kidd on his daily tutorial at the Steamboat Springs Ski Resort.
- Dip into the delightful hot spring pools of Strawberry Park near Steamboat Springs.

"Pike's Peak or Bust" lured many prospectors into that first boom and bust cycle. The cry then was for gold but other treasures quickly screamed as loudly: silver, coal, uranium and oil shale. By the time World War II was over, the Colorado mountains were busted again and waiting for the next big boom.

That explosion came not with a bang, but with a whisper. The skiable serenity of powdery snow lulled the

Centennial State out of the sleepy, backwoods category into the world-class, world-famous, star-studded ski capital of the world. Coloradans defend this distinction with fierce pride, going ski-tip-to-ski-tip and snowboard-to-snowboard with all challengers.

Yet snow is only half the story—the drafty, winter half, say non-skiers. Colorado's Rockies are corralled with dude ranches, galloping with horses, laced with vista-laden biking and hiking trails, steaming with hot springs, roiling with rivers full of fish and rubber rafts and Victorian-era towns that explode with shops and restaurants.

The North Forty

The north central portion of the Colorado Rockies, from Berthoud Pass (near U.S. Interstate 70) north to the Wyoming state line—called the north forty because U. S. Highway 40 skirts the area—is a land of glistening mountain pinnacles contrasted with broad valleys. These wide-open swaths ring with simple, geographically descriptive names like Middle Park and North Park, while the cities that anchor them take on the monikers of local geologic wonders: Steamboat Springs and Grand Lake. The Vasquez, Rabbit Ears and Never Summer ranges define these parks and provide backdrop for the high-country towns.

Winter Park's Ski Train

A couple "heads for the hills" on the ski train

Every Saturday and Sunday (and some weekdays) from mid-December to early April, passengers board the Ski Train (303-296-4754), a 17-car choo-choo that carries 750 passengers. The train departs from Denver's Union Station at a bright and early 7:15 a.m. and arrives two hours later a mere 50 yards from the lifts at Winter Park Resort (970-726-5514). Then, after a day of snow play, travelers board the train at 4:15 p.m. and, following another two-hour ride, they arrive at Union Station in the very heart of trendy LoDo, just in time for dinner.

Along the 56-mile route, the train gains 4,000 feet of elevation and passes through 29 tunnels, including the nation's fourth longest, the 6.2 mile-long Moffat Tunnel. That's not all they pass through; the train wends its way through sweeping vistas rarely accessible by any other means.

The views aren't the biggest advantage. "Our trip is a relaxing jaunt right from central Denver," explains general manager Jim Bain. "Two hours is the same length of time it takes to get to Winter Park in a car. But we dish up food, drinks and relaxation."

Winter Park

Winter Park Resort (970-726-5514) is Denver's winter playground. In addition to a stunning array of downhill ski terrains, they've become interested in the new snowshoe technology, developing trails and offering rental equipment and guide packages. Nearby lie miles of cross-country trails. At the National Sports Center for the Disabled (970-726-1540), physically and developmentally disabled men and women learn the fine art of flowing down snowy slopes. Volunteers have instructed more than 2,000 challenged skiers every year since the program started in 1970.

Come summer, folks ride mountain bikes along 600 miles of single and double track, bounce across Rollins Pass in four-wheel-drive vehicles or blaze down the Alpine Slide (970-726-5514); at 3,030 feet, this is the longest slide in the state.

Winter Park's visitor center is located at 78841 U. S. Highway 40; call 970-726-4118.

Colorado River Headwaters Scenic and Historic Byway

Coloradans view the Colorado River as a million-gallon-a-minute recreational vehicle, thoroughly enjoying the pastimes it bubbles up. The scenic byway follows the river's headwaters, beginning in Grand Lake, tracing through Hot Sulphur Springs (with its renovated hot springs facilities), past Kremmling (keep an eye out for pronghorn) and into the Upper Gore Canyon (home to mule deer and bald eagles). All along it are dude ranches, backcountry hiking expeditions, hunting organizations, and rafting and kayaking outfitters.

Grand Lake

Near the Colorado River's headwaters lies Grand Lake, the western gateway to Rocky Mountain National Park. Ringed with fir and spruce, Grand Lake is the largest natural body of water in the state. The shops-behind-wooden-facades feel of Grand Lake harkens back to the Wild West. A stroll atop the boardwalk and a visit to Spirit Lake Marina (970-627-8158) to catch a paddleboat or sailboat for a spin around the lake makes for a wonderful, high-altitude afternoon. Every summer, yachts compete for the Lipton Cup, a solid silver extravaganza donated by English tea baron Sir Thomas Lipton. On July 4th each year, thousands of people congregate for one of Colorado's largest fireworks displays, which explodes across the lake after sundown.

If one lake is "grand," three must be better, right? Enter Lake Granby and Shadow Mountain Reservoir—both man-made, both teeming with fish; both abreeze with sailing and motorboating opportunities and ringed with campsites and hiking trails. The lakes border the Indian Peaks and Never Summer wilderness areas, both laced with trails and bursting with wildlife. If Estes Park is the shopping center for Rocky Mountain National Park, then the Grand Lake area is undoubtedly its recreational backyard.

Heart Spring at Steamboat Springs

Grand Lake's visitor center is at U.S. Highway 34 and Grand Avenue; call 970-627-3402 or 800-531-1019.

Steamboat Springs

U.S. Highway 40 reaches its peak atop Rabbit Ears Pass and skirts the Gore Range on its way into Wyoming. Cuddling into a broad bend of the

We Kidd You Not

Billy Kidd brought home the first ever U.S. Olympic medal for alpine skiing from the 1964 Winter Olympic Games at Innsbruck, Austria. Actually, he brought home two–a silver in the slalom and a bronze in the alpine combined.

In 1970, Kidd captured the world championship, too. That same year he came to Steamboat Springs, Colorado to become the director of skiing for the then-fledgling ski resort. He still holds that title, and his job allows him to sneak away from his desk at 1 p.m. to host his informal training clinic.

Indeed, nearly every afternoon, Kidd shows up in his signature pheasant-feathered Stetson cowboy hat to guide a group of skiers down the mountain. Along the way, the Vermont native offers gentle advice on how to perfect your technique.

"I just love what I do here," says Kidd. "I was always afraid I'd have to get a 'real' job. It turned out to be this."

This "real" job is providing a sense of the wonder of skiing, not only for guests at Steamboat, but for the downhill industry around the world. Kidd offers ski clinics and has promoted skiing in Iran, Scotland and Antarctica.

Cowboys on a cattle drive near Steamboat Springs

mountains that parallels the farm-flanked Yampa River Valley, Steamboat Springs prides itself on dimming down the glitz and glamour quotient of Vail and Aspen. Here, the main street—Lincoln Avenue—is as likely to host hay trucks and horse trailers as high-tech downhillers.

Steamboat has been a quiet agricultural community since 1885 when James Crawford, the region's first homesteader, laid out the township. It didn't take long for skiers to start showing up however. In 1913, Norway's Carl Howelsen first titillated crowds with a 110-foot ski jump. By the 1940s, skiing was a popular class in the local high school and Steamboat Ski Area opened in 1963. It's no wonder the town's nickname is "Ski Town U.S.A."

Today, agriculture and hosting out-of-towners mixes nicely. Farm-implement stores downtown line up with tack shops packed with fishing and hunting gear. Banks with old-fashioned, cast-iron teller cages share the block with upscale craft stores proffering handmade log-and-branch furniture. The Steamboat Springs Resort (970-879-6111) itself is actually located three miles east of town.

More than 100 hot springs bubble up hereabouts. Half a dozen spritz the heart of downtown and a two-mile walking tour, navigated with a brochure's help, rounds them up. One of these, the "steamboat" spring, once made chugging noises reminiscent of a Mississippi sternwheeler, hence this land-locked mountain town's nautical moniker.

The Steamboat Springs Health and Recreation Association (970-879-1828) utilizes hot spring water, cooled with crystal-clear snow runoff, to form two soaking pools and two lap pools. But the finest mineral spring in the area (some say in the state) bubbles up six miles north of town. At Strawberry Park (970-879-0342), earth-heated mineral water gurgles out of the valley wall at 146° Fahrenheit. They blend it with the chilly runoff from Hot Springs Creek, then fill four stone-lined pools with the mineral elixir. Water temperatures range from frigid to frying and the pools inch down the valley like stepping stones set among fragrant fir and quaking aspen. Be forewarned—after dark, clothing is optional.

Ample local and Native American history is on display at the Tread of Pioneers Museum (970-879-2214) on Oak

Steamboat Springs Annual Festivals and Events

January
Cowboy Downhill—Suffice it to say that participants must be rodeo professionals and that horses, skis, cowboys, snow and silliness are all involved; call 970-879-6111

June-August
PRCA Summer of Pro Rodeo—weekly rodeo events throughout the summer; call 970-879-0882

July
Cowboy Roundup Days—A three-day rodeo event celebrating the fourth of July; call 970-879-0882
Strings in the Mountains—Internationally known musical artists perform classical music; call 970-879-5056

August
Vintage Auto Race and Concours d'Elegance—Vintage auto racing on the streets of the mountain village; call 970-879-0882

Street. The other popular museum in town is historic too; the Depot Art Center (970-879-4434) enlivens the turn-of-the-century train station, providing changing exhibits of local artists as well as a gift shop with locally made crafts.

For bicyclists, the Steamboat area is a northern Colorado pedaling paradise. The ski resort rents bikes and helmets so visitors can gondola to the top of Mt. Werner for a bone-jarring ride down. Others spin the nearly level 20 miles from Rabbit Ears Pass to Buffalo Pass while more urban folks pedal along the four-mile-long Yampa River Trail in town.

Fly fishing takes place right

SuperAmerica Guide's Idaho Springs Area Recommendations

- Drive to the top of Mt. Evans and hike to the very crest; "bag" a Colorado "14er."
- Climb aboard the Georgetown Loop Railroad for the exhilarating ride to Silver Plume.
- Shop for ornaments and gifts while sipping hot chocolate at Georgetown's Christmas Market in early December.
- Search for Rocky Mountain bighorn sheep at the Georgetown Wildlife Viewing Area. Even in the middle of the day, these nimble creatures can often be seen.
- If time permits, skip driving through the Eisenhower Tunnel. Instead, cross the Rockies via Loveland Pass for an alpine tundra experience.

Ride the Rockies

Georgetown Loop at Devil's Gate Viaduct

High-altitude vista-viewing draws visitors to the Georgetown Loop (303-569-2403), an eight-mile restored portion of the one-time Colorado & Southern Railway 60 miles west of Denver. The line's name stems from the engineering marvel constructed to enable trains to climb the nearly eight percent grade from Georgetown to Silver Plume.

Designers conquered the steep ascent by installing a "loop," calling it "Devil's Gate Viaduct," which takes the train on a corkscrew course around and across the narrow valley. At one time, long trains loaded with ore, food and crusty prospectors passed over this viaduct, a spindly bridge built 100 feet over Clear Creek. Old timers used to say the bridge swayed under the locomotive's weight.

Not to worry, there's a solid new trestle in place these days. It easily carries passengers in open-air cars, pulled by a coal-fired steam locomotive, on the two-hour tours. Purchase tickets in either Georgetown or Silver Plume.

Back in the early 1900s, tourists from Denver often boarded the Colorado & Southern Railroad for sightseeing trips from Denver up into Clear Creek Canyon. At the town of Silver Plume, they transferred to the Argentine Central Railway for looks at one of Colorado's "14ers," Mount McClellan. Today, a company called Trails and Rails (303-569-2403) invites bicyclists to coast down the roadbed of that now-defunct railroad. The path follows the old tracks descending 4,500 feet to Silver Plume. Riders may then board the Georgetown Loop for the rail trip to Devil's Gate Viaduct.

Bighorn sheep frequently peer down from the rocky heights in these parts. They're used to the train's whistle filling the valley with lonesome wails.

Silver mining brought these panting trains into this valley, and today there are some flecks left at the Lebanon Mine where passengers may disembark for tours. Hardy Cornish and Italian miners removed a fortune in ore before the 1893 silver crash crippled the area.

People looking for shiny stuff these days do better to cast an eye up to the surrounding hills while the train hisses through the forest. Fall color speckles the crumbled cliffs with shimmering stands of aspen.

Georgetown

along the Yampa, too, but most of the casting hereabouts takes place on the many lakes and reservoirs in the region. Steamboat Lake State Recreation Area north of town, and Stagecoach Reservoir, south of town, are well stocked throughout the summer. Dozens of lakes are brimming with fish at the nearby Flat Tops Wilderness Area.

Hikers head to the Flat Tops, too, as well as to the Routt National Forest and the Mt. Zirkel Wilderness Area. Refreshing Fish Creek Falls is only a three-mile hike from town and Mt. Werner operates a lift during the summer so day-hikers can be whisked up and stroll down.

Those who take horseback riding seriously—or want to—should trot over to one of the stellar guest ranches in this area. At both the Home Ranch (970-879-1780) and Vista Verde (970-879-3858), wannabe-dudes are assigned their own horses for a week-long stay guaranteed to improve their riding skills.

It's no coincidence that Steamboat Springs is where the term "champagne powder" originated. The snow is so dry, it simply sparkles. Steamboat Ski Resort (970-879-6111) boasts 2,500 acres, a 3,600 foot drop and a world-class skier, Billy Kidd. Kidd hosts informal downhill clinics on many winter afternoons.

Nightlife in Steamboat slaloms the course from Strawberry Park for a good soak to a pub crawl from the Old Town Pub to the Steamboat Brewery.

The Steamboat Springs visitors center is at 1255 S. Lincoln Ave.; call 970-879-0880

The Heart of the Rockies

From old-age mine shafts to new-age meditation gardens, from the largest ski area in the world at Vail to the largest swimming pool in the world at Glenwood Springs, from the world-renowned Food and Wine Magazine Classic at Aspen to the music of Vail's Bravo! Colorado, from white-water rafting on the Arkansas headwaters to the bike trails threading Summit County—here lies the vibrant heart of a spectacular state.

Idaho Springs

The first stop for most sightseers heading into the Rockies is Idaho Springs. The main street here—aptly called Miner Avenue—is lined with shops selling Colorado memorabilia, antiques and mountain clothing. The Underhill Museum (303-567-4709) pays tribute to mining's assayers. Across the street stands Beau Jo's (303-567-4376). This wood-walled emporium fills up every Saturday and Sunday evening with folks devouring custom-designed pizza masterpieces.

Across U.S. Interstate 70 (or rather, under its overpass) stands the Indian Springs Resort (303-567-2191). Utes and Arapahos fought for ownership of the warm waters here, but now you're more likely to see couples cuddling in the pool, which is covered greenhouse-style. Downstairs, "vapor" caves, bored out of Saddleback Mountain, splash with mineral-water pools.

The Argo Gold Mill and Museum (303-567-2421) is listed on the National Register of Historic Places and features mining machinery, mine tours and a "real" gunfight. For a real hard-rock mine tour, head up-valley on the frontage road to Trail Creek Road, then south to the Phoenix Working Mine (303-277-0129).

Idaho Springs' visitor center is located at 2200 Miner St.; call 303-567-4382 or 800-685-7785.

Mount Evans Scenic and Historic Byway

Mount Evans is the snow-crested peak visible in all those eye-widening photographs of Denver. Ascending 7,000 feet to 14,264 feet above sea level, the road is said to be the highest automobile road in North America. The paved two-lane (Colorado 103 and 5) loops 28 miles round trip to a summit parking lot, and a 600-foot-long path attains the peak itself. All in all, it's the easiest way in the state to "bag" a "14er."

Georgetown

To bag a wildlife view, exit at the Georgetown Wildlife Viewing Turnout. This is an odds-on bet for spotting Rocky Mountain bighorn sheep—the state animal. A herd of nearly 200 of the rock-walkers teeters among the rocks visible from a viewing area near Georgetown Lake.

Georgetown's delightful downtown is a gathering of Victorian jewels akin to San Francisco's. A brochure available at the information center leads walkers through the National Historic District. Dozens of homes delight the eye with color and composition, but two buildings sum up the Victorian era best. The first is Hamill House (303-569-2840). William Hamill was a silver magnate as well as a magnet for good taste. He installed marble fireplaces, hand painted wallpaper and walnut and maple paneling. The highlights here, though, are the glass conservatory and the triple-seater, cupola-covered outhouse. Not to be outdone in the elegant materials category, Louis Dupuy sheathed the dining room floor and walls in his Hotel De Paris (303-569-2840) with walnut and silver maple, too. Today, visitors may see exquisite furniture, books and diamond-dust mirrors.

Georgetown puts on its holiday finest during the first two weekends in December for Georgetown Christmas Market (303-569-2840). Carriages ply the streets, carolers warble and old St. Nick strolls about greeting children.

The Georgetown

A Bristlecone pine still stands in Arapahoe National Forest

Colorado Climate: What to Wear

Summer

Colorado's dry air means that temperatures can rise and fall up to 40 degrees Fahrenheit on any given day. This explains why layering is the perfect packing strategy for the high country. On a sunny morning, you might need a long sleeved shirt or jacket until 10 a.m. or so. Then, a shirt alone will be fine. That extra layer is a definite must after the sun goes down, as the mercury drops as well.

Rainstorms are quite common on summer afternoons, so an umbrella or raincoat is a definite plus.

Winter

Layer, layer, layer. Its amazing how warm you can feel at the base of a ski mountain and how freezing cold you end up at the top. Be prepared to add and shed clothing all day. Most experts suggest starting with polypropylene underwear and adding T-shirts, shirts, turtlenecks, sweaters, fleece, jackets and coats to suit your taste. Covering face and hands is important to prevent frostbite. Sunglasses prevent damage to eyes and sunscreen inhibits harmful rays from hitting your nose.

Spring

Dress as you would for winter, though the snow can be much wetter. Be prepared for rain, too.

Autumn

The fall can be warm and mild—even summerlike—for days on end. Then, Mother Nature can pitch a winter hissy. Be prepared for sudden changes with a variety of clothes.

Dillon Reservoir

information center is at 404 6th St.; call (303-569-2888).

Guanella Pass Scenic and Historic Byway

Spanning the mountains dividing Georgetown and Grant, Guanella Pass Road slides above timberline and provides golden vistas during autumn's color change.

The 22-mile route is lined with aspen and fir interspersed with vistas of Mt. Bierstadt. A trailhead from the pass' summit starts a scenic hike up the west face of Mt. Evans.

Altitude Adjustment

Many people's health is mildly affected by the higher altitudes and the thinner air of Colorado's high country. It's not unusual at all to develop mild symptoms of nausea, headache, fatigue, or to have trouble sleeping. This is called acute mountain sickness.

For most people, these discomforts pass away in a couple days. If they continue or get worse, proceed to a lower elevation and consult with a physician.

If you find you've got a wet cough, your shortness of breath is worsening or you feel like your lungs are filling with fluid, see a doctor immediately. You may be experiencing high altitude pulmonary edema. This is usually easily treated, but may be quite serious if not attended to.

Here are some suggestions to relieve high-altitude discomfort:

- Drink plenty of liquids such as water and juice. Staying hydrated is extremely important at higher elevations.
- Stay away from caffeine and alcohol for the first couple days of your visit. Then, use them only in moderation.
- Stay at a more moderate altitude (5,000–6,000 feet above sea level) for a couple days before hitting the hills. This should help attune your system.
- Lower your intake of salt.
- Keep physical activity down for a couple days. Take a nap if you crave it.
- Eat smaller meals and keep them low in fat and salt.

Summit County

Three words summarize Summit County: year-round recreation. Summer means biking, hiking, ballooning, four-wheeling, fishing, rafting, sailing, golfing and ordinary lazing around looking at the views. Autumn calls up casual drives through golden aspen glades. When the snow piles up, plan on downhill and cross-country skiing, snowshoeing, snowmobiling and ringing sleigh bells as a team of horses pulls through piles of wintry white. Springtime? Schedule a quiet hike.

The centerpiece of the county is Dillon Reservoir, ringed with the towns of Silverthorne, Dillon and Frisco. Each has a smattering of hotels, restaurants and activity outfitters. To the west lies Copper Mountain Resort

(970-349-2333) and eastward rises Keystone Resort (800-258-9553), both year-round destinations. South of the lake glitters Breckenridge, with its mining town ambiance.

Miles of bikeways connect the various cities of Summit County, making it one of the most enjoyable—and scenic—mountain bike and touring capitals in the nation. Vail Pass Bikeway scurries from Copper Mountain over Vail Pass. Nine miles long, the Blue River Bikeway connects Breckenridge and Frisco. The Frisco to Copper Mountain link is called Tenmile Canyon Bikeway. On the south edge of Dillon Reservoir, there is even a campground for bikers and hikers, the Peninsula Recreation Area, where no motorized vehicles are allowed.

Arapaho National Forest envelops amoeba-shaped Summit County. The Forest Service publishes a hiking booklet, the Summer Trailhead Guide, which is available at visitor centers throughout the county. It lists a dozen or so trails ranging from piece-of-cake, hour-long strolls to day-long, darn-difficult excursions into the backcountry.

Two short hikes sparkle with mountain and water vistas. For an easy one-mile-long hike, trek around to the Sapphire Point Overlook off Swan Mountain Road. The Old Dam Trail, off Dillon Dam Road near Heaton Bay Campground, is a little steeper but offers spectacular views of both the old lake and the new.

Eleven major roads were built to connect the mining areas in the late 19th century and most now jostle four-wheeler drivers. Georgia Pass links Breckenridge with South Park and Webster Pass unites Montezuma (above Keystone) with Handcart Gulch.

Running north and south through the county, the Blue River was dredge-mined during mining days, leaving deep pools for trout and brookies to hide and grow huge. The county's Gold Medal run—catch and release only—is the stretch of the Blue between Dillon Dam and Green Mountain Reservoir about 12 miles north. Cast for trout at Dillon Reservoir, or for kokanee salmon in Green Mountain Reservoir.

The same stretch of water that provides Gold Medal fishing provides rafting opportunities along the Blue River. Outfitters offer half-day and full-day adventures.

The near-constant breeze on Dillon Reservoir assures sailors of the wind they need to explore the lake's serene nooks and crannies. Two marinas access the lake, Frisco's (970-668-5573) on the west side and Dillon's (970-468-5100) on the easterly edge. Dillon Marina even sports a sailing school.

There is only one open-to-the-public, Jack Nicklaus-designed golf course in the world: the Breckenridge Golf Club (970-453-9104). It plays through trees, gullies, along mountains and among beaver ponds. Remember, balls go farther in the high altitude. Other courses are the Copper Creek (970-968-2339) course (the highest elevation P.G.A. course in the world) at Copper Mountain, and Eagle's Nest (970-468-0681) in Silverthorne with

Outlets on the Summit

No doubt about it—the most popular vacation activity is shopping. And while Breckenridge and Frisco burst at the windows with great merchandise, Silverthorne has something a lot of people love—an outlet mall.

Actually, the Silverthorne Factory Stores (970-468-6440) have three separate villages. The "Green Village" (with its green roof) has two buildings adjacent to the Blue River and contains twenty shops including a London Fog, OshKosh B'Gosh, a Levi's Outdoor Store and, a Colorado favorite, Miller Stockman Westernwear. The "Blue Village" sports a Bugle Boy, Jockey, J. Crew and Anne Klein as well as an amphitheater for frequent events. "Red Village" shines with Gap, Tommy Hilfiger and Carole Little.

SuperAmerica Guide's Summit County Recommendations

- Walk around to Sapphire Point Overlook off the Swan Mountain Road on the south side of Dillon Reservoir. The views of water and mountains are otherworldly.
- Shop for an afternoon among the very-Victorian stores lining Breckenridge's Main Street; savor an open-air lunch.
- Glimpse into the past at the Frisco Historic Park on Main Street in Frisco. These old cabins, homes and buildings give a good idea of life here a hundred years ago.
- Pick a ski resort—any ski resort—for a downhill fling.

its great views.

Summit County must be doing something right. Its four ski areas host more than three million visitors every winter. The Breckenridge Ski Resort (970-453-5000) itself comprises 1,600 acres which slope into two base areas, one right in town. Breckenridge's greatest strength, outside its terrain diversity, is its Victorian, mining-era feel. Copper Mountain's (970-968-2882) drawing card is its accessibility from Denver and its smart division of expertise levels. Plus, the runs are just plain fun. Keystone Resort (970-468-2316) has great all-around skiing as well as the stellar food, accommodations and ambiance of an upscale, family-oriented destination resort. Arapahoe Basin (970-468-0718) sits high in the hills, so high it can stay open till June every year. But this is not an area for beginners; it's steep going.

The Breckenridge Nordic Ski Center (970-453-6855) is perhaps the oldest cross-country ski center in the state, grooming more than 20 miles of trails and offering lessons. At the Copper Mountain/Trak Cross-Country Center (970-968-2882), they'll give you any level of lesson you want—including telemarking tutoring. The Frisco Nordic Center's (970-668-0866) trails were designed by Olympic silver medalist, Bill Koch.

For backcountry cross-country skiing, Summit County offers Boreas Pass, Peru Gulch Trail, Quandary Peak and Saint John trails. All are off the beaten path, all are advanced trips, all offer great views, plenty of mining ruins to spot and terrific snow. Beware of avalanches on any of these backcountry expeditions.

All the ski areas now have snowshoe rental. In addition, many of the cross-country areas encourage snowshoeing.

After all those activities, it may be time for a little relaxation. Several sleigh companies take groups and couples out in the evening for a ride among the trees, followed by a sumptuous dinner in either a cabin or heated tent.

The Frisco visitor center is at 409 Main St.; call 668-2051. The Breckenridge visitor center is at 309 North Main St.; call 970-453-6018.

Barney Ford

Barney Ford was a runaway slave who arrived in Breckenridge in 1860 in the hope of striking gold. Since blacks could not file land claims, Ford hired a Denver lawyer to file them for him, but the attorney swindled him.

Undeterred, Ford started working as a bellhop in Denver, soon bought a barbershop and before long, he owned several restaurants and hotels in the region.

In 1866, when Colorado first applied for statehood, Ford traveled to Washington D.C. to lobby for inclusion of voting rights for blacks, a provision that was actually included in the 1876 constitution. In 1873, he became the first black Coloradan to run for the legislature.

Ford built a house for himself in Breckenridge in 1882 near Washington and Main streets. The successful black businessman died in 1902 and is buried in Denver.

A photo of Ford hangs at the Edwin Carter Museum (970-453-9022) on the corner of Ridge St. and Wellington Rd. in Breckenridge. Edwin Carter was a naturalist who gathered nearly 10,000 flora and fauna specimens and donated them to the state.

Breckenridge

Breckenridgers are quick to blush over their name change, which occurred nearly 140 years ago. They originally named themselves after then-Vice President John Breck-inridge, apparently hoping to secure a post office. Unfortunately, dear John sided with the Confederates during the Civil War, so local Unionists sweet talked Congress into re-spelling the burg's moniker to Breck-en-ridge.

Breckenridge today melds its mining-era heritage with a decidedly modern-day ski image. Nestled at the base of the gnarly Tenmile Range at 9,600 feet above sea level, the town contains only 1,600 hale and hearty year-round residents. Yet they host up to 23,000 skiers on busy winter weekends. Their string of ski mountains are simply named Peak 7, Peak 8, Peak 9 and Peak 10.

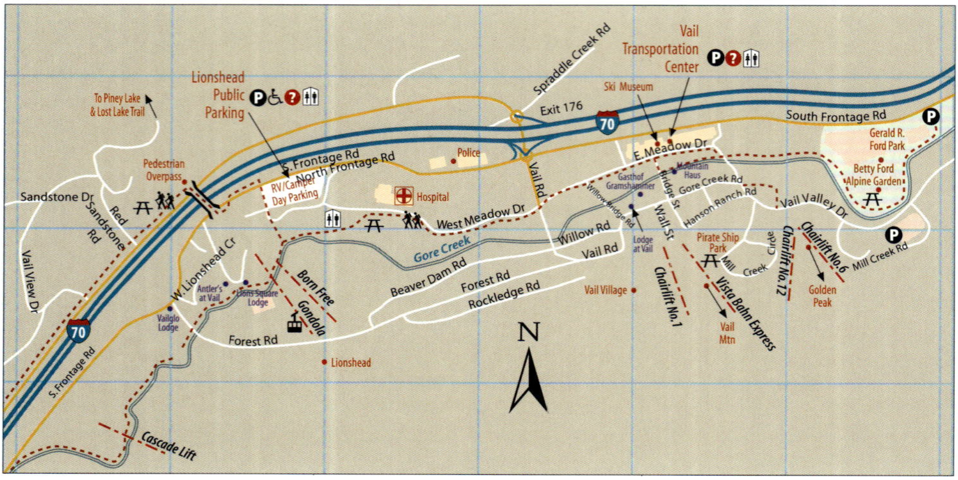

Street map of Vail

One of the state's largest historic districts, 200 buildings in a 16-block area, has been lovingly maintained with a riot of color. Two-hour guided walking tours run weekdays during the summer with a stop at the Edwin Carter Museum (970-453-9022). Mining tours of either the Washington Gold Mine or Lomax Placer Gulch (970-453-9022) dig deep into history too. Both tours journey underground to demonstrate hard rock mining. In Summit County, hard rock means minerals, not raucous restaurants.

Not that Breck can't get raucous. It certainly can. Enter Ullr Fest (970-453-6018), a week-long January celebration of snow and all things chilly that pays party-style homage to Ullr, the Norse god of winter. Then there's the International Snow Sculpture Championships (970-453-6018) held every January. A dozen teams from icy spots around Mother Earth carve short-lived but stunning works of art out of 12-foot-square blocks of packed snow.

Perhaps now and again they carve a likeness of "Tom's Baby." In 1887, the largest gold nugget ever unearthed in Colorado was discovered near Breckenridge by one Tom Groves. The hunk of heaven weighs in at 14 pounds, 10 ounces. Legend says it

Nature in the Vail Valley

Vail's snow is world-renowned, but it covers the ground only six to eight months a year. During the warmer seasons, the valley is blanketed in wildflowers.

Located on Gore Creek near Gerald Ford Park, the Vail Nature Center (970-479-2291) has been established to provide information on the where-to-gos and how-to-get-theres for the valley's nature enthusiasts.

They also provide guided excursions. For novice hikers, hour-long strolls along the creek focus on indigenous flora and fauna. Stronger hikers join full-day treks (offered twice a week) that head to the top of nearby mountains. On the Notch Mountain Hike, a nine-miler, walkers reach 13,000 feet encountering primrose, fireweed, wild violets and edible twinberries and thimbleberries.

The center also offers riverbed ecology tours and moonlight strolls to look for great-horned owls. An unusual "edible plants hike" ends up with a cooking lesson using indigenous plants.

Devoted wildflower enthusiasts head for the Betty Ford Alpine Gardens (970-476-0103) in Ford Park to visit the highest public alpine garden in the world. Over 1,500 varieties of flora populate the Perennial Garden, including flowers, shrubs, conifers and heathers. The Meditation Garden takes its design inspiration from rocks and water. Throughout June, the Vail Valley Festival of Flowers (970-476-0103) hosts workshops centering around the challenges of high-altitude gardening.

"Downtown" Vail

Vail's Betty Ford Alpine Gardens

originally tipped the scales at nearly 16 pounds, but, as the story goes, miners fondled a pound off of it while repeatedly caressing the gorgeous stone. Today, the rock is the centerpiece of the mineral exhibit at the Denver Museum of Natural History.

The Breckenridge Visitor Center is at 309 North Main St.; call 970-453-6018.

Vail Summer Festivals and Events

June–August

Bravo! Colorado Vail Valley Music Festival—Music aficionados and casual concert-goers enjoy the opportunity to hear world-class performances against the backdrop of the Rocky Mountains. Bravo! presents 60 events, 50 soloists, three orchestras, a jazz ensemble and a musicians' program. The Detroit Symphony takes up residence in the village for 10 days each July. Call 970-827-5700.

August

Vail International Dance Festival—This dance festival takes place during early August each summer, bringing together a wide range of dancers, styles and troupes as well as workshops. Performances have included ensembles from the Bolshoi and the Stuttgart ballets, dancing excerpts and complete classic and contemporary selections. The festival also stars principal dance couples from stellar companies like the American Ballet Theater and the Zurich Ballet, executing pas-de-deux from a wide repertoire. Call 970-949-1999.

July

Vail Arts Festival—More than 100 artists gather to meet buyers and show off their work. A similar event takes place in Beaver Creek in August. Call 970-827-5299.

September

EXPLORE—Designed for adults aged 50 and over, this popular collection of seminars assembles people for discussion of global issues, history, astronomy, music and art.
Call 303-777-6873 or 800-298-4242.

Vail

Until Gerald Ford's ascension to the White House in 1974, Vail was a sleepy, if luxurious, ski resort (970-476-5601). Ford, a congressman, spent his Christmas holidays and summer weekends at his home hereabouts.

But when the Michigander came to power, he brought along a veritable blizzard of publicity with him on his seasonal jaunts into the Vail and

SuperAmerica Guide's Vail Recommendations

- Savor the beauty and setting of the Betty Ford Alpine Gardens early one morning.
- Feel the rhythm of the Rockies during a Bravo! Colorado concert.
- Stroll along the river from Gerald Ford Park to downtown.
- Ski Vail's astonishing back bowls; from professional to strong intermediates, skiers find these pistes to be among the best skiing in the state.
- Take an evening to play on Adventure Ridge: ice skating, tubing, snowbiking, even sledding.

Beaver Creek area. Consequently, millions of people around the world saw pictures of Colorado's high country sheathed in winter's glorious powder, summer's dappled greens and autumn's gilded golds. Ford still maintains a home in Beaver Creek (he's one of Colorado's easiest-to-spot celebrities), and Vail has blossomed into the largest ski area in the world.

The city sets astride the gurgling Gore Creek with its serenity-inducing background babble. And the main thoroughfare, open only to pedestrians, is lined with shops proffering first-class merchandise, great restaurants and a generous number of amiable people.

Beaver Creek

Vail Mountain forms the backdrop. From early November to early May, 30 lifts, quads and gondolas whisk skiers up to the 4,644 acres of terrain. Wisely, the area has been divvied up equally for beginner, intermediate and advanced schussers. The longest ski run, from "Flapjack"

Glenwood's Canyon Grand

Question: What took 13 years and $500 million to build, consumed 60 million pounds of steel and devoured 1.6 billion pounds of concrete?
Answer: The Glenwood Canyon stretch of U.S. Interstate 70, the costliest ribbon of interstate highway in the nation.

Glenwood Canyon stretches for 12.5 miles east of Glenwood Springs. Carved by the Colorado River, it's a glorious 1,800-foot-deep gash into 570-million-year-old Precambrian granite. Sheer walls rise up out of the river, barely supporting trees and shrubbery. Bighorn sheep pick their way among the rocks while elk and deer use lengths of it to graze and migrate. All in all, it's one of the most ruggedly beautiful stretches of river and scenery in the state.

Cyclists enjoy the Colorado River in Glenwood Canyon

So how to build a road through it? "Very carefully," insisted environmentalists. To meet the Department of Transportation's (DOT) Interstate Highway requirements, a four-lane freeway had to be constructed to match the curvature of the canyon. The DOT was required to raise a good portion of the road on pylons to protect animal migration paths. Any rock blasted out had to be resculpted, replanted and even recolored to camouflage with surrounding areas. In all, 300,000 cubic yards of dirt and rock were shuffled hither and yon.

As well, they threw in a few amenities. More than 150,000 bushes were planted and four rest stops were built. One, the Grizzly Creek, even has a kayak and raft put-in. But the highlights for ever-active Coloradans are the 16-mile-long, paved recreation path that runs the length of the canyon out of Glenwood Springs and the extremely scenic hike up to Hanging Lake from the Hanging Lake rest area.

through "Riva," runs 4.5 miles. The Back Bowls, nearly twice as much mountain as you see from the valley floor, sprinkle powder among 2,743 acres.

But success in winter means more than just skiing nowadays. Vail has upped the ante at Adventure Ridge (970-476-9090). Here, they have dedicated an area at the top of the mountain to alternative winter activities. There's an ice-skating rink near the new gondola building, a snowboard halfpipe with a dedicated surface lift, a tubing and sledding park (remember sledding as a kid?) as well as snowmobile excursions along Eagle's Nest Ridge. All this is accessible from a heated, lighted, high-speed gondola. The area is open after sundown so winter funsters can play under the stars.

Plain old ordinary skiing still draws the crowds too, and one of the reasons is the new high technology approach to the skis you strap on your feet. At three "New Technology Centers" (970-476-9090), Vail offers a way to try several different kinds of sticks. Skiers may rent different equipment by the hour: powder skis, shaped (or parabolic) skis, and mogul skis from many different manufacturers.

Vail also offers spectacular Nordic skiing at the Vail Nordic Center (970-476-8366), the Golden Peak Cross-Country Center (970-479-4390) or McCoy Park (970-845-5313) at nearby Beaver Creek. The Shrine Pass Trail starts at the peak of Vail Pass, heads up for three miles to the top of Shrine Pass then descends eight miles into Redcliff. Try a midweek run to avoid snowmobilers.

Ski aficionados pay a call at the Colorado Ski Museum/Ski Hall of Fame (970-476-1876). Displays capture the excitement of a developing sport from its beginnings in the 1800s right up to a look at snowmobiles and snowboards.

There is also much to recommend Vail in the summer months. Not only are prices less astronomical, the village is less crowded and the surrounding Gore and Sawatch ranges are covered with wildflowers, hiking trails, mountain bikers and wildlife. And since they allow bikes on the gondolas, the mountain becomes a cycler's dream.

Vail has a visitors center, located atop the Vail Village parking structure on South Frontage Road and another on the Lions Head parking structure; call 970-476-1000.

Beaver Creek

Beaver Creek is upscale Vail's even tonier next door neighbor. Residing high above the Vail Valley, 10 miles west of Vail itself, this deluxe group of European-style stone and stucco condos and hotels meanders along the bubbling Beaver Creek. The architecture is so sensitive to this delightful water feature that if the brook takes a little turn, you can be certain the adjacent building has turned along with it—

Mount of the Holy Cross

Historical shot of Holy Cross

South of U.S. Interstate 70, as it winds its way into the plateaus of the Western Slope, rise the wind-swept peaks of the Holy Cross Wilderness Area. Made famous when an Air Force pilot crashed his A-10 into Gold Dust Mountain in April of 1997, the area was used by Coloradans as a hiking and stream-fishing getaway long before the area was declared wilderness in 1980. The spot's original claim to fame is the 14,005-foot Mount of the Holy Cross. In 1873, photographer William Henry Jackson captured the snow-filled cross etched on the mountain's face on film. The photograph became one of the most famous of its time.

The viewing platform for the cross is a moderately difficult, six-mile (one-way) hike along Fall Creek Trail from the end of County Road 707, approximately two miles south of Minturn.

probably using a cone-topped corner turret to accomplish the trick. A brick-paved pedestrian avenue forms the village's central artery, replete with high-end restaurants and shops. The surrounding hills are draped with quaking aspen and nail-straight lodgepole pine. Among the trees, trails accommodate horses, cyclists and hikers.

The swank resort was planned with the 1976 Winter Olympics in mind, but environmentally conscious voters vetoed the state's bid. With the addition of much terrain and many lifts over the years, the resort, owned by Vail Resorts, has grown into a destination in its own right.

Some of the best (and easiest) elk viewing is to be found near Beaver Creek at the junction of U.S. Interstate 70 and U.S. Highway 24. The Dowd Junction Elk Viewing Area was established for the United States Forestry Service to manage the hundreds of elk that make these aspen-coated slopes their winter home.

Beaver Creek's visitor center is in nearby Avon at 260 Beaver Creek Place; call 970-949-5189 for information about Beaver Creek.

Glenwood Springs

If you ask Glenwood Springs residents what there is to do around town, many actually answer, "Drive to Aspen." Indeed, celebrity central is only a few miles south on U.S. Highway 82, but Glenwood has several major drawing cards of its own.

The first is the Glenwood Hot Springs Pool (970-945-7131). This immense warm-water plunge is said to be the largest swimming pool in the world. At 405 feet long by 100 feet wide, it's certainly the biggest in Colorado. This more-than-a-million-gallon tub easily accommodates up to 1,000 swimmers summer and winter in its 90 degrees Fahrenheit water. A

A Teddy for Teddy

In 1905, the Hotel Colorado (970-945-6511 or 800-544-3998) hosted President Theodore (Teddy) Roosevelt for a bear hunt. When Mr. President returned empty handed, eager-to-please hotel maids sewed fabric scraps together into the shape of a bear. The press broadcast these bare facts worldwide, and kids have been snuggling up to "Teddy" bears ever since.

The town of Aspen and the Aspen ski area

smaller pool (a mere 100 feet by 100 feet) is for more therapeutically minded soakers at 104 degrees Fahrenheit. It even sports coin-operated hydro jets.

Next door are the Yampah Spa and Vapor Caves (970-945-0667). The spa offers standard treatments and massages. The steamy caves provide a unique opportunity to warm weary bones 10 feet below ground level. They are heated by the warmth of hot mineral water. The temperature runs about 112 degrees Fahrenheit, and the humidity hovers near 100 percent. Keep in mind that *yampah* is a Ute word meaning "big medicine."

Glenwood is fraught with history, too. Doc Holliday, the pistol-packing, card-dealing *bon vivant* of Gunfight at the OK Corral fame, is buried in Linwood Cemetery overlooking the spectacular junction of the Colorado and Roaring Fork rivers. The headstone, engraved with a perfect four-aces poker hand, is often decorated with decks of cards and whiskey bottles.

The Glenwood Springs Visitor Center is located at 1102 Grand Ave.; call 970-945-6589.

SuperAmerica Guide's Aspen Recommendations

- Attend a musical event in the Bayer-Benedict tent at the Aspen Music Festival.
- Sigh at the beauty of Maroon Bells Wilderness Area early in the morning or late in the afternoon when the deer are out and the crowds are gone.
- Taxi through town in the ULTIMATE Taxi, Jon Barnes' fun-filled vision of Aspen through the seventies, eighties and nineties.
- Shop for gorgeous glassware and jewelry in the stores on Aspen's mall.
- Watch art being crafted by artisans at the Anderson Ranch Arts Center in Snowmass.
- Visit the ghostly remains of Ashcroft; shop for handmade crafts at Toklat Gallery.
- Mush huskies through the snow, then feast on a gourmet lunch at Krabloonik Kennels.

Aspen/Snowmass

Some folks think that you might as well be leaving Colorado when you head south from U.S. Interstate 70 onto U.S. Highway 82 into the broad sweep of the Roaring Fork River Valley. They insist that things are so different here that it's not really Colorado at all. Others argue exactly the opposite, that Aspen and its environs are the quintessential Colorado experience.

Truth be told, things are a little different here. For one thing, the price of the average single-family house in Aspen hovers near the two-million-dollar mark. For another, the airport here is as likely to be lined with private jets as commercial airliners. And the owners' registrations are likely to carry names like Trump and Streisand.

On the other hand, there is something quintessentially Colorado about a Victorian-style hamlet, with its roots dug deep into mining, placed in a spectacular mountain setting of aspen and evergreen, surrounded with wilderness and inhabited by interesting, active men and women who sneak away from work to schuss or pedal—depending on the season—down sun-dappled slopes. In that sense, Aspen could just as well be Telluride, Crested Butte, Durango, Breckenridge or Steamboat Springs.

So why do so many people spend their time here summer and winter? It could be the ambiance; Aspen has an air about it that lets one savor the sweet life. It could be intellectual; the Aspen Institute (970-925-7010) hosts seminars attended by the likes of Margaret Thatcher and

Robert McNamara. Or it could be the feeling of being at the heart of it all: after all, Aspen was the first ski-oriented mountain town to host international design, music and dance events.

The city itself glitters at the east end of a canyon like pure

Aspen's Galaxy of Stars

There are two kinds of people in Aspen: The people who live there and the rest of us, who go to look at the people who live there. Check out these neighborhoods if you want to see how the stellar half lives.

Starwood
Picture names like Sally Field, Chris Evert and Prince Bandar bin Sultan looking across both the Aspen and the Maroon Bells areas from this gated enclave of homes, which sport price tags in the $3.8 million category.

The West End
Right in town—between 8th and Mill streets—folks like actor Jack Nicholson and writer Jim Salter cozy up to their fireplaces in getaways that run a mere $1.8 million.

Snowmass Village
Elk still make occasional appearances on the grounds of these $1.5 million homes. It's nice to know that celebs like Michael Eisner, Michael Douglas, Goldie Hawn and Kurt Russell are getting in a little wildlife-watching.

Woody Creek
Well-knowns like Hunter S. Thompson, Ed Bradley, Don Henley and Don Johnson live in this neighborhood. Supposedly, Thompson and Henley hang out at the Woody Creek Tavern.

Aspen Recreational Opportunities

With easy access to three designated wilderness areas—Maroon Bells/Snowmass, Hunter/Fryingpan, and Collegiate Peaks, as well as the 260,000 acre White River National Forest—Aspen has lots to offer beyond skiing.

Winter Activities

Dogsledding
Krabloonik Kennels (970-923-4342) outfits full or half-day trips into the Maroon Bells Wilderness Area via teams of 13 dogs.

Ice Skating
Aspen glitters with two ice rinks; Aspen Ice Gardens, a 16,000 square foot indoor rink, (970-925-7485) and the outdoor Silver Circle (970-925-6360).

Sleighrides
Aspen Carriage Company (970-927-3334) offers scenic and historic tours in their sleighs parked at the corner of Galena and Cooper. Snowmass Stables (970-923-3075) takes riders to a cozy cabin, where dinner and entertainment are provided.

Cross-country Skiing
Nearly 48 miles of no-cost, groomed cross-country trails connect Aspen and Snowmass. Aspen's two visitors centers (in the Wheeler Opera House and at Rio Grande Place) provide trail maps. Roaring Fork Transit Agency buses will even drop skiers off at several trailheads. Either Ute Mountaineer (970-925-2849) or Aspen Cross-Country Center (970-925-2145) rent equipment. Ashcroft Ski Touring Center (970-925-1044) keeps nearly 20 miles of trail groomed in the stunning Castle Creek Valley. After skiing, you might enjoy a fixed price, gourmet meal at the Pine Creek Cookhouse (970-925-1044) before you ski back to your car.

Summer Activities

Hiking
Maroon Bells: At Maroon Bells, an extensive set of trails leads from the shuttle drop-off. One popular path is the 1.5 mile Crater Lake Trail. Another runs 3.5 miles downhill to East Maroon Portal, where the shuttle will pick you up.

Aspen: The Rio Grande Trail begins at Mill St. (right on the river) and winds along the Roaring Fork for nearly ten miles all the way to Woody Creek. Braille Trail provides just what the name implies, a nature walk guided by nylon rope with Braille information kiosks along the quarter-mile path.

Biking
The Rio Grande Trail mentioned above is also a terrific bicycle trail, as is Richmond Road off the Aspen Mountain gondola. Owl Creek Trail runs along Colorado Highway 82, joining Aspen with Snowmass. Heartier souls trek the road to the Maroon Bells Wilderness Area.

Fishing
The Fryingpan River east of Basalt is a Gold Medal stream famous for ease of access to the river and the sheer size of catch available. Ruedi Reservoir is good lake fishing.

Picnicking
Along Independence Pass, eight miles east of Aspen, look for "The Grottos" turnout. This popular spot has many tables to eat at, as well as caves to explore.

Downtown Aspen

Aspen's ULTIMATE Transport

The ULTIMATE Taxi is Jon Barnes' high-tech flash back—in a taxi. For $75, Barnes takes up to five people on half-hour spins through Aspen.

But this is no ordinary taxi. Barnes bills his rolling side show as the only "music studio, theater, nightclub, planetarium, toy store, Internet connected taxi on the planet."

The cab is indeed Internet connected. At www.ultimate-taxi.com, his site spreads out two dozen colorful pages with sound and motion. There are message boards, a chat room, views of the taxi, pictures of passengers, information on Barnes and his mobile enterprise and a list of the famous people who have hailed him.

This being Aspen, no opportunity is lost to drop a name or two: Clint Eastwood, Bill Bradley, Pierce Brosnan, Dudley Moore, George Hamilton, Ringo Starr, Michael Douglas and Jerry Seinfeld.

The tour may take in Aspen highlights, but the cab itself is the biggest attraction. A disco ball swings from the ceiling, a fog machine spews smoke and spinning red lasers dazzle the eyes.

The cab is equipped with state-of-the-art-sound but fares are as likely to hear the cabbie himself banging on the dashboard or fingering the organ—Barnes' musical tastes run from Stevie Wonder to Dire Straits.

Barnes occasionally stays live on the Internet as he drives through town, sometimes pulling over to exchange messages with interested parties around the world.

To make a reservation, call 970-927-9239 or search him out on the World Wide Web. Every person who takes a ride gets a free page on his site for 90 days. Or, if you just want to chat, Barnes says he's often online live from around 7:30 p.m. to 1 a.m. on summer nights.

gold settled out into the bottom of a miner's pan. Its story is the same as many mining camps in Colorado: prospectors hit silver in the late 1870s, boom times played until the government quit guaranteeing silver prices in 1893, then bust times ruled until the close of WWII, when skiing brought the current boom.

But Aspen comes with a twist. When the first lift started swaying skiers up the west face of Aspen Mountain on January 11, 1947, film star Gary Cooper was among the dignitaries, as were a number of millionaires and world-class skiers. Aspen's future was cast forever that day as an expensive, celebrity-oriented getaway with some of the best skiing—and skiers—in the world.

Interestingly, there is no single ski area here—there are four, each with its own flavor. Aspen Highlands (888-290-1325) is the all-around area, mixing expert, intermediate

Aspen Summer Festivals and Events

June

International Design Conference—brings world-class designers together to line out the future of architecture and related design fields; call 970-925-2257.

Food and Wine Magazine Classic—whips together chefs and wine experts along with thousands of guests; call 888-794-6398

July/August

Aspen Music Festival and School—a staggering variety of classical and jazz events; call 970-925-3254 for a schedule, 970-925-9042 for reservations.

following pages: the Maroon Bells are one of Colorado's most famous sights

and beginner runs. The views from the Olympic chairlift are wondrous and high-glamour clothing is optional on this bit-of-a-rebel peak. Aspen Mountain (888-290-1325) is called Ajax by locals, no doubt to honor the silver mine there and because the runs are pure sterling. All are expert or strong intermediate—beginning skiers beware. At Buttermilk (888-290-1325), the 410 acres are mostly groomed into long, gentle slopes. Snowmass (970-925-1220) is really a separate, family-oriented resort 12 miles down-valley with four peaks comprising 2,655 acres.

For visitors who want to spend a day off the slopes, Aspen offers splendid diversions. The downtown area is rich with interesting shops. Many contain art, clothing and furniture that would as easily stock shops in Manhattan or Beverly Hills. The jewelry and artistic glass stores (and there are lots of them) compete with each other to offer the most sophisticated designs.

The region is extremely culture conscious—that's part of its allure—so it's no surprise to find galleries downtown offering the works of major artists. The Aspen Art Museum (970-925-8050) exhibits well-known artists from around the world, and Anderson Ranch Arts Center in Snowmass (970-923-3181) not only displays established artists but offers dozens of workshops. The Wheeler-Stallard House Museum (970-925-3721) shows off collectibles from another age.

Aspen boasts several think tanks that welcome visitors, too. The Aspen Center for Environmental Studies (970-925-5756) was founded to preserve Hallam Lake, and they offer a number of programs focused on the environment as well as year-round wildlife tours. Rocky Mountain Institute (970-927-3851) seeks to educate visitors about the blessings of architecture in tune with Mother Nature. Their building, which is in Snowmass, is used to demonstrate solar-powered heating and cooling principles. The Aspen Institute (970-925-7010) hosts conferences throughout the year that are focused on international issues.

No town could come this far down the culture highway without offering first-rate nightlife. The Crystal Palace Dinner Theater (970-925-1455) takes advantage of their multitalented serving staff to do a musical revue that satirizes local celebs and issues of the day. At the J Bar (970-920-1000) in the Hotel Jerome autograph hounds sometimes spot celebs. The Wheeler Opera House (970-920-5770) is the site of year-round theater, music, dance and film.

One Aspen visitor center is at the corner of Hyman and Mill; call 970-925-5656. Another is at 425 Rio Grande Place; call 970-925-1940.

Ashcroft

Not many ghost towns still have this much to offer: First, the 13-mile drive from Aspen is through the scenic Castle Creek Valley rife with shaking aspen; second, the town itself is well-marked, well-preserved and well-maintained. Now a National Historic Site, Ashcroft was founded in 1880 by miners hunting silver. And they found it. By 1883, the town had 2,000 occupants, a court house, a school and 20 saloons. Many of those buildings still stand, in various states of disrepair. The site is manned by volunteers who answer questions, lead tours and sell books. Across the highway is the Toklat Gallery (970-925-7345), displaying fine, handmade crafts. Up-valley another couple miles is the Pine Creek Cook-house

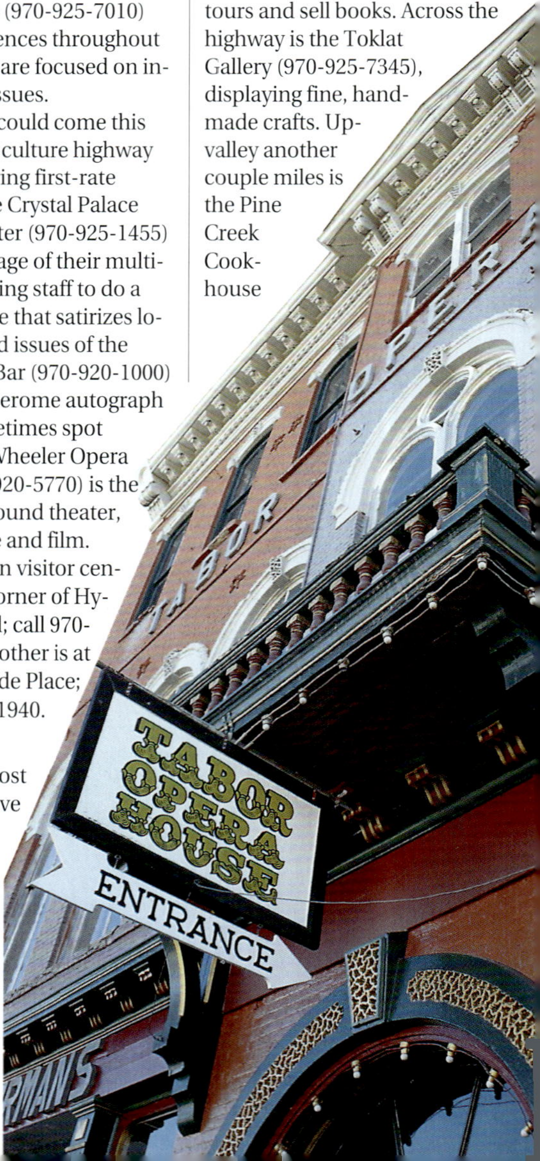

Leadville's Tabor Opera House

(970-925-1044), a small restaurant with big views serving well-prepared game dishes.

Maroon Bells Wilderness Area

Aspenites say "The Bells" are the most photographed scenic site in Colorado. Indeed, with their splendid massing of granite peaks reflecting into Maroon Lake, it is hard not to become a shutter bug.

Maroon Bells is so popular in summer (the road is open only to snowmobiles during winter) that the road is restricted to county buses (and campers with passes) from 8:30 a.m. to 5:00 p.m. The buses are operated by the Roaring Fork Transit Authority; call 970-925-8484 for rates and frequency.

Independence Pass

The shortest route between Aspen and Leadville crawls across Independence Pass topping out at 12,095 feet above sea level. Opened in 1881, the roadway was banked gracefully so stagecoaches could take the tight turns without slowing down. The trip required five changes of horses, and trained dogs ran ahead to clear the way. Still, that adventure took between 10 and 25 hours to complete.

The disparity in those two lengths of time is perhaps due to riders' insistence that the driver pull over to let them admire the views. Today, the 50-mile drive takes more like two hours (and is open only during summer), but that can still be extended substantially because of the sheer scenic wonder of this, the highest passenger car crossing of the Continental Divide. The highway stretches along vistas of both the Roaring Fork Valley to the west and the Sawatch Range spiking the eastern horizon.

Two of the peaks dominating that eastern vista are Mt. Elbert and Mt. Massive. At 14,433 and 14,421 feet above sea level, they are the highest peaks in Colorado.

Leadville

Leadville—population 3,200—is a small town with a big history. Shortly after gold was discovered here in 1860, the tented camp exploded to 5,000 inhabitants. Most of them passed right through town, though, for the gold here was difficult to mine. In 1875 two metallurgists, finding traces of silver, started restaking claims and soon a few miners came to

Earth Quakies

Speaking of Aspen...
Coloradans are crazy about aspen, or "quakies" as they are affectionately called because of the tendency of the leaves—and the trees themselves—to quake in the gentlest breath of air. Urban dwellers buy clusters of them (they thrive only in groves), along with columbine and Indian paintbrush to create mountain meadows in their flatland backyards.

Many believe the aspen groves to be the oldest living organism on earth. You see, aspen don't seed, they spread from root growth. And since the conditions for seeding haven't existed here since the last glacial epoch, around 20,000 years ago, all the aspen we see must have rooted from a tree, or trees, alive at that time. So, in essence, that grove is still alive.

Aspen are the first tree to grow after an avalanche, landslide or fire has ravaged a landscape. So aspen thickets are often evidence of a fairly recent natural disaster. In fact, many of the old mining towns that boast so many aspen have them simply because the original growth of pine and fir were clearcut by the miners.

The Terrifying 10th

From 1942 till 1944, a military unit—the 10th Mountain Division—trained for winter military maneuvers at Camp Hale in the Pando Valley between Leadville and Minturn. This elite group of 14,000 trainees was composed of men from around the country who knew how to ski and were willing to serve out their military obligation doing dangerous duty in extreme cold and high altitude.

Carrying 90-pound rucksacks on their backs, these men skied up—and down—the nearby mountains. They developed special boots for use on both skis and snowshoes as well as for hiking and climbing. They even had a way to attach their packs to their skis in case they needed a toboggan.

The division saw action in Italy; they scrambled up the sheer cliffs of Riva Ridge in April, 1945 to overtake the Germans on Mt. Belvedere.

Many of these winter warriors returned to Colorado after the war. Several started winter-oriented businesses here. In fact, many opened ski resorts.

town hoping for a big silver strike. Horace Tabor was one of the lucky ones (see box), but his wealth vaporized after the 1893 silver crash.

Much of the history of mining in Colorado—indeed, of the nation—may be extracted from the variety of museums and home/museums in Leadville. The National Mining Hall of Fame and Museum (719-486-1229) educates visitors about mining technology, ores and production rates throughout the United States. The Matchless Mine and Baby Doe's Cabin (800-933-3901) is 1.5 miles east of town and worth the drive if you want to get a feel for Tabor himself and the woman he ran off with. Self-guided tours of the Healy House and Dexter Cabin (719-486-0487) tell the tale of the Daniel Healy, an engineer who ran a boarding house and James V. Dexter, a rather rakish fellow who built this luxurious "cabin" as a social club. The Heritage Museum and Gallery (719-486-1878) uses artifacts and dioramas to tell the story of Leadville in great detail.

After walking through museums, visitors to Leadville may hop aboard a train. The Leadville, Colorado and Southern Railroad (719-486-3936) chugs out of town two times a day during summer and early fall for two-hour excursions up to the Climax Molybdenum Mine.

Trucks haul supplies in these parts nowadays, but back in mining times, burdens were lugged by burros. Leadville honors these gentle-spirited pack animals each year during Boom Days (719-486-3900), a riotous revelry held in early August featuring parades, mucking and drilling contests, "painted" ladies and the International Burro Race up Mosquito Pass.

Leadville's visitor center is located at 809 Harrison Ave.; call 719-486-3900 or 888-LEADVILLE.

Top of the Rockies Scenic and Historic Byway

Leadville is the largest city on this 82-mile loop—but not its only attraction.

Colorado Highway 91 weaves along the headwaters of the Arkansas River and passes the Climax Mine—one of the largest in the state—before topping Fremont Pass and dipping into Frisco.

U.S. Highway 24 courses northwest, twisting past Ski Cooper and descending into the Pando Valley—the locale of Camp Hale where the 10th Mountain Division trained.

Minturn, near U.S. Interstate 70, has become a mountain-home decorator's dream, as it hosts many antique and furniture emporiums.

South Park

Leadville isn't the only high-country host for a burro race. A short but strenuous mule—or four-wheel-drive—ride across Mosquito Pass from Leadville

Colorado's Mining Royalty

When silver surfaced in Oro City, later Leadville, in the late 1860s, the postmaster there was Horace Tabor, a onetime prospector who had given up on digging and taken to shopkeeping.

He hadn't given up on gambling, so he often traded equipment, food and liquor to prospectors in exchange for a percentage of any silver they discovered. Two German shoemakers were among these, and after a swig of swill one day, they went up the hill and located a vein of silver so rich that Tabor's share alone amounted to $500,000. (At the time, miners toiled a 12-hour day for $3.) Tabor parlayed his cache into a $12 million fortune.

While Tabor was living high on the hog, he divorced his long-suffering wife Augusta to marry the young divorcée Elizabeth McCourt Doe–affectionately called "Baby Doe" by admiring miners. Horace and Baby tied the knot in a lavish Washington D.C. ceremony held during Tabor's 30-day tenure as Colorado's junior senator. Dozens of men attended, including President Chester Arthur, but their wives were too scandalized to show up.

When the U.S. government stopped underwriting the price of silver in 1893, Tabor's wealth evaporated. He died in Denver, instructing Baby Doe to hang on to the Matchless Mine, once rich in ore. Indeed, she died there, found frozen to death, 35 years later.

In 1956 the Central City Opera staged *The Ballad of Baby Doe*, an opera by John Latouche that weaves the tale of Horace, Augusta and Baby Doe, three people that symbolize the dreams and downfalls of Colorado's mining days.

brings travelers to South Park, the 1,200-square-mile bowl that sunk as the Rockies rose around it. In late July every summer, a dozen or more burros and their human attendants gather on Fairplay's Main Street for a jaunt up and down Mosquito Pass—provided the cantankerous hoofers are willing to giddy-up, that is.

Hundreds of race fans gather to watch the send-off and then stroll Fairplay's streets during the long wait for the victor to return. With mules on their minds, some pay respects to "Shorty," a miner's four-legged friend whose bronze monument stands on the courthouse lawn.

History buffs head to South Park City Museum (719-836-2387) to poke around 30 historic buildings. All were moved to this locale from other spots in South Park and assembled to recreate the activities of life in these parts between 1870 and 1900. Each represents some relevant aspect of local history: There are doctor's instruments in the doctor's house, tack and a stagecoach in the barn, even a narrow-gauge steam engine in front of the railway station.

At a population of 400, Fairplay isn't the only town in South Park; it is simply the largest. Guffey and Hartsell both claim to be the geographic center of the entire state. Hartsell sits within casting distance of Spinney Mountain Reservoir, some of the best Gold Medal fishing around.

U.S. Highway 285 ladles through South Park, scooping up other interesting recreational diversions. The 90-mile stretch of the Upper Arkansas River from Granite, southeast to Cañon City might well be called "River Rat Row." Nearly a hundred river outfitters operate excursions in these roiling waters. They offer everything from hour-long, barely-get-wet floats to multi-day free falls down Class V rapids. In fact, the entire 148-mile length between Granite and Pueblo is designated the Arkansas Headwaters Recreation Area. Their offices in Salida are full of useful information on rafting, boating and kayaking the Upper Arkansas (719-539-7289).

The U.S. Forest Service information center at the junction of U.S. Highway 285 and Colorado Highway 9 handles Fairplay requests; call 719-836-4279.

Ghost Towns in Colorado

Ashcroft, near Aspen
In the 1880s, Ashcroft was a bigger town than Aspen. When Horace Tabor's new wife, Baby Doe, made an appearance in town, he was so glad to see her that he closed the mines and bought everybody drinks. Nowadays, it boasts nearly two dozen well-preserved buildings connected by a boardwalk.

Independence, near Aspen
Halfway up the difficult Independence Pass, this town couldn't decide on a name. It has been called Chipeta, Mt. Hope, Mammoth City, Farwell and Sparkhill. Drivers along the pass can pull off at a turnout to visit the ruins which are in good condition.

Lulu City, west side of Rocky Mountain National Park
At the end of a three mile walk, Lulu City, once a town with many homes, a hotel and several saloons, displays nothing but eerie foundations.

Nevadaville, near Central City
Only a handful of brick building shells remain from this city that once was home to 2,000 ambitious miners. One of the buildings was the Colorado Territory's first Masonic lodge.

Saint Elmo, near Buena Vista
Despite its saintly name, St. Elmo had a rough reputation. Miners came from miles around every Saturday night to drink and fight. This town is in good shape–for a ghost town. Some of the cabins are still occupied during the summer.

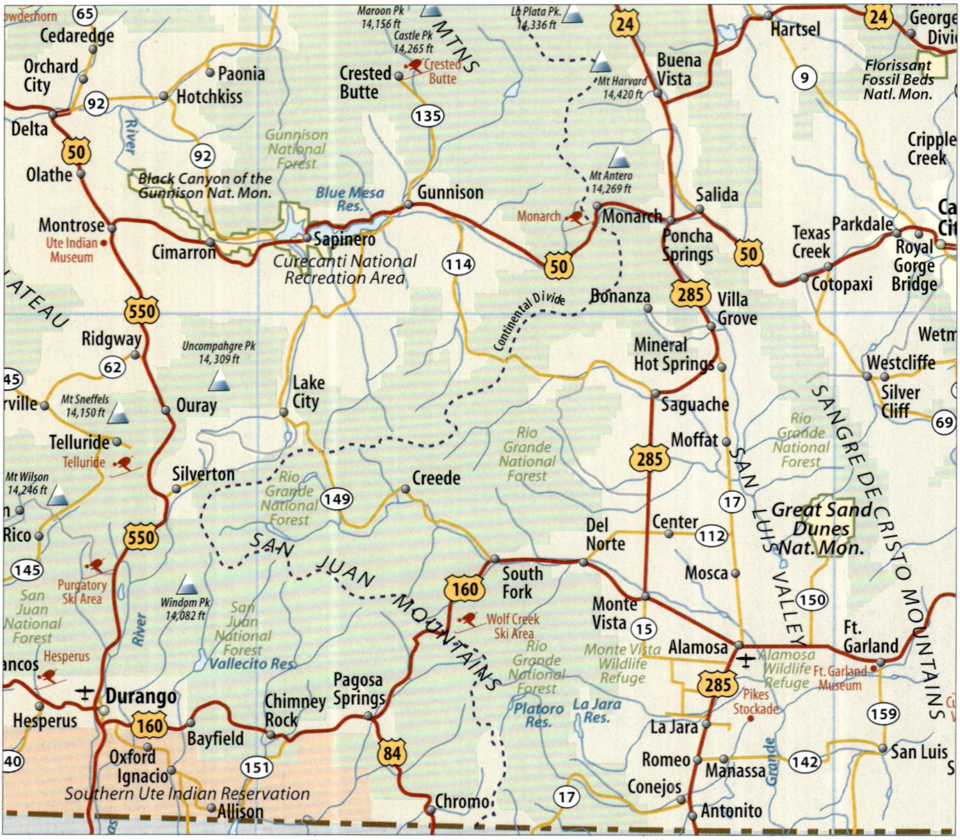

The southern section of Colorado's Rockies

The San Luis Valley

Ringed by the Sangre de Cristo, La Garita and San Juan Mountains, this 125-mile-long by 50-mile-wide cameo-shaped domain may be one of the largest valleys in the world. At an average of 7,000 feet above sea level, it is certainly the largest alpine valley in this country. Don't expect alpine meadows adrift in flowers, though, for this valley is awash with barley (used mostly for Coors beer) and potatoes, as well as a rich, multi-cultural history.

Ute bands had free range for centuries, even though Spaniards arrived in 1694. Ranchers and farmers settled spots here and there as the bowl changed ownership from Spain to Mexico and ultimately passed to the United States after the Mexican-American War. In 1851, the first community in Colorado was formed, San Luis, at the base of the Sangres in an eastern crook of the valley.

SuperAmerica Guide's San Luis Valley Recommendations

- Play beach bum on the extensive sand dunes at Great Sand Dunes National Monument. The short trail that loops around the visitor center is a great way to learn about these sand piles.
- Stroll the trail overlooking the river at the Rio Grande Wildlife Refuge to be amazed at the quantity and diversity of wildlife in the middle of a farming region.
- Roman Catholic or not, walk the trail to absorb the heartfelt love that went into the making of the Stations of the Cross in San Luis.
- Sit in an open-air car of the Cumbres and Toltec Scenic Railroad as it winds its way through the wilderness.

Los Caminos Antiguos Scenic and Historic Byway

This 129-mile route—circuiting together Colorado highways 17, 150, 159 and 142—combines the glories of nature at the Great Sand Dunes National Monument with the traditional ways of several Hispanic communities.

In addition to Antonito and Conejos, this history-laden two-lane passes through Ft. Garland, San Luis and Alamosa.

Fort Garland

The Utes didn't see all that early growth in quite the same light as the white and Hispanic settlers did, and harassed homesteaders until the construction of Fort Garland in 1858.

Today that fort, at the intersection of U.S. Highway 160 and Colorado Highway 159 (719-379-3512), offers peeks into this pre-railroad past. Several rooms are filled with objects from the various groups that have called the valley their own: Native Americans, Spanish, Mexicans and Europeans. The restored adobe structures surround a courtyard that flaunts stagecoaches which used to cross the valley nearly a century-and-a-half ago.

The Commander's Quarters—once home to Kit Carson—are set up as if the famous scout still occupied them. Another building displays dioramas of life in the San Luis Valley. In the old theater, there are art objects including an unusual straw representation of Our Lady of Guadalupe.

The Cumbres and Toltec Scenic Railroad

Cumbres and Toltec Scenic Railroad

The San Luis Valley has strong railroad ties. In fact, the Denver and Rio Grande Railroad's (D&RG) arrival in 1878 spurred much of the farming development in the valley. In 1880, the D&RG completed a track that ran from Antonito, Colorado to Chama, New Mexico.

After decades of neglect, that route is running again. The new railroad is called the Cumbres and Toltec Scenic Railroad (719-376-5483). The 64-mile line is the longest and highest narrow-gauge steam run on the continent. Trains trace the route daily during the summer from one end to the other, after which riders return to their starting city via a one-hour bus ride. Many riders, though, turn around at the halfway point, Osier, Colorado, to ride the train back to their starting point.

Great scenery is guaranteed either way as the cars whisk through tunnels, over trestle bridges and along valley walls.

San Luis

South of Fort Garland lies the oldest town in Colorado—San Luis—established April 5, 1851. San Luis may not be the largest city in the valley, but it is certainly its spiritual heart. Here, the Catholic Hispanic community worships in several adobe churches. A set of 15 bronze sculptures representing the last hours of Christ's life line a path leading to a domed, adobe church. The San Luis Museum and Cultural Center (719-672-3611), even has a rare *morada* (a chapel of the *penitente* sect) on display along with a wide variety of photographs and objects.

The San Luis visitor center is at the intersection of Colorado Highway 159 and Colorado Highway 142; call 719-672-3611.

Alamosa

Along the banks of the legendary Rio Grande River lies Alamosa, which translates into "Cottonwood Grove." With a population of about 10,000 people, the largest city in the San Luis Valley boasts Adams State College. The college's Luther Bean Museum and Art Gallery (719-589-7151) contains a European porcelain and furniture collection along with many ancient Native American and Hispanic artifacts.

Every spring, Alamosa bulges with birders eager to sight the sandhill cranes and their endangered cousins, the whooping cranes, that land at the Alamosa National Wildlife Refuge (719-589-4021). The 11,168-acre refuge, located southeast of town on El Rancho Lane, contains a 2.5-mile-long panoramic walk along the Rio Grande River. Another refuge, the nearby Monte Vista National Wildlife Refuge (719-589-4021), hosts as many as 35,000 ducks during the fall migration.

Another wildlife attraction just might be the most unusual venue in the state: the Colorado Alligator Farm (719-378-2612). It seems the spring waters here run at the perfect temperature to farm tilapia, an African perch popular on menus

Great Sand Dunes National Monument

Great Sand Dunes National Monument

Thirty-eight miles northeast of Alamosa ripples one of Colorado's most unusual geological features. The Great Sand Dunes National Monument (719-378-2312) comprises 39 square miles of sand dune, some of which top out at 700 feet high—higher than a 70-story building.

The dunes formed when sand (picked up by wind blowing across the Rio Grande River's sandy streambed to the southwest) dropped at the base of the Sangre de Cristo mountains to the east.

A visitor center provides a good introduction before heading across Medano Creek and out onto the dunes. Books, brochures, maps and information about guided hikes, camping and after-dark programs are available at the center. A three-quarter mile path past illustrative panels is accompanied by views of the dunes themselves.

While the mountains of grit may appear easy to climb, looks can be deceiving. They are actually shifting constantly and walking around on them is reasonably strenuous. And while you might be tempted to head out barefoot, keep in mind that the particles can reach daytime temperatures of 140° Fahrenheit. Trips in the morning or evening are less work and much cooler. The dunes are also quite dry so carrying water is recommended.

As for wildlife, keep your eyes peeled for six kinds of insects found only here, including the great sand dunes tiger beetle and the dunes circus beetle. Watch for kangaroo rats, too. These clever creatures survive on negligible amounts of water.

around the South. But what to do with the leftovers after the fish are cleaned? Enter 80 alligators ranging in weight from babies fresh out of the egg to 700-pound swamp monsters. Visitors may feed the 'gators themselves or merely watch them wallow.

The Alamosa Visitor Center is at Cole Park; call 719-589-3681.

The San Juan Mountains

While Coloradans enjoy the easy-going prosperity of Vail, the shiny celebrity of Aspen and the down-home goodness of Steamboat Springs, many feel most at home, most Western, most in touch with their Colorado-ness in the San Juan Mountains.

San Juan mountains

Perhaps it's because this area is a microcosm of the state itself. The area is a geological patchwork of sedimentary layers and volcanic cones. Its cultural history is more layered still: Ancestral Pueblo ruins, Ute Indian ownership, Hispanic settlements, mining, mining, and more mining along with doses of railroad construction. Granite-topped mountains stretch beneath azure-blue skies.

Recreation abounds: river running, world-class mountain biking, ski areas bragging more than 300 inches of powder a year, free-wheeling four-wheeling, hikes both simple and strenuous, and eye-popping scenic drives.

Stationed in San Luis

San Luis—Colorado's oldest town—may only claim 800 full-time residents, yet it boasts nearly 100,000 visitors each year. Catholic pilgrims come here to walk along a cactus-strewn trail and reflect on Christ's last hours on earth.

The Hill of Piety and Mercy, covered with stands of juniper, yucca and mesquite, rises from the edge of San Luis. Strung along the mile-long path stand 14 bronze sculptures representing the agony and death of Jesus. Each illustrates a significant event in Christ's last few moments such as Pilate's condemnation, falling three times, being helped by others, meeting his mother and being nailed to the cross.

Chapel of All Saints

Fourteen is the usual number of illustrations in such "Stations of the Cross," but the sculptor of this group, local artist Huberto Maestas, wanted to finish the tale with something uplifting, so he showed Christ's resurrection as a fifteenth station.

At the top of the mesa stands a church—the Chapel of All Saints—handcrafted by the local faithful from adobe and stucco.

Catholics come from around Colorado and New Mexico to make the pilgrimage up this hill. Many pray at each statue, meditating on how Christ's agony relates to their own, some stop in at the chapel and finish their pilgrimage by praying at the altar.

The Rio Grande Headwaters

In New Mexico and Texas, the Rio Grande is thought of as being wide and lazy, but its first 100 miles are a romp through narrow canyons and scenic valleys.

The Rio Grande National Forest (719-852-5941) is blessed with all the recreation activities for which the Centennial state is deservedly famous. Hikers and backpackers step lively into the Weminuche Wilderness, the state's largest pristine area. Fishers cast flies into miles of the Rio Grande near South Fork. Cyclists pedal the single-tracks encircling Del Norte. Scenic and popular campsites and dude ranches dot the areas surrounding Creede and South Fork. Rock

SuperAmerica Guide's San Juan Skyway Recommendations

- Drive the 236-mile Skyway itself and ogle the vistas.
- Wave at the cars on the road and the cows in the fields as you rock along the tracks aboard the Durango and Silverton Narrow Gauge Railroad; one of the most enjoyable activities the state has to offer.
- Get wet on a raft trip out of Durango.
- Sign on for a jeep excursion in Ouray to bounce across the mountains, and head to Telluride for lunch.
- Join the happy people of Telluride for a festival, a hike, a bit of shopping or a fine meal; simply being there seems to make people relax.

Thar's Zink in Them Thar Hills

Ed Zink is an industrious man. In addition to running his bicycle shop on Durango's Main Street (The Mountain Bike Specialist, 970-247-4066), this third-generation Durango native builds hiking and biking trails around the region.

In 1972, Zink founded the Iron Horse Bicycle Classic. A mountain biking event, it started with a few riders pedaling to Silverton. Now 2,000 heavy-pedalers join the world-class extravaganza. Since 1988, Zink has been on the board of trustees of N.O.R.B.A–the National Off-Road Bicycle Association. In 1990, Zink was the promoter for the World Mountain Bike Championships. In 1996, he was an official for the first Olympic mountain biking events at the Atlanta games. So it's probably no surprise to find him installed in the Mountain Bike Hall of Fame.

Then there's the ski patrol–Zink saved fallen skiers for twenty years. Plus, he raised money and donated land to form a city park in Durango–Durango Mountain Park. Recently, he started helping the Bureau of Land Management to coordinate tourism initiatives.

Manassa's Mauler

Jack Dempsey, World Heavyweight Boxing Champion from 1919 to 1926, was born in Manassa, Colorado in 1895. Although the fighter died in 1983 and was buried in Long Island, New York, the people of Manassa remember him well.

They honor his memory at the Jack Dempsey Museum (719-843-5207). Here in a small log-sided building no bigger than a boxing ring, Dempsey was born on June 24, 1895. Today, his boyhood home holds memorabilia of the "Manassa Mauler's" career: old newspaper clippings and vintage ticket stubs, photographs, and well-scuffed boxer's gloves and boots. They tell the rough-and-tumble tale of a small-town boy who made good.

"Fame and fortune didn't go to his head," says Laverne King, who runs the Jack Dempsey Museum. "He wasn't the kind of person to put on airs." This despite the fact that the fighter earned some $3.5 million in purses during his career, appeared in movies, did numerous exhibition bouts in Europe, and was cited by the U.S. House of Representatives as "one of the worthiest Americans of our time."

opposite: Chimney Rock

climbers inch up the bolted cliffs in Penitente Canyon. Fans of Hispanic history enjoy the San Juan Art Center in La Garita (719-589-4769), housed in an adobe chapel listed on the National Register of Historic Places or the Rio Grande County Museum in Del Norte (719-657-2850). Geology-buffs enjoy Lake San Cristobal, the Slumgullion Earthflow and the soda-bottle-shaped stone wonders of the Wheeler Geologic Natural Area.

Silver Thread Scenic and Historic Byway

Colorado Highway 149 connects the cities of South Fork, Creede and, after crossing three passes, Lake City.

South Fork is the town at the junction of the South Fork and Rio Grande rivers. Being loaded to the rafters with useful information, its visitors center is one of the finest in the state. Creede is a mining town perched between the Rio Grande's headwaters and sheer cliffs. The Creede Historical Society, in the rail depot, offers glimpses into the past. More interesting is the Underground Mining Museum (719-658-0811), where local miners carved actual tunnels out of sheer rock to accommodate the exhibits. Lake City has a historical museum too; the Hinsdale County Museum (970-944-9515) houses several exhibits on Lake City's most famous visitor, Alferd Packer.

The South Fork visitor center is at the intersection of Colorado Highways 160 and 149; call 719-873-5512. The Creede visitor center is on Main between Third Avenue and Wall St.; call 719-658-2374 or 800-327-2102. Lake City's visitor center is at 306 Silver St.; call 970-944-2527 or 800-569-1874.

Chimney Rock Archaeological Area

The Chimney Rock Archaeological Area (970-883-5359) splays out about 20 miles west of Pagosa Springs off U.S. Highway 160 on Colorado Highway 151. Two-hour walking tours, conducted by well-informed volunteers, show visitors many of the structures that once housed up to 2,000 Ancestral Puebloans. The site contains two chimney-like towers—hence the name—and archaeologists aren't certain whether they were used as ancient trading-center signposts or star-gazing platforms.

The San Juan Skyway

Colorado is blessed with 21 state-designated Scenic and Historic Byways. One of these, The San Juan Skyway, was judged by the U.S. government's byway commission in 1996 to be so exceptional that the committee named it to be one of the first ever United States Scenic and Historic Byways.

The 236-mile loop, often simply called the San Juan Skyway, drapes in and out of spectacular volcanic calderas, glacial valleys and box canyons. The five main cities on the trail—Durango, Silverton, Ouray, Telluride, and Cortez—offer a range of activities from archaeological digs to mining and railroading history to hot springs to river rafting and grind-your-teeth jeeping.

Durango

Durango, usually the jumping off point for a three- to six-day excursion, is a city of 15,000. Many people serve the active travel business, many provide support for farming along the Animas River Valley, others administer to the needs of the students and faculty of Fort Lewis College.

The city exists merely because of the snobbery of the now-extinct burg of Animas City. When the short-sighted city fathers there refused to pony up funds to build a depot for the Denver and Rio Grande Railroad, General Palmer, the train line's owner, simply decided to build one a little farther south. Animas City was deserted within a decade and Durango is still profiting from their depot.

Only a handful of cities in the state have more spectacular settings. Rock mesas define the east and west edges of town, to the south are

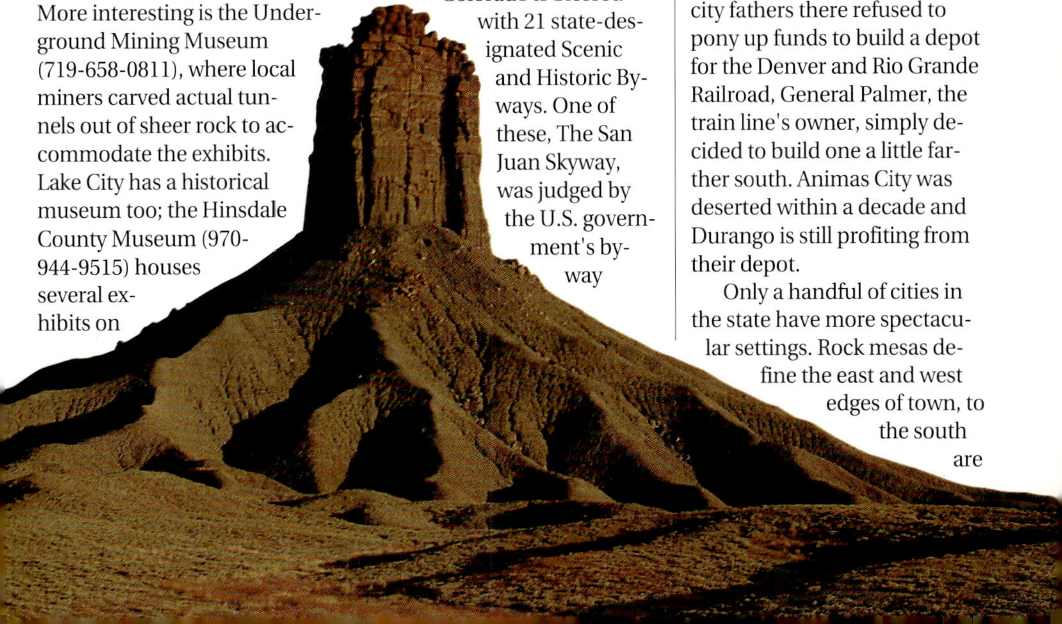

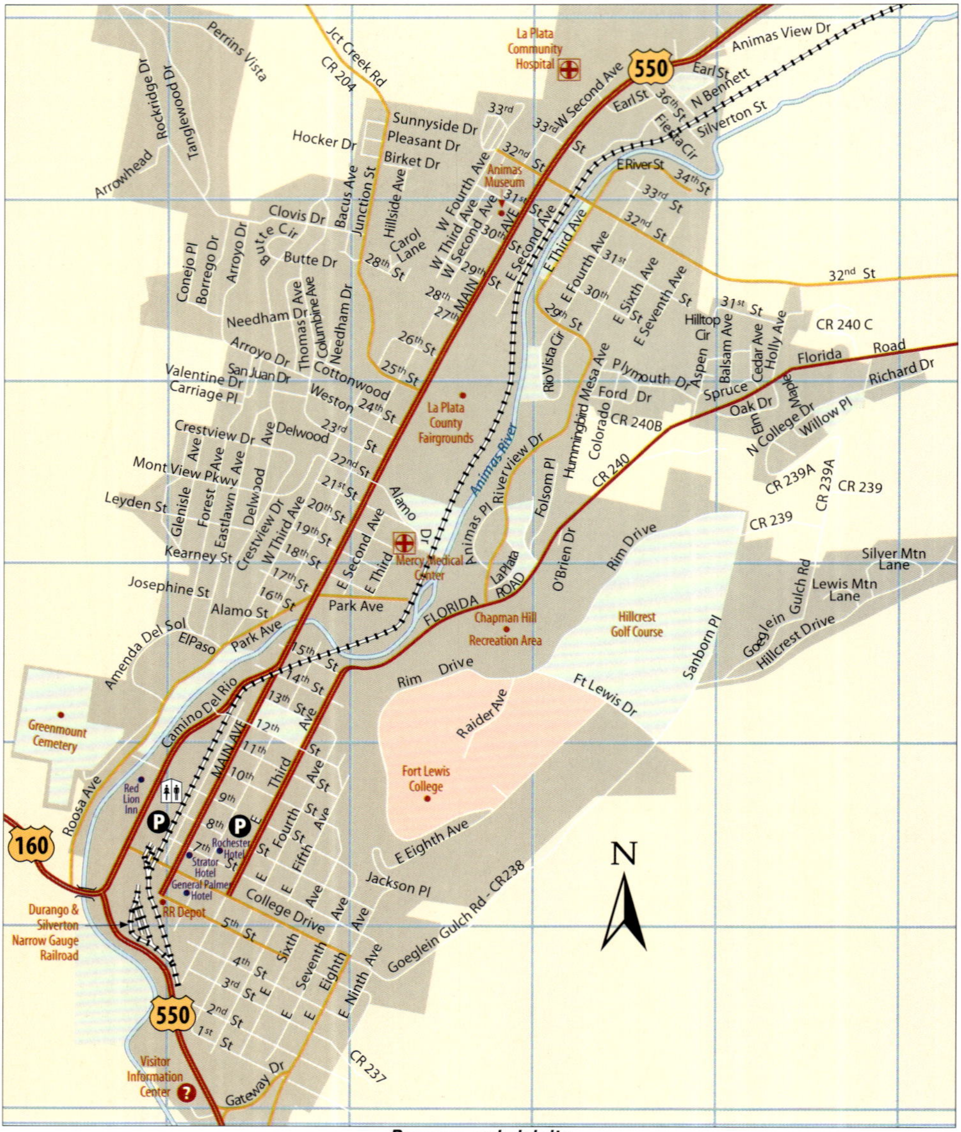

Durango and vicinity

the mesas and valleys defining the high desert ecological zone (which includes Mesa Verde National Park), and northward spreads the verdant valley of the Animas River.

Running parallel to the river is Main Avenue, one of the reasons so many people pay Durango an extended visit. Lined with fine stone and brick Victorian commercial buildings, the blocks from 13th Street south to the train depot comprise one of the two National Historic Districts that Durango enjoys.

The quarter contains two renovated, historic hotels. The Strater (970-247-4431), on the corner of 7th Street and Main Avenue, was built in 1897 for the then-exorbitant sum of $70,000. Completely renovated in 1990, the hotel now has 93 rooms. The Diamond Circle Theater right off the lobby dollops up a cornier-than-corn melodrama on summer nights, and at the Diamond Belle

Strater Hotel, Durango

Saloon right next door, waitresses don Gay '90s garb such as garters and fancy skirts. Nearer the train station, the General Palmer Hotel (970-247-4747), a Victorian vision, was named for the cavalry general that brought the railroad into town.

More recently—and creatively—renovated, the Rochester Hotel (970-385-1920) struck passersby as a down-in-the-dumps flop house for years. Now it has been transformed into 15 large rooms, each based on a Wild West theme in the style of *Butch Cassidy and the Sundance Kid* or *How the West Was Won.*

Durango's downtown runs the gamut from rock shops to rock-climbing shops to rock-and-roll record shops. Restaurants span the taste range from pizza to sit-down, up-scale dining. Western clothing, excursion equipment and ice cream and coffee emporiums round out the shopping experience. Mixed in are a variety of river rafting outfitters. Some have established booking windows in the mountain goods stores. Others simply set up booths on the street. Both offer half- and full-day whitewater excursions on the three nearby waterways; the Animas, the Dolores and the Piedras rivers.

The very south end of the historic district is anchored by the depot that handles the thousands of rail fans who come to Durango to climb aboard the Durango and Silverton Narrow Gauge Railroad (970-247-2733).

The north end of town is

Training the San Juans

However compelling Durango's spectacular setting, shopping and recreation opportunities, visitors come here primarily for two reasons–as a base for an expedition into Mesa Verde National Park and for a ride on the Durango and Silverton Narrow Gauge Railroad (D&SNGR) (970-247-2733) to the remote old mining town of Silverton.

The D&SNGR is Colorado's–perhaps the nation's–most famous excursion train. Whether you book into the first-class "Alamosa" parlor car, an enclosed coach or an open-air excursion car, the wood-paneled rail cars are reminiscent of another age. The engine is run by steam power; coal tenders manually shovel thousands of pounds of coal per run. The moaning whistle haunts every rider and the scenery that goes by the windows (along with gray smoke and the occasional cinder) is miraculous–the lush greenery of the San Juan National Forest, the deep chasms carved by the Animas River and finally, the immense tea-cup-like valley holding Silverton.

Such an adventure is bound to be popular: More than 200,000 train buffs ride these rails each summer. The railroad's managers strongly recommend making reservations 30 to 60 days in advance, but many people make it onto the train by simply walking up to the window and asking for tickets.

lined with motels and free-standing restaurants. On Main Avenue at 31st St. is the Animas Museum (970-259-2402), showcasing artifacts from as far back as the Ancestral Puebloans' use of the area around 1,000 A.D. to farmers' implements of only 100 years ago. Six miles north is Trimble Hot Springs (970-247-0111), the mineral soak of choice for occasionally over-active Durangoans and their guests.

The Durango Area Chamber Resort Association information center is at 111 S. Camino del Rio; call 970-247-0312 or 800-525-8855.

Silverton

In its silver-mining heyday, Silverton was dubbed "the mining town that never quit" because of the carousing that went on day and night. In fact, Bat Masterson was invited to rid little Silverton—so named because it produced silver by the ton—of its more notorious citizens.

Not to worry; it's a lot tamer today. As close as you'll get to a gun is the smoke that drifts off the blanks that fire each summer evening at 5:30 p.m., when locals stage a gunfight.

For another experience of the area, take the Old Hundred Gold Mine tour (800-872-3009). Guides point out ore lines and tell anecdotes as a railcar descends 1,500 feet into a mine that closed in 1961. The chill and constant drip of water make visitors keenly aware of the difficulty of mining.

Silverton is the county seat of San Juan County, and the San Juan County Historical Museum (970-387-5838) occupies the old jail. The museum displays a variety of mining and historic artifacts and has even renovated the women's cells. In a way, all of Silverton is a museum, for the entire city is on the National Register of Historic Places.

Silverton's visitor center is located at 414 Greene St.; call 970-387-5654 or 800-752-4494.

Ouray

The 23-mile length of road that crests at Red Mountain Pass and switchbacks its way north into Ouray is termed the "Million Dollar Highway" for several reasons. First, the cost to make it passable for autos in the late 1950s ran about a million greenbacks; second, miners once estimated (after it was too late to extract it) that a million dollars of gold ore was used in the road's gravel base; and finally, that an early traveler said she wouldn't accept a million dollars to cross the cliff-hanging highway via stagecoach.

Ouray itself was named after the Ute chieftan who reluctantly signed all the land

Colorado's Cannibal: Alferd Packer

Alferd–yes, Alferd–Packer stumbled out of a blizzard in 1873 at the Los Piños Indian Agency near present-day Lake City. He said he'd been left behind by his five companions on their journey from an encampment near Delta to Los Piños.

Oddly, despite six weeks "alone" atop a blizzard-swept mountain range, Packer didn't appear the least bit gaunt. And why was he packing so much cash?

The gruesome answers came when five bodies turned up in August–picked clean. Here's the story as Packer told it: The party of six men–Packer, Frank Miller, James Humphrey, Israel Swan, George Noon, and Wilson Bell–got lost about ten days into their excursion. When Swan died, they diced and devoured him. Next they served up Humphrey, then Miller. Packer swore that while he was away hunting game, Bell murdered Noon and came after him with a hatchet. In self-defense, Packer had to kill Bell.

The jury at his first trial, held nearly 10 years later, believed otherwise. They found him guilty of murder. Judge Melville B. Gerry, delivering a sentence destined for Colorado folklore, has been reported as saying:

> *Stand up, yah voracious man-eatin' SOB and receive your sintince! There was seven Democrats in Hinsdale County and yah et five of thim! I sintince you to be hanged by th' neck ontil yer dead, dead, dead, as a warnin' ag'in reducin' the Democratic population . . . ye Republican cannibal!*

Packer didn't hang though. He was eventually released, but Coloradans still believe that Packer added new meaning to the expression "having a friend for lunch."

Ouray

hereabouts over to the whites. Yet, it is often referred to as the "Switzerland of America," because of its high-altitude setting in a narrow valley cleft, surrounded by sky-tickling summits.

The town might more accurately be called the four-wheeling capital of the world—the mountains surrounding Ouray are literally laced with jeep trails. In fact, jeeping is so popular on the narrow gravel and rock byways that during the colorful autumn season, traffic jams actually develop on the more popular jeep routes such as Imogene, Engineer and Black Bear Passes.

Oddly, Ouray is one of the only towns in Colorado bubbling over with hot springs that does not have the term "Springs" attached to its name. It probably ought to. The Ouray Hot Springs and Pool (970-325-4638) soothes visitors with a huge pool partitioned into different sections, each with a different temperature. All have views of the peaks in the background. The

Hope Springs Eternal

Tom Walsh was poking around the supposedly useless silver tailings outside Ouray one day after the silver crash of 1893. What many miners saw there as worthless quartz, Walsh knew to be gold embedded in tellurium. He started snapping up unused mining claims.

One day in 1896, he walked into one of those mines and discovered a vein of tellurium three feet thick. "Daughter," he yelled excitedly to his daughter Evalyn, "we've struck it rich." Indeed, that vein turned out to be six miles long. By 1900, Walsh was bringing in $3 million a year.

The family moved to Washington, D.C., built a mansion in the ritzy Dupont Circle neighborhood and became socialites. When Walsh told Evalyn to buy herself something pretty for her wedding, she went out and purchased the 92.5-carat Star of the East diamond. Not long after her father's death, she treated herself to the 67-carat rare, blue—and supposedly dangerous—Hope Diamond.

Evalyn Walsh McLean donned the rock frequently for parties and social events; she refused to believe it carried any curse. Yet the rest of her life was filled with tragedy. Her son was run down by a car, a daughter ate an overdose of sleeping pills, a granddaughter expired from alcohol/barbiturate poisoning and her husband died in a mental institution.

Jewelry baron Harry Winston snapped up the gem after Evalyn's death—her family desperately needed the cash. Winston donated it to the Smithsonian Institute where it sparkles every day for thousands of visitors.

Telluride

Weisbaden Hot Springs (970-325-4347), located in the heart of town, features water spritzing right out of the mountain into a screened-off hot tub as well as a steamy vapor cave.

Need some culture? The Chamber of Commerce (970-325-4746) has published a 30-page vacation guide which includes an historic walking tour. The Ouray Historical Museum (970-325-4576) contains several period rooms of interest—a hospital ward, a general store and a legal office.

Many people stay the night here on their way around the Skyway, so there is a broad range of accommodations, restaurants and nightlife. From Memorial Day to mid-October, the Chipita Emporium Theater (970-325-0357) froths up nightly musical productions. The Wright Opera House (970-325-7277) features the Silver Legacy Players in live performances.

Telluride

Telluride boasts a number of claims to fame. Oprah Winfrey thinned down here once at what is now The Peaks at Telluride, and she still owns a home here. Stars such as Tom Cruise and Oliver Stone have places nearby, preferring the laid-back feel here to the hustle and bustle of Aspen. Butch Cassidy (without the Sundance Kid) pulled his first heist here in 1889, walking calm as can be into the Mahr Building, demanding the payroll stored there, and hightailing it out of town with $20,000.

Nowadays, folks aren't in such a hurry to leave. In fact, development is a hot topic here. Locals want to keep the local flavor, as well as reasonable housing prices. Developers want to create even more local flavor with new structures in the gingerbread style of yesteryear, but with much larger price tags.

In any case, the setting is spectacular with the San Juans looming all around, light as sprites in sunshine, hunkering bunkers during the often wicked winters. The skiing at Telluride Ski Area (970-728-3856) is geared to the advanced skier. Hiking runs from a steep stroll along with the jeeps heading up to Bridal Veil Falls (at 365 feet, Colorado's highest) to extended overnight trips in the

Free Skis! Free Appliances!

Every town is abundant with two kinds of people: the "haves" and the "have-lesses." In Telluride, those that have more help those who have less in a most unusual way–the Telluride Free Box.

The "box" is a set of outdoor bins on the corner of Colorado and Pine Streets. Folks wanting to clean out the garage or attic bring stuff and drop it off. Those who are a little more needy rifle through the goodies and take what they want. Call it an open-air Salvation Army–but everything is free.

Sometimes, pretty great items show up. After the ski season, you're sure to find skis and snowboards–usually well worn. At summer's end, bicycles line the street. Clothing, some sporting well-known labels, and small appliances are also common.

San Juan National Forest. The jeeping is focused on the routes heading east to Ouray. Fishing, kayaking and white-water enthusiasts savor the San Miguel River.

Telluride Festivals

May

Mountain Film
Filmmakers, writers, and outdoor enthusiasts celebrate mountain life; call 800-525-3455.

Steps to Awareness
Thirty workshops devoted to holistic healing. Topics include numerology, tarot and shamanism; call 800-525-3455.

June

Invitational Balloon Rally
Balloonists float over the Telluride Valley; call 800-525-3455.

Theater Fest
Celebrated artists and directors perform new works; call 800-525-3455.

Bluegrass Festival
The most intense four-day display of American music in the country; call 800-624-2422.

Wine Festival
Wines and their makers from around the world; call 800-525-3455.

July

Fireman's Fourth of July
Parade, picnic, fire trucks and fireworks; call 800-525-3455.

Talking Gourds
Cross-cultural gathering of regional poets, storytellers and artists; call 800-525-3455.

Celebration Arts
Street fair with arts and crafts, jugglers and buskers; call 800-525-3455.

Classics in the Park
Live theater in Town Park. Plenty of Shakespeare and Molière; call 800-525-3455.

Nothing Festival
Nothing going on, absolutely nothing. No banners, no events, nothing; there's nobody to call.

Rotary 4x4 Tour
Local experts conduct off-road history and wildflower tours; call 800-525-3455.

Joffrey Ballet Summer Residence
Two to three performances a week by the world renowned ballet troupe; call 800-525-3455.

August

Jazz Celebration
Legends of jazz in intimate settings; call 800-525-3455.

Melée in the Mines
Off-Road Bicycle Association race; call 800-525-3455.

Rocky Mountain Playwriting Festival
New works by up-and-coming playwrights; call 800-525-3455

Chamber Music Festival
Six "bring-your-own-picnic" concerts in Town Park; call 800-525-3455.

Mushroom Festival
This cook-and-taste feast features hunts, lectures and workshops; call 800-296-9356.

Film Festival
Some call it the best film fest in the world. It is certainly the definitive Telluride event; call 603-643-1255.

September

Hang Gliding Festival
World Aerobatic Hang Gliding Championships; call 800-525-3455.

Performing Arts Festival
Local talent from a variety of genres; call 800-525-3455.

Wild West Weekend
Telluride celebrates the Old West; call 800-525-3455.

Brews Festival
Homemade beer and live music; call 800-525-3455.

Behind Closed Doors Home Tour
A glimpse into Telluride's luxury homes; call 800-525-3455.

The Western Slope

Carp Lake, Grand Mesa National Forest

Technically, the Western Slope of Colorado begins at the Continental Divide, the imaginary line meandering along the spine of the Rocky Mountains that determines whether rivers flow east or west. Westward from the Rockies' summits, the landscape drops and splays out into an expansive highland, the Colorado Plateau. To the north lie the verdant forests of White River and Routt National Forests, which descend northwest into scrubby high prairie toward the intersection of Utah and Wyoming. The Colorado Plateau's midsection encompasses a diverse geography etched with evergreen-blanketed mesas, deep ravines, stark canyonlands and broad, fertile valleys. The volcanic San Juan Mountains interrupt the plateau's southward sweep, then give way abruptly to juniper-covered mesas pawing into the arid, high desert region of the Four Corners.

Northern Plateau

Northeast of Grand Junction tower the Book Cliffs, gray, desolate-looking mesas with striped vertical rims. Rising from the Colorado River Valley, the country gains altitude, traversing the Grand Hogback into the forests of the White River Plateau. Westward, the plateau spreads into high desert scrublands, an area that appears bleak and disheartening, and is in fact thinly populated except with herds of pronghorn. Beneath the soil, however, lie immense deposits of oil shale and coal. Dozens of oil pumpjacks nod up and down along the highway. Company towns such as Craig and Rangley testify to extreme northeastern Colorado's working-class economy, set amidst the endless and humble starkness of sagebrush and sky.

Flat Tops Trail

Meeker and Yampa frame the scenic byway, the Flat Tops Trail, which cuts 82 miles via a series of county

left: Colorado National Monument

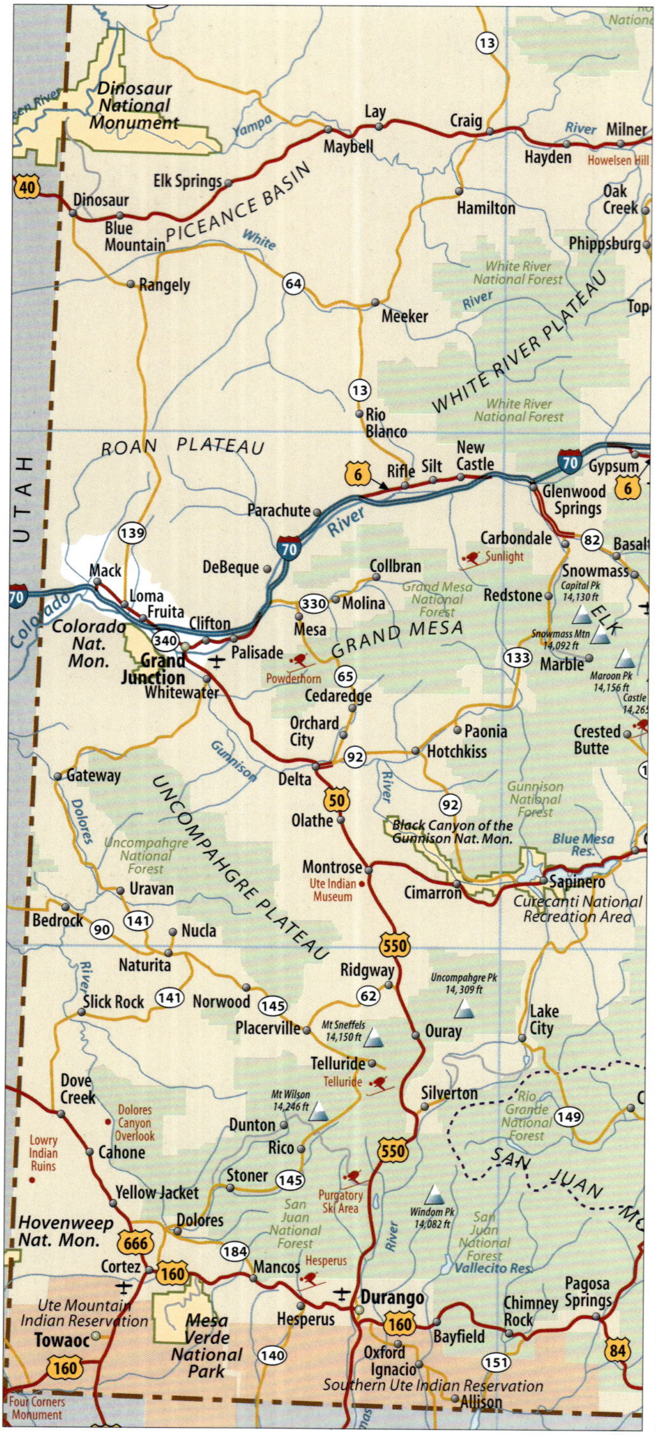

The Western Slope of Colorado

Western Slope Festivals and Events

February

Pinto Bean Cooking Contest—Bean aficionados indulge in favorite recipes. Cortez; call 970-565-3414.

June

Ute Mountain Bear Dance—Traditional powwow and arts and crafts show. Towaoc; call 970-565-3751.

July

Cattlemen's Days—One of the state's oldest rodeos celebrates the area's ranching heritage. Gunnison; call 970-641-1501

Fat Tire Bike Week—Mountain bike race competitions and the Pearl Pass Classic to Aspen. Crested Butte; call 970-349-6438.

Dinosaur Days—Dinosaur lectures, raft races, T-Rex T-Off, Pteranodon Ptrot 5K run and Stegosaurus Stomp. Grand Junction; call 970-242-3214.

September

Colorado Mountain Winefest—Music, food and wine tasting of Colorado's finest blends. Grand Junction and Palisade; call 970-243-8497.

Meeker Classic Sheep Dog Championship Trials—Working sheep dogs take on challenging courses and reluctant sheep. Meeker; call 970-878-5510.

Native American Lifeways—Two days of Native American dancing, storytelling, arts and crafts, fry bread and buffalo burgers. Montrose; call 970-249-3098.

roads through the White River National Forest. This was once prime timber land, and still is to a great extent, but less so since the 1964 Wilderness Act protected tracts of the Flat Tops from development. Pristine and idyllic Trapper's Lake, for instance, deserves its designation as the "Cradle of Wilderness."

Meeker, itself, looks every bit the part of a solid Colorado ranching town. Pretty historical buildings—especially the Meeker Hotel and St. James Episcopal Church—line the main street. The town's simple quaintness belies its notoriety as it is the site of the bloody Meeker Massacre (see box page 142).

Cañon Pintado Historic District

Rangley, a coal town, probably won't figure on most visitors' itineraries, though Cañon Pintado (painted canyon) should. Situated south of town on Colorado Highway 139, some 50 rock art panels line the canyon along the Douglass Creek Valley. The sites date from the Fremont Culture, which occupied the territory from 600 to 1300 A.D. East Fourmile Canyon (mile 10.5) displays polychrome concentric circles, and the main Cañon Pintado section features a "Kokopelli," the humpbacked, flute-playing imp of Native American legend.

The Rifle Area Chamber is located at 200 Lions Park Circle; call 970-625-2085. The Meeker Chamber can be reached at 970-878-5510. The Rangley Area Chamber of Commerce is located at 209 E. Main Street; call 970-675-5290.

Central Plateau

From the Elk Mountains west, and south of the Colorado River to the lower Gunnison River, the Rocky Mountains ease gently from high country to broad tablelands. Situated in the lush strip of the Colorado River Valley, Grand Junction with its 38,000 residents is the largest town between Denver and Salt Lake City. Agriculture and farming are the city's mainstays, though tourism increasingly defines the economy.

It's understandable: the town is centered in a territory pinched between montane forest and desert flatlands. Southwest of the city is the Colorado National Monument, and farther west are the canyonlands of the Uncompahgre Plateau. Grand Mesa, the world's largest mesa, corrals 53 square miles and reaches altitudes of 11,000 feet as it ascends west of Grand Junction. East and southeast of

SuperAmerica Guide's Western Slope Recommendations

- Explore Colorado's dinosaur past at Devil's Canyon Science and Learning Center and Dinosaur National Monument.
- Take Rim Rock Drive through the Colorado National Monument to see a miniature version of the Grand Canyon.
- Peer into the depths of a narrow 2,000-foot-deep gorge at Black Canyon of the Gunnison.
- Tour Colorado's wineries along the Grand River Valley and North Fork of the Gunnison.
- Wonder at the Ancestral Puebloan cliff dwellings and artifacts at Mesa Verde National Park, the Anasazi Heritage Center and Hovenweep National Monument.

Dinosaur National Monument Facilities

Most of Dinosaur National Monument's land sits within Colorado, and the main entrance is located two miles east of the little town of Dinosaur, Colorado. On the Utah side is the entrance to the Dinosaur Quarry, which is seven miles north of Jensen, Utah.

The park itself has no restaurant or overnight accommodations other than campgrounds, and several of these are considered primitive with no potable water. The closest motels are located in the town of Dinosaur, though there is a greater range of choices in Vernal, Utah, which is 20 miles from the Dinosaur Quarry.

Dinosaur National Monument is open year-round, but both the main visitor center (970-374-3000) and Dinosaur Quarry are closed on Thanksgiving, Christmas and New Years. During the summer, the visitor center is open from 8 a.m. to 4:30 p.m., seven days a week, but closed weekends the rest of the year. Dinosaur Quarry keeps the hours of 8 a.m. to 7 p.m. from Memorial Day to Labor Day, and from 8 a.m. to 4 p.m. the remainder of the year. Admission to the monument is $10 per car, which also allows access to the Dinosaur Quarry.

following pages: Split Mountain Canyon and the Green River in Colorado National Monument

Dinosaur National Monument

Colorado and Utah share the 300 square miles of Dinosaur National Monument, clearly some of the West's most stunningly stark scenery. Rumpled by unusual east-west oriented hills, the Uinta Mountains, the rugged territory is incised with deep gorges. Carved by the Green and Yampa rivers, they converge at Echo Park near the monument's center.

More than 140 million years ago, another river washed through the southwestern section of the monument. This was the Jurassic period, when dinosaurs ruled the earth. The sandy river bottom of this ancient river proved ideal for preserving their remains.

The monument's existence stems from the fantastic finds that Earl Douglass and other paleontologists scraped from the earth here around the turn of the century. Over time, the quarry sites yielded more than 350 tons of fossils and attached rock, representing 10 dinosaur species. Their reconstructed skeletons now grace exhibition halls throughout the world.

Dinosaurs aside, the allure for many people who venture into this arid badland is, ironically, water. The wild Green and Yampa rivers throw a fit while coursing through the Uinta Mountains. Torrents and whirlpools raging through cramped 2,000-foot-deep chasms are pure rapture to river-running enthusiasts. Several river rafting outfits regularly receive permits to offer one- to five-day trips down the rivers. See chapter three, Rocky Mountain Recreation, for details.

Dinosaur National Monument

Dinosaur Quarry

This is the only place within the monument where visitors can actually see fossilized dinosaur bones. An entire hillside has been excavated and enclosed within the visitor center, allowing guests to view protruding skulls and skeletal fragments trapped in the rock. Excellent displays throughout the complex complete the story of the monument's Jurassic past.

Harper's Corner Drive

This is the main road into the monument, which leads from the headquarters' visitor center off U.S. Highway 40, located on the Colorado side. Harper's Corner is paved and winds north for 31 miles offering access to several trailheads. Noteworthy ones are Harper's Corner and Ruple Point trails, which lead to spectacular views of Green River Canyon.

Echo Park Road

While Echo Park Road is unpaved and impassable to RVs and trailers, most high-clearance cars can make the 13-mile journey. That said, it's best to check with rangers before heading out, as this branch off Harper's Corner Road is steep and impassable if it has been raining.

Those who make the effort can inspect ancient petroglyphs at Pool Creek and step inside Whispering Cave before arriving at Echo Park, where the turbulent Green and Yampa rivers come together. At one time, the area was known as Pat's Hole. Irishman Pat Lynch didn't much care for folks, preferring the solitude of echoes to the drone of others' voices. Lynch got along quite nicely, living a good part of the late 1800s here until he passed away at the respectable age of 98.

Park rangers answer guests' questions at Dinosaur Quarry

Yampa Bench Road
Only people with a vehicle designed for off-road driving should attempt Yampa Bench Road, which veers off Echo Park Road approximately eight miles from its intersection with Harper's Corner Road. All together, it's 38 miles of rough going to reach Elk Springs, but it rewards visitors with splendid views of Yampa Canyon. From Elk Springs, it's 38 miles back to the monument's headquarters on U.S. Highway 40.

Cub Creek Road
As Cub Creek Road is paved and only 10 miles long, it's a popular route for visitors who have been to the nearby Dinosaur Quarry. The road leads to the onetime cabin of Josie Morris. Around 1914, Morris moved here, and stayed for 50 years to raise crops and livestock on her homestead in the shadow of Split Mountain. Only the occasional visit from relatives and friends disturbed her peaceful retreat.

Jones Hole Road
Four miles south of Dinosaur Quarry, the paved but narrow Jones Hole Road proceeds west, then north for 48 miles to reach the Jones Hole Fish Hatchery (303-789-4481). The hatchery is open for tours, but most people come to hike the four-mile length of Jones Hole Trail into Jones Hole. This beautiful canyon is one of the Green River's few remote access points reachable by foot rather than by kayak or raft.

Island Park Road
Like Echo Park Road, the 17-mile unpaved Island Park Road can be a tough trip. Rainbow Park, and farther on, the Ruple Ranch are the destinations along this route to the Green River.

Gates of Lodore
Although Missouri fur trader William H. Ashley floated through the intimidating Lodore Canyon with mountain men Jim Bridger, John Colter and Jim Beckwourth in 1825, it was left to Major John Wesley Powell to name the place in 1869. The Green River's tortuous assault on the Uinta Mountains and the 2,300-foot-deep fissure struck Powell as being "beyond the power of the pen to tell." The Gates of Lodore refer to a poem by Robert Southey, verses from which Powell recited to his men while braving perilous river rapids. Colorado Highway 318 travels 50 miles north from the town of Maybell to the Gates of Lodore campground and ranger station, where a short hike leads to views of the gorge.

Grand Mesa, the land dips into river valleys before climbing to the cordillera of the Rocky Mountains.

Grand Junction

With the expulsion of the Utes in 1881, ranchers and farmers soon settled the area at the confluence of the Gunnison and Grand (now the Colorado) rivers, hence the name Grand Junction. The fertile valley sliced with irrigation canals spawned farms and many orchards. Western Slope peaches, cherries and apricots have long been summertime favorites for Coloradans.

Cross Orchards Historic Site (970-434-9814) recaptures Grand Junction's early days with tours of a late 1800s-era working apple orchard, which at one time covered 250 acres. On a hot summer afternoon, it's a wonderful place to relax amid a nostalgic atmosphere.

The Museum of Western Colorado (970-242-0971) operates Cross Orchards in addition to the Main Museum and Dinosaur Valley (970-241-9210). The Main Museum chronicles the area's geological past and Native American culture, while Dinosaur Valley steps back in time to the days when *T-Rexes* and *Stegosauruses* stomped through the land.

Of late, Grand Junction has become one of the nation's definitive "dinosaur towns." The region's shale and sedimentary rock expanses have yielded truckloads of important fossils. And with the popularity of movies such as *Jurassic Park* and *Lost World*, dinosaur quarries have emerged as top tourist destinations. Three trails in the Grand Junction area—Rabbit Valley Research Natural Area, Dinosaur Hill and Riggs Hill—offer quick self-guided explorations of former dinosaur dig sites via maps available at Dinosaur Valley.

A dinosaur extravaganza awaits at Devil's Canyon Science and Learning Center

28 Hours of Fame

Eight thousand pounds of orange nylon fabric, 142,000 square feet in all, fluttered between the cliffs of Rifle Gap on August 10, 1972. Voilà, Christo and Jeanne-Claude.

It was another crowning moment for the husband-and-wife team of environmental artists, world renowned for their immensely scaled, packaged and draped creations. Their works have included many altering-the-familiar installations such as *Surrounding Islands in Biscayne Bay* and *Wrapped Museum of Contemporary Art, Chicago*.

The Valley Curtain, as it was called, took 28 months to complete, but was short-lived. Gale-force winds slamming through the Rifle Gap terminated the project 28 hours after its unveiling.

The Meeker Massacre

Nathan Meeker got his start in Colorado while leading the founding of Greeley on the Front Range. In 1878, he became an Indian Agent at the White River Agency on the Western Slope, with a goal to "Americanize" the Utes into farmers. Long accustomed to a nomadic hunting and gathering lifestyle, the Utes didn't easily take to agrarian ways. Meeker's stern demeanor and wholesale disregard for Ute customs and values quickly alienated the people he was charged with helping.

During the summer of 1879, many of the Utes abandoned the reservation. Those who stayed found Meeker unrepentant in his oppressive pursuit to "civilize" them. When Meeker ordered the plowing of their horse-racing field and pastures, the Utes had had enough.

Fearing imminent reprisal, Meeker called for troops, and Major Thomas T. Thornburgh was dispatched with a small force of men. The Utes learned of the approaching cavalry, went into action and surprised Thornburgh's unit at Mill Creek. In the skirmish, Thornburgh was killed along with 13 soldiers. Enraged, the Utes next went for Meeker himself, killing him and 11 other men at the White River Indian Agency. Meeker's wife, Avilla, his daughter, Josephine, and a Mrs. Shadrack Price and her two children were abducted and held captive for more than a month on Grand Mesa before they were released.

The government's response to the incident echoed the cry of newspapers of the day, "The Utes Must Go." In 1880, Chief Ouray and other Ute leaders reluctantly agreed to forsake their lush valleys and forests for dusty reservations in Utah and extreme southern Colorado.

(800-DIG-DINO), located near the town of Fruita. This multi-million-dollar facility emphasizes education for kids with scores of hands-on exhibits and remarkable full-scale growling and screeching animated dinosaur replicas. Devil's Canyon also offers on-site expeditions whereby participants join paleontologists on actual dinosaur digs.

The Grand Junction Visitor and Convention Bureau is located at 740 Horizon Drive; call 970-244-1480 or 800-962-2547. A Colorado Welcome Center is located at Fruita on Highway 340; call 970-858-9335.

Colorado National Monument

Perhaps nowhere in Colorado is the contrast between urban bustle and solitary backcountry more dramatic than in the short trip from downtown Grand Junction to the Colorado National Monument (970-858-3617). Thirty minutes is all it takes to leave parking lots and stop lights behind to reach yawning canyons guarded by monolithic and whimsical sandstone formations sculpted by wind, rain and time.

A scribbling, socialist-minded hermit by the name of John Otto is credited with spurring the preservation of the geological phenomena. Otto doggedly extolled the virtues and importance of the area in numerous missives dispatched to politicians. Finally, in 1911, President William Howard Taft granted the area national monument status. Otto became its first superintendent.

The monument's access road, 23-mile Rock Rim Drive, is one of Colorado's most

Vintage Colorado

Grapes are no strangers to the orchards dotting the Grand River Valley and North Fork of the Gunnison. The fruit has been grown here for over a century, and there was even a winemaker or two way back then. Prohibition drained the prospects of the budding industry, and the vineyards were replaced with orchards.

All that changed a couple decades ago, when classic wine-grape varieties were reintroduced on the Western Slope. Modern vintners were drawn to the area's favorable climate and distinctive shale soil conditions—essential ingredients for interesting chardonnays, sauvignon blancs, merlots and pinot noirs. Over the years, Colorado wines have come into their own,

Western Slope Vineyard

garnering more than two dozen gold medals in various competitions with California and other world class wines.

The Colorado Wine Industry Development Board (970-523-1232) lists more than a dozen wineries that offer complimentary tours and tastings. Here's a sampling.

Vineyard / Location	Wines	Contact
Carlson Vineyards / Palisade	Reds, Riesling, Gerwurztraminer, Fruit Wines, Blends	970-464-5554
Colorado Cellars Winery / Palisade	20 wines, 35 wine-made foods	800-848-2812
Columbine Cellars Ltd. / Palisade	Chardonnay, Cabernet Sauvignon, Merlot, Riesling	970-464-0559
Grand River Vineyards / Palisade	Merlot, Chardonnay, Meritage Red & White, Syrah	970-464-5867
Plum Creek Cellars / Palisade	Chardonnay, Merlot, Cabernet Sauvignon	970-464-7586
Rocky Hill Winery / Montrose	Chardonnay, Cherry, Merlot	970-249-3765
Terror Creek Winery / Paonia	Gewurztraminer, Riesling, Chardonnay, Pinot Noir	970-527-3484

scenic. The route's vistas are nothing short of spectacular, like seeing Arizona's Grand Canyon—only in miniature. Twists and turns define the route, and the many pullouts are ideal for picture-taking or short walks to view rocky wonders bearing evocative names such as "Kissing Couple."

Uncompahgre Plateau

Some eight million years ago, the Colorado and Gunnison rivers careened through the lowlands southwest from Grand Junction. Then the land began to rise, forming the Uncompahgre Plateau and diverting the mighty rivers to the north. The remnants of those rushing torrents chiseled and gouged the soft-red sandstone country, creating a harshly beautiful backdrop laced with the green ribbon of the Dolores River.

The Unaweep/Tabeguache Scenic & Historic Byway meanders through the plateau, picking up Colorado Highway 141 at Whitewater and progressing for 133 miles through Gateway, Uravan and Naturita. It ends at Placerville on Colorado Highway 145.

At 29 miles south of Gateway, look for the "Hanging Flume" clinging to the canyon's wall 400 feet below the rim. From 1889 to 1891, a steady stream of workers hung precariously by ropes to construct the six-by-four foot, six-mile trough designed to carry water to the Lone Star Placer gold mining operation.

It was radioactive ore, however, which ignited the state's scientific mineral boom. In 1898, several tons of Colorado earth were sent to France, where Pierre and Marie Curie processed it into the rare luminescent element called radium. In the 1940s, the little town of Uravan on the Uncompahgre Plateau supplied uranium for the Manhattan Project, which lead to the development of atomic weapons.

Uncompahgre Plateau

Grand Mesa

An old Ute legend recounts how ill-tempered thunderbirds created Grand Mesa's 300-plus lakes. As the tale goes, the thunderbirds tore apart a hefty serpent while flying high above the mesa, and with each scrap that fell to earth, huge pockmarks erupted which eventually filled with water. Utes referred to the land as *thigunawat,* "home of departed spirits."

The Grand Mesa Scenic and Historic Byway, 63 miles in length, skirts across the mesa, rising from Plateau Creek at the town of Mesa to roll through a cool evergreen forest to Cedaredge. Near Skyway, Land's End Road is a summertime alternative backtrack to Grand Junction off the western edge of Grand Mesa. Note: It's not for the faint-hearted, for it plunges down

Chief Ouray

For a generation in the late 1800s, Chief Ouray's eloquence guided the Utes through the most difficult period of their history. Versed in both Spanish and English, his cool-headed demeanor earned the respect of government negotiators. His sage advice of tolerance helped assuage his people's anger at the incursions of settlers and fortune-seekers. Sadly, his determined efforts couldn't forestall the inevitable deportation of Utes from their homeland.

Mt. Crested Butte, Crested Butte

the rim for 14 miles (only seven miles of which is paved), delivering dizzying views of the Colorado River Valley 5,000 feet below.

West Elk Loop

At Carbondale, Colorado Highway 133 veers up the Crystal River Valley, by many accounts one of the state's most beautiful. It's only the beginning to a memorable scenic byway, the West Elk Loop. The route heads through the White River and Gunnison national forests, treks along the Curecanti National Recreation Area and Black Canyon of the Gunnison National Park, then circles north to the little towns of Hotchkiss and Paonia.

Although the circuit is only 205 miles, (31 of which is gravel road) the drive can easily take eight hours. The varied topography ranging from alpine high country to sagebrush valleys, interspersed with numerous worthwhile stops, calls for a leisurely pace.

John Cleveland Osgood, a coal mining millionaire, certainly enjoyed relaxation. In 1900 he built the fabulous Cleveholm Manor, 42 rooms replete with Morrocan leather wall coverings, Tiffany chandeliers, Persian carpets and yards of stonework. Power brokers such as John D. Rockefeller and President Theodore Roosevelt were his guests. Cleveholm was the "castle" for his model "worker's community," Redstone, which is today a resort town. Cleveholm Manor (970-963-3463) is now an upscale lodge, and the Redstone Inn, where Osgood's bachelor workers bedded down, offers comfortable accommodations and first-rate meals.

About 10 miles south of Redstone are the Yule Marble Quarries. In the 1930s and 1940s, the lightly veined, diamond-hard stone was shipped around the world—including Italy—for use by noted architects and sculptors. The Lincoln Memorial is sheathed in Colorado marble and Washington D.C.'s Tomb of the Unknown Soldier in Arlington National Cemetery was carved from the largest single block of stone ever cut from the earth—100 tons.

Crossing over gravel Kebler Pass on Colorado Highway 135, the West Elk Loop calls at Crested Butte. Once a thriving gold camp, this pretty Victorian town now banks on skiing in the winter and mountain biking in the summer. In fact, Crested Butte rightly deserves its stature as one of the world's mountain-biking capitals. The sport was practically invented here, and numerous old logging and mining roads around town make it ideal not only for serious competitions but for also easy-going spins. In fact, the Mountain Bike Hall of Fame (970-349-7382) is located downtown.

Gunnison, too, has its share of mountain bikers; it's the home of Western State

Hot News

First published some 30 years ago in Lander, Wyoming, the often- controversial *High Country News* (HCN) now calls Paonia its headquarters. Billed as "A Paper for People who Care about the West," the bi-weekly HCN is largely supported by subscription. This frees the publisher to tackle sensitive issues without concern that their coverage might conflict with the viewpoints of advertisers. Mining, logging and government policy interests regularly hear the concerned voice of this press on a variety of subjects: rampant land development for ski resorts and golf courses; habitat loss for endangered wildlife; and the plight of the West's low-paid immigrant workers.

College. This youthful town of 5,700 dates back to Colorado's mining days, but it was ranchers who put it on the map. The broad Gunnison Valley cut by the swift Gunnison River is a cattleman's pasturing paradise.

Outdoor enthusiasts think it's paradise, too. Rafters and kayakers won't be disappointed in the Gunnison River's thrilling whitewater. Four-wheelers spend entire summers gearing over high-mountain passes. Anglers have a creel-full of fishing choices, starting with the Gunnison River itself, plus several other reservoirs, especially the 20-mile-long Blue Mesa Lake, part of the Curecanti National Recreation Area.

The Curecanti is the result of a massive water project which hemmed in the Gunnison River with three separate dams to provide irrigation water and hydroelectric power. At its heart, the Gunnison is a wild river, and no more so than through the Black Canyon of the Gunnison.

The Utes who occupied the area avoided Black Canyon, which they called *tomichi,* "land of high cliffs and plenty water." It is just that: 53 miles of raging torrent choked by a narrow gorge with sheer 2,000-foot-high walls of dark gneiss and schist. In 1933, President Herbert Hoover declared the most stunning 12 miles of the abyss the Black Canyon of the Gunnison National Monument (970-249-7036). Drives on both the north and south rims of the canyon have many pullouts to take in vertigo-inducing views to the chasm's bottom.

Black Canyon of the Gunnison

West of the Black Canyon of the Gunnison, the terrain opens into the northern reaches of the Uncompahgre Plateau. This is farming and orchard country. Agricultural communities—Paonia, Hotchkiss, Delta and Montrose—produce some of the state's best harvests of fruits and vegetables.

Citizens are deservedly proud of their land's bounty, and have even devoted several walls of old buildings to lavish murals depicting their agricultural achievements, scenic attractions and history. Paonia, Delta and Montrose each have "mural walks," where strollers can marvel at oversized paintings such as *Homage to Delta's Diversity, West Elk Wilderness, Fruit Box*, and *Dominquez-Escalante Expedition, August, 1776.*

For details on the region's past, the Delta County Historic

Museum (970-874-9721) presents an eclectic collection of dinosaur bones, Native American artifacts, cowboy crafts and even old bells. At Delta's pretty Confluence Park, the Fort Uncompahgre Living History Museum (970-874-8349) recreates the lives and times of trappers and traders from 1826 to 1844. Burly buckskin-clad mountain men who act as interpreters give the place an authentic feel. Early settlers are the focus at the Montrose County Historical Museum (970-249-2085), housed in the original Denver and Rio Grande Railroad depot.

The Ute Indian Museum (970-249-3098) outside Montrose occupies the former homestead of Chief Ouray and his wife Chipeta. Operated by the Colorado Historical Society, the museum chronicles Ute culture and their forced exile from their ancestral lands. Delta is the site of the "Ute Council Tree," an 85-foot-tall, 200-year-old cottonwood where Ouray and other chieftains met with whites to resolve conflicts.

The Gunnison County Chamber can be reached at 970-641-1501 or 800-274-7580. The Delta Chamber is located at 301 S. Main; call 970-874-8616. The Montrose Chamber of Commerce is located at 1519 E. Main; call 970-249-5000 or 800-873-0244.

The Four Corners

Colorado, Utah, Arizona and New Mexico come together at Four Corners. In this land of mesa and canyon, the Colorado Plateau drifts into the realm of high desert. Piñon, juniper, rabbitbush and yucca spread across the landscape. Nearly always within sight on the northeastern horizon stand the sparkling La Plata Mountains. In the foreground rests Sleeping Ute Mountain, the signature landmark of the region.

Native American heritage is the principal draw of the Four Corners, specifically the magnificent archeological legacy of Ancestral Puebloans. For over a hundred years, the area has attracted scientists from many disciplines who are eager to excavate and interpret the remains of a civilization that flourished for generations, then mysteriously vanished. Mesa Verde National Park, with its fascinating cliff dwellings, is deservedly world famous, though it is but one site that recounts the wonder of this ancient culture.

Outdoor recreation beyond exploring ancient sites shouldn't be overlooked. The San Juan National Forest covers a large portion of the territory, and there are large tracts of undeveloped acreage managed by the Bureau of Land Management (BLM) and the national park system. Hiking and biking trails are abundant, as are opportunities for excellent whitewater rafting and superb cold and warm water fishing.

The best way to experience the Four Corners is by driving the Trail of the Ancients Scenic and Historic Byway. The 114-mile route encompasses three highways, using the town of Cortez as the base. Colorado Highway 145 heads north past Dolores to Colorado Highway 184, which leads to

Four Corners Monument

Colorado, New Mexico, Arizona and Utah come together at a point 38 miles southwest of Cortez, where a flag-bedecked plaza commemorates this cartographic happenstance. As it's the only place in the U.S. where the borders of four different states meet, visitors invariably gather to crouch on all fours (right knee in Colorado, left knee in New Mexico, right hand in Utah, and left hand in Arizona) to capture a memorable vacation photo.

The monument is also somewhat of a shopping mart where Native American vendors have set up booths, or *ramadas,* for displaying handicrafts, in addition to offering snacks. Buy a Navajo taco in Utah, try on rings in Arizona, peruse pottery in New Mexico, then bargain for blankets in Colorado.

Four Corners Monument

The Ancestral Puebloans

Native Americans have inhabited the Four Corners area for thousands of years, occupying lands stretching from Utah's Abajo Mountains and Comb Ridge to Arizona's Montezuma Valley and into Colorado's upper San Juan River Valley. Early archaeologists used the Navajo term *anasazi* to refer to these early peoples, believing that it meant simply "ancient ones." Recently, the word has been more accurately translated to "enemy ancestor," a term not favored by modern Puebloan people. For example, the Hopi prefer the word *hisatsinom,* "those who came before," while the more general phrase "Ancestral Puebloan" is becoming more common.

10,000 to 6,500 B.C.
Known simply as Paleo-Indians, these early nomadic hunter-gatherers roamed over the Four Corners area preying on bison and mammoth. Evidence of their existence comes from surface campsites and projectile points.

6500 to 1500 B.C.
During this "Archaic" period, hunter-gatherers camped in natural shelters throughout the San Juan region. Using the "atlatl" (a throwing board) and darts, they successfully hunt small game, in addition to foraging for edible plants.

1500 B.C. to 50 A.D.
In the "Early Basketmaker II" period, a primitive farming society emerged that used natural floodplains to cultivate corn and squash. Natural shelters were used more seasonally for camping and sometimes, for burial. Coil and twined baskets were used for storage and transport.

Cliff Palace at Mesa Verde National Park

50 to 500 A.D.
During this "Late Basketmaker II" time, shallow pithouses were built for storage and habitation, though caves and other shelters were still used. Dryland farming, in addition to floodplain agriculture, was underway to grow crops and supplement hunting and gathering activities.

500 to 750 A.D.
The "Basketmaker III" period saw the development of more elaborate pithouses, occasionally gathered into small villages. Plain gray pottery was used for cooking and storage, and the bow and arrow replaced the atlatl as the preferred hunting device. Farming now included bean cultivation.

750 to 900 A.D.
The "Pueblo I" period is characterized by large villages with deep pithouses and separate storage areas. Some above-ground rooms made in a wattle and daub method were used for storage and living. "Great Kivas," circular underground ceremonial centers, graced some communities. Gray pottery is abundant, though some black-on-white and decorated red ware were also crafted.

900 to 1150 A.D.
In the "Pueblo II" time, masonry "unit" pueblos in the form of blocks of living and storage rooms appeared like mini apartment buildings for groups of villagers linked by kinship. Corrugated and black-on-white pottery became widespread. Roads connected some communities, and these clusters of pueblos acted as trading and ceremonial centers for surrounding villages. Several communities held in excess of 1,000 residents. Indeed, the population of the San Juan drainage system at the time was twice its present number.

1150 to 1350 A.D.
The "Pueblo III" period saw the emergence of cliff dwellings tucked beneath sandstone overhangs. Some structures reached up to five stories in height. Up to 60 different kin groups shared relatively close quarters, saving the open mesas above for farming. Within two generations beginning in the late 13th century, the mesas and valleys were abandoned. Archaeologists speculate that a variety of reasons—drought, over-farming, pestilence, disease and tribal rivalry—led to their exodus and dispersion to central Arizona and western New Mexico.

Hovenweep National Monument

Hovenweep National Monument. Southward, U.S. Highway 160 leads to the Four Corners Monument and continues into Utah. U.S. Highway 160 east out of Cortez takes in Mesa Verde National Park. The entire trip may be driven in three to four hours, but with the wealth of worthwhile stops, a week may seem like too little time to cover the distance.

Anasazi Beans

The small town of Dove Creek, 35 miles north of Cortez, is the undisputed "Pinto Bean Capital of the World." That said, a number of farmers also grow Anasazi beans, a large mottle-colored purple bean with a sweet taste. Some say it is less flatulence-inducing than carbohydrate-rich pinto beans. Adobe Milling (970-677-2620 or 800-542-3623) is the place to pick up a sack to test out the theory.

Cortez

The town of Cortez, population 8,000, functions largely as a ranching and agricultural center for the Montezuma Valley. The area is fertile drainage of the San Juan River, first platted by farmers in the late 1800s. During the summer, the town also becomes the staging ground for Four Corners' visitors eager to experience the area's Native American culture.

The Cortez Center (970-565-1151), through a partnership with the University of Colorado, has a small museum that displays artifacts primarily from the Yellow Jacket site. Free evening programs held here cover a range of Native American subjects including archaeology and astronomy, and arts such as Navajo sand painting.

A Colorado Welcome Center is located in Cortez at 928 E. Main Street; call 970-565-4048. The Cortez Chamber of Commerce can be reached at 970-565-3414.

Anasazi Heritage Center

The BLM operates the Anasazi Heritage Center (970-882-4811) as a museum, in addition to a site for research with laboratories and a library. The collection contains some two million artifacts, and many excellent examples of pottery and basketwork on display were culled from more than 125 excavations in the Dolores River Valley. A half-mile from the center is the Dominguez and Escalante Ancient Puebloan site, dating from the 12th century. Franciscan friars Frailes Francisco Atanasio Dominguez and Silvestre Vélez de Escalante camped near here in 1776 while scouting a route from Santa Fe, New Mexico to missions in Spanish California.

Crow Canyon Archaeological Center

The Crow Canyon Archaeological Center (970-565-8975 or 800-422-8975), four miles north of Cortez, puts the thrill of working on an actual Southwest archaeological dig into the hands of everyday people. Through a series of innovative fee-based "volunteer" programs, visitors can sign up for a day tour of the facility and its various operations, or stay a week to scrape with a trowel alongside trained scientists. Crow Canyon also offers several "Cultural Exploration" activities whereby scholars lead excursions to seldom-seen Ancestral Puebloan sites.

Dolores

The town of Dolores, 12 miles north of Cortez, thrived as a

stop on the Rio Grande Southern Railroad until the early 1950s, when the line was discontinued.

Hard times were not new to the community. During the lean years of the 1930s Great Depression, the Rio Grande Southern Railroad employed seven gasoline-powered, auto-like contraptions fitted to narrow gauge railroad tracks to keep the line running between Durango and Lizard Head Pass. The odd, truck-like locomotive hybrids were dubbed the "Galloping Geese," and old Number 5 stands outside the Galloping Goose Museum (970-882-7717).

Today, Dolores is the gateway to high plateau and mountain recreation. Anglers come to cast their lines in the Dolores River, and McPhee Reservoir is just outside town. Hikers find miles of trails leading into the Lizard Head Pass Wilderness Area.

Hovenweep National Monument

Hovenweep is a Ute word meaning "deserted valley" and it accurately describes this 785-acre rocky arroyo landscape that straddles the Colorado-Utah border.

Photographer William Henry Jackson came here in 1874, took pictures and introduced the world to Hovenweep's distinctive sandstone square, oval, circular and D-shaped towers. The Smithsonian Institute excavated here, and due to their efforts the site was declared a national monument in 1923.

Six individual Ancestral Puebloan sites can be explored, although only one, Square Tower, is easily visited. The other archaeological locations—Holly, Cutthroat Castle, Cajon, Horseshoe and Hackberry, aren't readily accessible by car, and therefore will require hiking over some difficult terrain. Hovenweep has limited facilities; only a ranger station and a small campground at Square Tower. For more information, contact Mesa Verde National Park at 970-529-4465.

Lowry Pueblo National Historic Landmark

In 1994, the remains of Lowry Pueblo underwent stabilization, opening the spot for better exploration. Located 20 miles north of Cortez on Colorado Highway 184, and then nine miles farther west on County Road CC, the site is secluded and serene. A self-guided walking tour leads to a kiva, a circular subterranean pithouse used for social and religious gatherings. This tour reveals one of the Four Corners' most interesting Ancestral Puebloan sites.

The 8th-century pithouse community developed into a large pueblo by the 12th century, with some structures reaching three stories in height. At least two distinct Puebloan groups occupied the area. Some construction bears a resemblance to classic Chaco-style masonry, so noted for its banded rows of light and dark stacked sandstone. The distinctive architecture led some researchers to contend that Lowry may have been a far-flung satellite community to the Chaco Canyon civilization in New Mexico. Later additions to the pueblo are more

Ernest House Jr.

In a sense, 18-year-old Ernest House Jr. is carrying on a family tradition.

Born to a Ute father and a Hispanic mother, House is descended from a Ute leader named Acowitz. Although it is seldom acknowledged, Acowitz was the one who confided to Richard Wetherill that deep within the twisting canyons of Mesa Verde were many ancient houses, one of which was fantastically large. In 1888, Wetherill and his brother-in-law Charlie Mason came upon the "Cliff Palace," thus "discovering" the magnificent cliff dwellings of the Ancestral Puebloans.

Today, House works as a part-time guide at the Ute Mountain Tribal Park. On half- and full-day tours, he escorts visitors up Mancos Canyon and into Lion's Canyon to view the timeworn ruins sheltered within the Ute Mountain Indian Reservation. One cliff dwelling, called simply "Tree House," contains an interesting artifact seldom seen by visitors. There, beneath a rock overhang etched upon the stone is the century-old signature of Richard Wetherill, who perhaps was first lead here by House's great-great grandfather.

Exploring a cliff dwelling

characteristic of Mesa Verdean-type architecture.

Lowry Pueblo is also well known for its "Great Kiva." A rare ceremonial painting (now housed at the Anasazi Heritage Center) was excavated here by the Chicago Field Institute in the 1930s.

Ute Mountain Indian Reservation

While the extreme southwestern Four Corners area was traditionally only ever a temporary home for the nomadic Utes, the U.S. government established a permanent reservation for the Weeminuche Utes here in 1895. Towaoc is the tribal center, 12 miles south of Cortez.

The enactment of the Indian Gaming Regulatory Act in 1988 opened the way for establishment of the Ute Mountain Casino, located off U.S. Highway 160 in the shadow of Sleeping Ute Mountain. From 8 a.m. to 4 a.m. daily, limited-stakes gambling in the form of keno, slot machines, blackjack and video poker keep locals occupied.

For a culturally rich experience, the Ute Mountain Tribal Park preserves numerous Ancestral Puebloan sites on 125,000 acres centered along 25 miles of the Mancos River south of Mesa Verde. Exploration of the area is under the guidance of Utes, who escort visitors to remote cliff dwellings and pueblos.

Tours are by reservation (800-847-5485 or 970-565-9653) and occur between June and October. Half-day tours visit roadside sites and Ute rock art panels, while full-day tours are more adventurous. Participants should be prepared to drive their own vehicls over some 80 miles of gravel road just to reach the sites, then scramble along hiking trails and climb ladders to the ruins.

Mancos

Mancos is the closest town to the entrance to Mesa Verde. Long a sleepy ranching community, the town has recently evolved into an arts center. Several Native American crafts galleries line Grand Avenue, and the Bounty Hunter (970-533-7215) run by clothier Steve King, is the place to be fitted for a custom cowboy hat. King's clients speak for his skill: actors Jack Nicholson and Robert Duvall, and country singer Barbara Mandrell.

The Mancos Visitor Center can be reached at 970-533-7434.

Mesa Verde National Park

The sheer cliffs, deep canyons and piñon-covered plateaus of Mesa Verde (Spanish for "green table") are scored with Ancestral Puebloan sites, explaining why archaeologists and visitors alike make this one of the American Southwest's most popular vacation areas. From 1190 to around 1300, the early Puebloans used their consummate masonry skills to craft massive cliff dwellings, some reaching five stories and 200 rooms. These perched villages literally cling to the underside of sweeping sandstone outcroppings, the condominium-type houses bunched together like honeycombs.

In what has become a conundrum that still baffles scientists, the cliff dwellings were forsaken during the 14th century, left to crumble and dissolve over time. The Utes came to the area in the 1500s, found the ruins too haunting and kept to the river valleys and tablelands. Spanish missionary Juan Maria Rivera journeyed here in 1765 to trade with Utes, and no doubt came upon evidence of past peoples. Several survey parties mapped the canyonlands in the late 1800s, and even William Henry Jackson took pictures of Two Story Cliff House in 1874.

It wasn't until 1888,

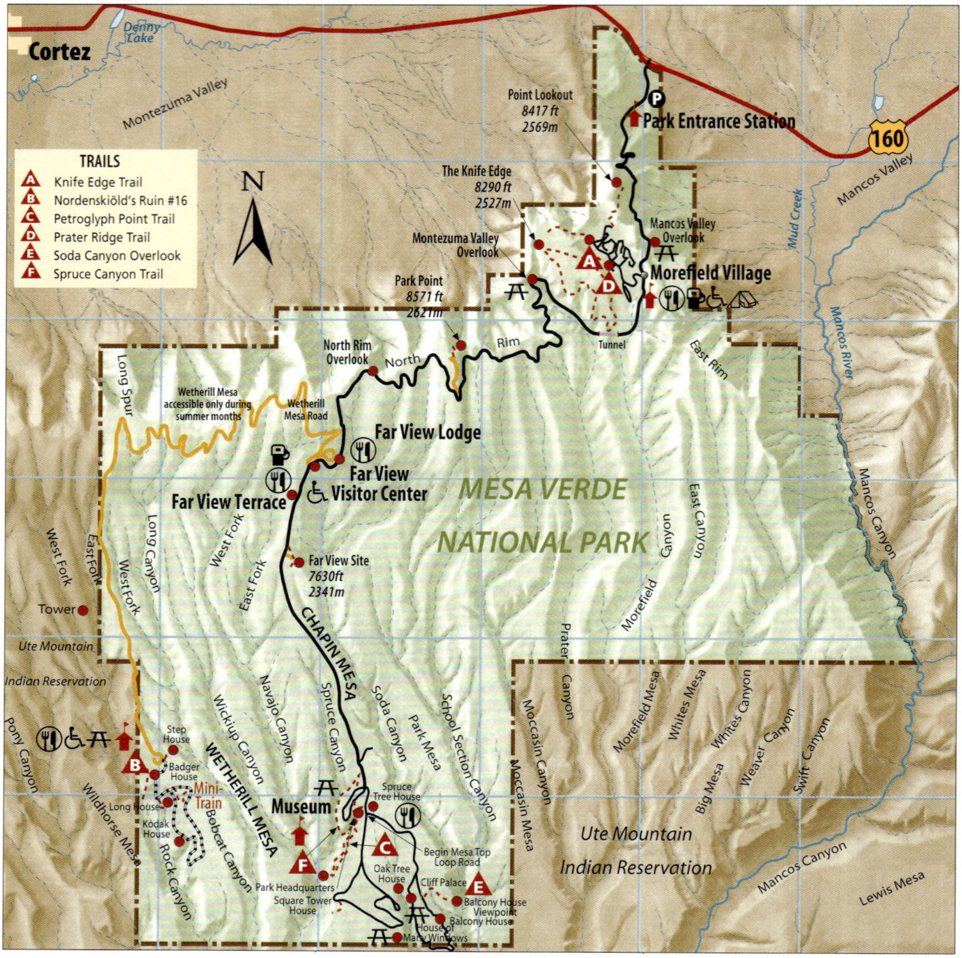

Mesa Verde National Park

however, when ranchers Richard Wetherill and Charlie Mason came upon the "Cliff Palace," that Mesa Verde's true wonders came to light. It was a cold December day when the cowboys paused while searching for strays on a slickrock overhang on Chapin Mesa and spied the massive structure with more than 200 rooms. Over the winter, Wetherill collected a number of artifacts that were later sold and exhibited. Soon, archaeologists and souvenir-hunters were combing the area, the more unscrupulous of which threatened in their collecting zeal to wipe clean any lasting record of the Ancestral Puebloans.

A wealthy son of a Swedish explorer, Gustaf Nordenskiöld, helped put Mesa Verde on a more scientific track. He traveled here in 1891, planning only to stay a few days. Instead, months went by while he explored the mesa, teaching his guides the rudiments of archaeological investigation. His illustrated *The Cliff Dwellers of Mesa Verde*, published in Swedish and English in 1893, outlined the scope of the area's vast architectural and anthropological treasure. By 1906, the U.S. Congress was nudged into creating the 82-square-mile Mesa Verde National Park, the first such park dedicated to preserving the works of humankind. In 1978, UNESCO designated Mesa Verde as a World Heritage Site.

Although the park contains a staggering 4,000 early Puebloan sites, travelers are restricted to two mesas. Far View Visitor Center (970-529-4421), located 15 miles within the park, is the access point to enter both tablelands. Orientation materials and exhibits here provide good overviews of the park's touring options.

Chapin Mesa

The Ancestral Puebloans obviously favored Chapin Mesa, as it was heavily used. The Chapin Mesa Archaeological Museum gives an excellent overview of the area and displays many artifacts from digs. Spruce Tree House, located in an arroyo behind the museum, is the most accessible site in the park. Tours of Spruce Tree House are self-guided in the summer and ranger-led in the winter. A reconstructed kiva allows visitors to descend into the quiet darkness of the covered pit structure that was once used for ceremonial purposes.

From the museum, Mesa Top Loop Road leads out onto the mesa in two one-way, six-mile driving loops that together take in more than 40 sites. Several roadside pullouts provide good vantage points to see the cliff dwellings. The west loop offers a stunning view of the Cliff Palace across the canyon, and a good look at Ancestral Puebloan life atop the mesa where pithouses once stood. The east loop covers two of the most visited sites, Cliff Palace and Balcony House, both of which require tickets for entry. Reservations and ticketing are handled out of the Far View Visitor Center, and participants need to be able to negotiate ladders perched over seemingly perilous heights, in addition to crouching through crevices.

Wetherill Mesa

Located in the western section of the park, the 12-mile Wetherill Mesa Road snakes its way into some of the park's less-frequented canyonland and is only open during the summer. Overlooks offer spectacular vistas into the Mancos River Valley, Sleeping Ute Mountain and, on clear days, the volcanic spire of Shiprock, New Mexico. The road terminates at a parking lot, where guests board a mini-tram for a four-mile loop around the mesa. Frequent stops are made to view the cliff dwellings, and rangers are on duty to answer questions. Long House (the park's second largest archeological site after Cliff Palace), and several surface pithouses, notably Step House and the Badger House Community, provide an excellent on-location review of Ancestral Puebloan development.

Mesa Verde National Park Facilities

The entrance to Mesa Verde National Park is located 10 miles east of Cortez, which is seven miles west of Mancos on U.S. Highway 160. From the highway, a paved road winds 15 miles to the Far View Visitor Center. Watch for rocks, deer and other animals on the narrow road. The park is open year-round, though several of the sites are closed during the winter. Summer hours are 8 a.m. to 6:30 p.m., and 8 a.m. to 5 p.m. the rest of the year. Park admission for a seven-day pass is $10 per vehicle, $3 for bicyclists.

Morefield Campground (open in the summer only) lies four miles from the park's highway entrance and contains 477 campsites that are occupied on a first-come, first-served basis. A cafe, general store, gas station, laundry and shower facilities are in the nearby Morefield Village. National Park Service (NPS) rangers hold evening programs at the Morefield Amphitheater throughout the summer.

At the Far View Visitor Center, the Far View Motor Lodge (closed during winter) offers 150 rooms, all with balconies overlooking 100-mile views past Soda Canyon, plus a lounge and an excellent restaurant, the Metate Room. Reservations are recommended; call 970-529-4421 or 800-449-2288.

The park concessionaire provides several daily, guided tours of Mesa Verde from May to October, departing from the Far View Motor Lodge. As road congestion can be a problem during the peak summer season, the nominal cost for the three-to-six hour tours is well worth the price of parking frustration. Call 970-529-4421 for information.

Finally, it's not uncommon to spot pottery shards and other artifacts lying among the archaeological sites in Mesa Verde. The Ancestral Puebloans left much of their culture behind when they left. While it may be tempting to procure these as souvenirs, the Antiquities Act prohibits the removal and destruction of historical items and the NPS strictly enforces the law. It's better to leave finds as they are, and let future generations enjoy the discovery too.

following pages: the Cliff Palace in Mesa Verde National Park

The Eastern Plains

"Ride'em lil' cowboy!" A young competitor clutches onto a sheep at a junior rodeo

Monotonous is the usual description applied to the vast, rolling landscape that covers the eastern third of Colorado. Grassland and tilled acreage seem to go on forever, with only the occasional clump of tall cottonwoods nurtured in small communities breaking the vista.

Explorer Major Stephen Long passed through the northeastern corner of the state in 1820 and wrote that it "would never be fit for human habitation other than by nomad races." He was wrong, of course. Homesteaders proved that the windswept reaches supported livestock and, with water, bountiful crops—at the expense of the Arapaho, Comanche, Cheyenne, Pawnee and Kiowa natives, who prospered here for generations.

Subtle may be a more apt description of the area, for the Eastern Plains divulges its diversity—culturally and topographically—in faint, almost imperceptible ways that are defined largely by latitude. In the south, the Arkansas River Valley cradles the beginnings of Colorado's Hispanic settlement and the rise of Anglo-American interests along the Santa Fe Trail. Place names like Las Animas and La Junta, coupled with terrain supporting sagebrush and yucca, relay a definite Southwestern flavor.

Northward, the land lifts slightly, opening into high prairie. U.S. Interstate 70 and a sparse network of back roads outline the region's tenuous ties to faraway urban centers. Farther north still, the South Platte River trickles toward Nebraska, irrigating thousands of acres of ranch and farmland. Many of Colorado's early prospectors and homesteaders let the South Platte lead them through the "Great American Desert" en route to the Rocky Mountains. Many found it far more hospitable than they had imagined and stayed to put down roots, which flourished into the archetype of small-town America.

Santa Fe Trail

With the independence of Mexico from Spain in 1821, commerce with the U.S. increased. Trappers and traders plied a route that became known as the Santa Fe Trail linking Santa Fe, Mexico (now

left: A dark sky looms behind Bent's Old Fort

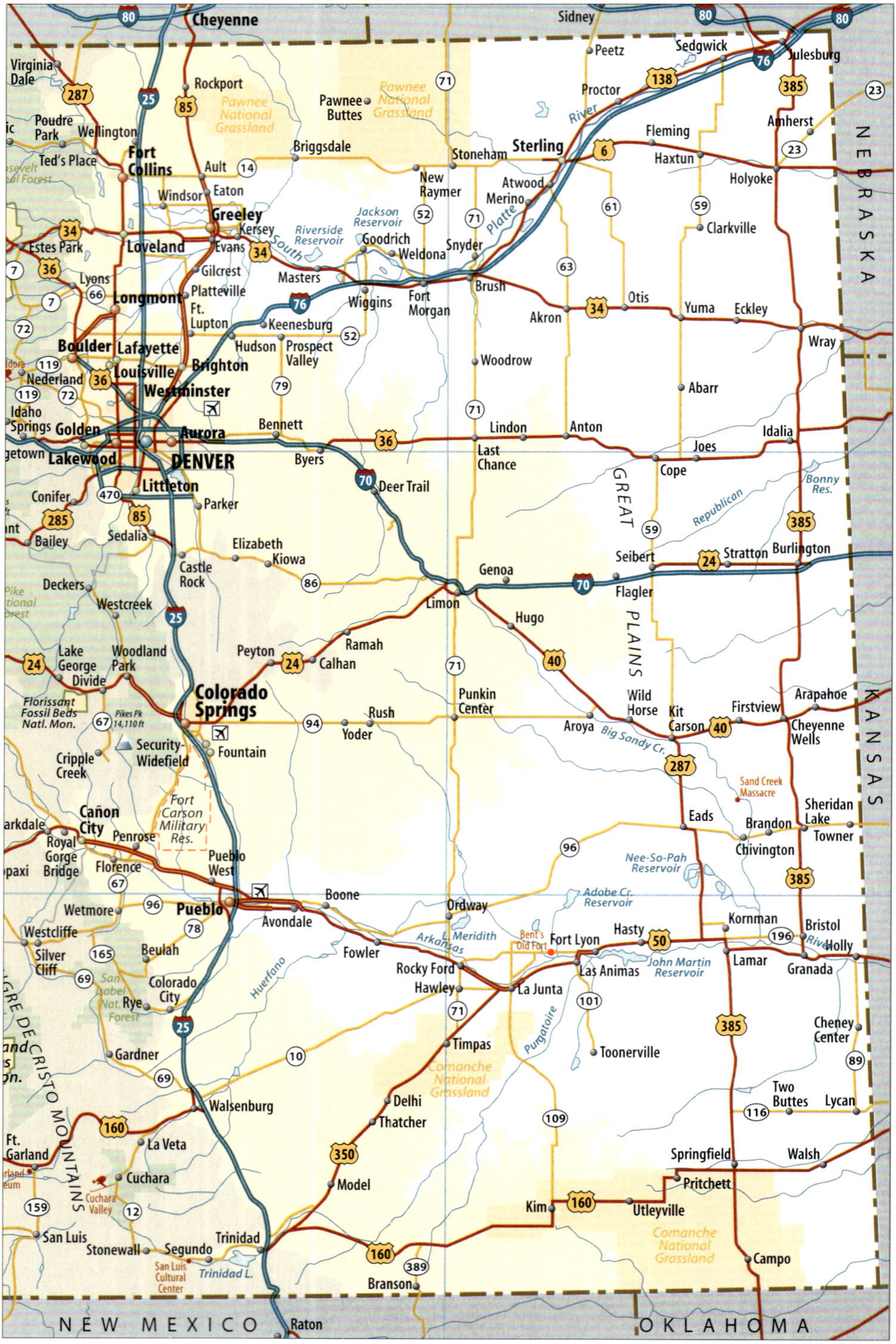

The Eastern Plains of Colorado

The courtyard in Bent's Old Fort

New Mexico) with Independence, Missouri. Originally, the route passed south of Colorado, but over time the "Mountain Branch" attracted travelers who preferred to cross the prairie via the relatively lush bottomlands of the lower Arkansas River.

For half a century until the 1870s, the Mountain Branch of the Santa Fe Trail was the highway of dreams for mountain men and settlers who were eager to stake a claim to the riches of the American West. Today, U.S. Highway 350 from Trinidad to La Junta, and then U.S. Highway 50 to the Kansas border parallel the Santa Fe Trail as a designated scenic and historic byway. The 188-mile, one-way drive traverses a cultural confluence marked by Plains Indian tribes, as well as the first strongholds of Hispanic and Anglo-American pioneers.

La Junta

In 1875, the Santa Fe Railroad made La Junta a stop on its track through the lower Arkansas Valley, connecting it with a line to Denver. *La junta* means "the junction" in Spanish. Even today, the town is an important transportation center for shipment of produce and cattle.

The Otero Museum (719-384-7500), located in the one-time Sciumbato Grocery Store, holds an impressive collection of artifacts dating primarily from the time of the railroad's arrival. Farming and ranching implements are the museum's principal items, though its exhibits of locally donated collections are remarkable. Don't miss the mustache cup display or the gallery of railroad calendar covers.

Native American arts and crafts are the centerpiece of the Koshare Indian Museum (719-384-4411). More than $5 million in artifacts reveal a range of items from Flathead buckskin moccasins to Hopi kachinas. The museum is also home to the Koshare Indian Dance Group, drawn from Explorer Scout Post 230. In its early days, the troop was known as "Buck's Brats" for their founder, James F. "Buck" Burshears. Their reputation for authentic recreation of Native American dances, however, is anything but the product of coarse youngsters. During summer Saturday evenings, performances are

SuperAmerica Guide's Eastern Plains Recommendations

- Drive the Santa Fe Trail, at least to Las Animas, then plan a half-day for exploring Bent's Old Fort National Historic Site.
- Take in the Koshare Indian Museum, as well as a performance of their Native American dances held on summer Saturday evenings.
- Stroll through Burlington Old Town's collection of historic buildings. Later, take a ride on the nearby Kit Carson County Carousel.
- Visit the impressive collection of pioneer artifacts at the Overland Trail Museum in Sterling.
- Explore the remote tracts of the Comanche National Grassland, especially Vogel Canyon. Hike to the Dinosaur Trackway for a strenuous adventure.

held at the "Great Kiva," a replica of an Ancestral Puebloan ceremonial center.

The La Junta Chamber is located at 110 Sante Fe Street; call 719-384-7411

Las Animas

The heyday of Las Animas was in the 1880s, when an English organization, the Prairie Cattle Company, ran 50,000 head of longhorn in the region. Las Animas was a stop for the Atchison, Topeka and Santa Fe Railroad, where cars loaded braying cattle destined for frying pans and stew pots throughout the Midwest. Ranching is still a part of the economy today, but not nearly as important as irrigated farming along the Arkansas River.

Two miles south of Las Animas is the townsite of Boggsville (719-384-8113), where Thomas Boggs and other pioneers settled in 1862.

Kit Carson moved here in 1867 with his wife and seven children, though his home has since been lost to a flood. Carson and his wife died within weeks of each other in 1868, and the Carson children were raised by the Boggs family.

The life and times of the famous frontiersman are remembered at the Las Animas Kit Carson Museum (719-456-2005), which was originally built as a security compound for WWII German prisoners of war. The simple museum contains a number of historic structures including a one-room steel jail, a carriage house, a one-room schoolhouse, a blacksmith shop and a stagecoach stop. Be sure to look for the "gallows" across the street.

A window at Bent's Old Fort

Bent's Old Fort National Historic Site (719-384-2596), 15 miles west of Las Animas, is by far the most fascinating stop on the Santa Fe Trail. In 1834, brothers William and Charles Bent and their partner, Cerán St. Vrain, established an adobe complex here that would become the focal point of a trading empire. In its prime, Bent's Fort controlled the movement of goods along the Santa Fe Trail.

Abandoned in 1852, the immense fort fell to its foundations but was faithfully reconstructed in 1976 from old drawings to depict what it was like during the 1840s. Costumed "living history" interpreters complete the picture of the recreated era. Mountain men and cavalry soldiers go about the daily tasks of the time—cleaning rifles and preparing hides—while

Comanche National Grassland

After the Dust Bowl disaster of the 1930s, the federal government began setting aside tracts of land to be protected from farming and grazing. The Comanche National Grassland, managed by the U.S. Forest Service (USFS), encompasses a total of 419,000 acres contained in two units. The Timpas Unit is south of La Junta and includes several easily accessible areas with sections of the Santa Fe Trail and archeological sites, whereas the Carrizo Unit south of Lamar is far more isolated.

Vogel Canyon, in the Timpas Unit, is a short, 13-mile drive south of La Junta on Colorado Highway 109. It's an ideal place for a picnic and there are short hiking trails to the canyon bottom. Native Americans once lived in the canyon, and there are many petroglyphs pecked into the canyon walls.

Southwest of Vogel Canyon is Picket Wire Canyon, which requires more effort to reach. Low clearance cars can only get within a mile of the entrance gate; then it's a two-mile hike to the trailhead. Five miles up the trailhead is the reward for the journey, the Dinosaur Trackway.

Here, approximately 150 million years ago, a herd of huge *Apatosaurus* left a quarter-mile trail of stubby footprints in the sand, which later fossilized. Look closely for tracks of the carnivorous *Allosaurus* too. Could it be that the lumbering *Apatosaurus* were being stalked by this smaller, yet equally vicious relative of *Tyrannosaurus Rex*?

A Comanche National Grassland ranger office is located at 1420 E. 3rd Street at La Junta; call 719-384-2181.

visitors inspect the blacksmith's shop, sleeping quarters, billiard room and warehouses.

The Las Animas / Bent County Chamber is located at 332 Ambassador Thompson Blvd.; call 719-456-0453.

Lamar

Normally, the quiet town of Lamar gets a shot of excitement each autumn as hundreds of hunters arrive to test out the town's claim as the "Goose Hunting Capital of the Nation." Few sharp-eyed marksmen leave disappointed.

Hunting has been a way of life in Lamar for decades. In the late 1800s, a disastrous infestation of jackrabbits threatened farmers' crops, and hunters took action. Large roundups were initiated where dozens of riflemen and clubbers encircled the bunny hordes, slaughtering thousands until the vermin were under control.

No doubt, rabbit stew was a favorite campfire meal for pioneers who inhabited a 25-mile stretch along the Arkansas River. Some of the area's colossal cottonwood trees' trunks measured 18 feet in diameter and reached 75 feet in height. Regrettably, most of the trees were felled for firewood and building material, but a few remain to recall what it must have been like to come across this leafy oasis in an otherwise arid terrain. The Big Timbers Museum (719-336-4379) recounts those pioneer days with a fine collection of historical photographs and exhibits.

The Lamar Chamber is located at 109 E. Beech in the old train depot; call 719-336-4379. It is also the site for a Colorado Welcome Center.

The howling of a coyote is as western as it gets

U.S. Interstate Highway 70 / U.S. Highway 40 Corridor

For expedience, U.S. Interstate Highway 70 is the preferred beeline out of Denver into Kansas. Truckers and long-distance travelers zip along the highway at breakneck speeds, rarely stopping to take in the sites, which are admittedly few and far between, but not without interest.

Limon

Limon may not warrant a stop for most people, but those who do pause here are in for a kooky diversion at the Genoa Tower (719-763-2309), located a few minutes from town. Built in the 1920s as a roadside cafe and lounge, the sprawling structure is now solely dedicated to displaying an incredibly kitschy array of artifacts. "If it ain't here, it doesn't exist" is the motto, and the place lives up to the claim. Expect to see ancient mammoth fossils, 20,000 arrowheads, old bottles, vintage guns, scads of curious ranching tools and bizarre natural animal mutations (i.e. two-headed calves). The tower, a mere 87 steps to the top, earned a mention in *Ripley's Believe It or Not.* It's said that six states can be seen from the summit on an exceptionally clear day.

On June 6, 1990, the sky was anything but clear as a violent tornado ripped through the center of Limon. Within 10 minutes, the town was devastated but miraculously, no one was killed. Countless hours of work and millions of dollars later, the town has recovered. The Limon Heritage Museum & Railroad Park (719-775-2373) shows a videotape recounting the tornado's destruction, in addition to

Rocky Ford

Located 11 miles northwest of La Junta, the tiny community of Rocky Ford has a big reputation. This is the "Melon Capital of the World." Honeydew, watermelon and especially cantaloupe thrive here. In August, when harvesting begins, roadside produce stands scattered throughout the area do juicy business.

other displays of the town's past.

The Limon Heritage Museum is located behind the Town Hall; call 719-775-2373.

Burlington

Burlington is the last town of note on U.S. Interstate 70 before the Colorado prairie seamlessly fades into the Kansas grasslands. At Burlington Old Town (719-346-7382 or 800-288-1334), remnants of the Wild West linger with a collection of 20 historic buildings, including a saloon with staged gunfights and can-can shows.

Old Town's wagon collection is impressive and during summer Saturdays, one of the vintage buckboards is pressed into service for peaceful tours of Burlington, ending at the Kit Carson County Carousel. Constructed in 1905 by the Philadelphia Toboggan Company, this classic wooden merry-go-round features 46 hand-carved animals, from mild-mannered ponies to snarling lions. Rides cost a quarter, and are worth every penny for the chance to spin joyfully around to marches that croon from a 1909 Wurlitzer Monster Military Band Organ.

The Burlington Chamber is located at 415 15th Street; call 719-346-8070. A Colorado Welcome Center is located behind Burlington Old Town off U.S. Interstate 70; call 719-346-5554.

South Platte River

Mark Twain summed up the South Platte in *Roughing It* as "a melancholy stream straggling through the center of an enormous flat plain, and only saved from being impossible to find with the naked eye by its sentinel rank of scattering trees standing on either bank."

A hundred-odd years later, his description still holds true. The river may be even harder to spot these days, as U.S. Interstate 76 streams past dozens of small towns and broad plots of sugar beets, alfalfa, wheat, corn, rye and soybeans.

Fort Morgan

Founded as the military post of Camp Tyler in 1864 to protect passing Overland Trail wagon trains, the name Fort Morgan was adopted two years later to honor a Civil War colonel from Cincinnati.

Great Western Sugar found the place to its liking in 1906 and erected a sugar beet processing plant. Even today, a good deal of the local economy is dependent on sugar beets. Fort Morgan has a prosperous small-town feeling, with charming Victorian-era houses located along the Sherman Street National Historic District.

The star attraction at the Fort Morgan Museum (970-867-6331) is Glen Miller, the famous Big Band leader who disappeared in 1944 while flying from London to France on a wartime concert tour. Miller graduated from Fort Morgan High School in 1921 before setting out to swing his baton to hits such as *String of Pearls.* As a youngster, Miller likely pulled up a stool at the Hillrose Drugstore soda fountain, which is re-created here.

The Fort Morgan Area Chamber is located at 300

Eastern Plains Events and Festivals

March

Spring Equinox Festival
Festival centered around an excursion to Crack Cave, where mysterious petroglyphs become illuminated at the equinox. Springfield; call 719-523-4061.

Winter Quarters—Bent's Old Fort—Recreation of winter life during the fur trading era by costumed interpreters. La Junta; call 719-384-2596.

April

Greater Prairie Chicken Mating
Sponsored weekend field trips by the East Yuma Historic Society seek out the "lek" and watch its curious mating ritual. Wray; call 970-332-5063.

June

Glenn Miller Festival
Presentations, tours, dinner and dancing to Big Band sounds. Fort Morgan; call 970-867-6121.

Little Britches Rodeo
Rodeo events and festivities for young cowpokes. Burlington; call 719-346-8070.

August

Arkansas Valley Fair
Coinciding with harvest time, attendees eat their fill of melons while taking in horse races and livestock shows. Rocky Ford; call 719-254-7483.

September

Sugar Beet Days
Lively festival to honor the region's favorite cash crop. Sterling; call 800-544-8609.

December

Old Town Outback Christmas
Traditional High Plains Yuletide in an historic setting. Burlington; call 800-288-1334.

Main Street; call 970-867-6121.

Sterling

Sterling bills itself as the "City of Living Trees" due to the creative sculptures of Brad Rhea, an artist from the nearby town of Merino. Rhea's eye for line and texture has brought new life to 16 dead treetrunks scattered around town by transforming them into craning-necked giraffes, sensuous mermaids and dreaming clowns.

The excellent Overland Trail Museum (970-522-3895) chronicles the famous route followed by thousands of prospectors, trappers and settlers who trekked across the route in the mid-1800s. Housed in a stone reproduction of Fort Sedgewick, the museum contains extensive displays of Native American and pioneer artifacts. Be sure to see the exhibit of branding irons, which is said to be the world's largest collection.

The Logan County Chamber (Sterling) is located at 109 North Front Street in the old train depot; call 970-522-5070 or 800-544-8609.

War Cry

The Eastern Plains were the stage for some the most tragic conflicts between Native Americans and encroaching traders and settlers defended by the U.S. military.

Sand Creek

White Antelope chanted his death song, "Only the mountains live forever" on November 29, 1864. Along with chieftain Black Kettle, Left Hand and a group of 500 Southern Cheyenne and Arapaho, he was encamped along Sand Creek near the present-day town of Chivington. They believed they were under the protection of U.S. authorities when Colonel John M. Chivington ordered the Colorado Third Regiment to open fire at dawn. When the massacre ended around noon, more than 150 Cheyenne and Arapaho lay dead, including many women and children. The "Bloody Thirdsters" collected scalps and later displayed them at a Denver theater.

Beecher Island

Cheyenne Dog Soldiers under the leadership of Tall Bull, Bull Bear, White Horse and the warriors of Pawnee Killer had been raiding homesteads in Kansas when Major George A. Forsyth, leading 50 scouts, picked up their trail on September 17, 1868. The Indian force, numbering some 600, lead Forsyth to the Arikaree Fork of the Republican River near present-day Wray, then turned on the soldiers. Vastly outnumbered, Forsyth's troops took refuge on a small island in the dry streambed, holding off repeated attacks for more than a week until reinforcements routed the Indians.

Summit Springs

On July 11, 1869, southeast of present-day Atwood, the U.S. Fifth Calvary along with Pawnee scouts engaged Chief Tall Bull and his Cheyenne Dog Soldiers. The Cheyenne had kidnapped two white women on a vengeful raid through Kansas, and the military had finally tracked them down. In the melée, Tall Bull was shot (allegedly by Buffalo Bill Cody), and 51 other braves were also killed along with an unknown number of women and children. Only one of the white women, Maria Weichell, was rescued, though she was badly wounded with a pistol shot to the chest. Susanna Alderdice, her companion, was tomahawked when the skirmish began. Summit Springs was the last major battle between U.S. military troops and indigenous Plains Indians.

Julesburg

When the Union Pacific Railroad reached Julesburg in 1867, it brought not only prospectors and traders but also a motley passenger list of land speculators, gamblers, outlaws and prostitutes. Julesburg soon sported a rag-tag collection of gaming parlors and brothels, and in short order was dubbed the "Wickedest City in the West."

The little town is far tamer these days, though it remembers its brief stint as a Pony Express station (15-year-old Buffalo Bill Cody worked the route) and the rest of its rough-and-ready past at the Depot Museum (970-474-2264). Southeast of town begins Colorado's shortest scenic byway, the South Platte River Trail at 19 miles in length. The route traces a portion of the path followed by "59ers" during the Pikes Peak or Bust Gold Rush. Markers along the way point out the sites of Julesburg #1, #2 and #3, the predecessors of present-day Julesburg.

The Julesburg Chamber is located at 122 W. 1st; call 970-474-3504. A Colorado Welcome Center is located at 20934 County Road 28; call 970-474-2054.

Reference

This reference section gathers together useful information on a variety of topics. General and specific subjects are listed alphabetically. Every attempt has been made to ensure accuracy, though it cannot be guaranteed.

ACCOMMODATIONS

ALAMOSA

Best Western Alamosa Inn, 1919 Main St., Alamosa, CO 81101; call 719-589-2567 or 800-459-5123, FAX 719-589-0767. Rates $$, 120 units. Indoor heated pool, HBO, non-smoking rooms, children under 12 stay free, senior and government discounts, restaurant and lounge.

Cottonwood Inn Bed & Breakfast, 123 San Juan Ave., Alamosa, CO 81101; call 719-589-3882 or 800-955-2623, FAX 719-589-6437. Rates $$, 8 units. Congenial hosts, comfortable furnishings and great breakfasts.

ANTONITO

Narrow Gauge Railroad Inn, Highways 17 and 285, Box 636, Antonito, CO 81120; call 719-376-5441 or 800-323-9469, FAX 719-376-5443. Rates $, 33 units. Closest lodging to Cumbres & Toltec Railroad depot, direct dial phones, in-room movies, restaurant next to motel.

ASPEN/SNOWMASS VILLAGE

Aspen Club Lodge, 709 East Durant, Aspen, CO 81611; call 970-925-6760 or 800-882-2582, FAX 970-925-6778. Rates $$$, 90 units. Complimentary full breakfast, restaurant, bar, health spa, outdoor pool and whirlpool, concierge, fireplaces, ski-in/ski out.

Beaumont Inn, 1301 E. Cooper, Aspen, CO 81611; call 970-925-7081 or 800-344-3853, FAX 970-925-1610. Rates $$$ to $$$$, 30 units. Bed and breakfast with mountain views, backyard BBQ, heated outdoor pool (summer), hot tub, sauna, pets welcome. Closed May.

Chalet Lisl, 100 E. Hyman, Aspen, CO 81611; call 970-925-3520, FAX 970-925-3580. Rates $$, 10 units. Economy non-smoking apartments with TV, hot tub and garden.

Crestwood Lodge, 400 Wood Road, Box 5460, Snowmass Village, CO 81615; call 970-923-2450 or 800-356-5949, FAX 970-923-5018. Rates $$ to $$$$, 120 units. Slopeside condos with kitchen, fireplace, balcony, BBQ grill, pool, hot tub, sauna and exercise facilities.

Fasching Haus Condominiums, 747 S. Galena St., Aspen, CO 81611; call 970-925-2260 or 800-321-7025, FAX 970-925-2264. Rates $$. Pool, hot tub, sauna and exercise room.

Grand Aspen Hotel, 515 S. Galena St., Aspen, CO 81611; call 970-925-1150 or 800-24-ASPEN, FAX 970-920-1090. Rates $$ to $$$, 150 units. Near Aspen Mountain gondola and downtown shopping area.

Heatherbed Mountain Lodge, 1679 Maroon Creek Road, Box 530, Aspen, CO 81612; call 970-925-7077 or 800-356-6782, FAX 970-925-6120. Rates $$, 20 units. Bed and breakfast with Maroon Bells in the distance and close to Aspen Highlands.

Hotel Lenado, 200 S. Aspen St., Aspen, CO 81611; call 970-925-6246 or 800-321-3457, FAX 970-925-3840. Rates $$$$, 19 units. Romantic bed and breakfast, distinctive interiors, hot tub, TV, bar.

Hotel Jerome, 330 E. Main St., Aspen, CO 81611; call 970-920-1000 or 800-331-7213, FAX 970-925-2784. Rates $$$$, 93 units. Mobile four star, AAA four diamond historic property in the heart of Aspen.

The Little Nell Hotel, 675 Durant St., Aspen, CO 81611; call 970-920-4600 or 800-525-6200, FAX 970-920-4670. Rates $$$$, 92 units. Signature Aspen property with grand-hotel amenities.

St. Moritz Lodge, 334 W. Hyman Ave., Aspen, Co 81611; call 970-925-3220 or 800-817-2069, FAX 970-925-8740.

Rates $$ to $$$; 30 units. European-style lodge, pool, whirlpool and sauna.

Silvertree Hotel, 100 Elbert Lane, Box 5550, Snowmass Village, CO 81615; call 970-923-3520 or 800-525-9402, FAX 970-923-5494. Rates $$$$, 250 units. AAA three-diamond rated, restaurant, nightclub, pool, sauna, whirlpool, health club, game room, laundry, ski in/ski out.

Stonebridge Inn, P.O. Box 5008, Snowmass Village, CO 81615; call 970-923-2420, FAX 970-923-5889. Rates $$, 95 units. Fifty yards from slopes; pool, sauna, hot tub and restaurant.

BOULDER

Alps Boulder Canyon Inn, 38619 Boulder Canyon Drive, Boulder, CO 80302; call 303-444-5445 or 800-414-2577, FAX 303-444-5522. Rates $$ to $$$$, 12 units. Bed and breakfast with fireplaces, private balconies, whirlpool tubs.

Prices

Accommodation listings are arranged alphabetically by city. Following the city roster are lodging associations, which can also recommend accommodations. Price classifications are based upon single-night summer rates, double occupancy and do not include taxes. Winter rates may be considerably higher for mountain and ski resort areas.

$...............under $50
$$.............$50 to $99
$$$...........$100 to $150
$$$$.........$150 and above

Best Western Boulder Inn, 770 28th St., Boulder, CO 80303; call 303-449-3800 or 800-233-8469, FAX 303-449-3800. Rates $$, 96 units. Mobil three stars and AAA two diamonds, mountain views, sauna, whirlpool, restaurant and lounge.

Best Western Golden Buff Lodge, 1725 28th St., Boulder, CO 80301; call 303-442-7450 or 800-999-BUFF, FAX 303-442-8788. Rates $$, 112 units. Centrally located, HBO/cable, pool, health club, whirlpool, sauna and restaurant.

Boulder Broker Inn, 555 30th St., Boulder, CO 80303; call 303-444-3330 or 800-338-5407, FAX 303-444-6444. Rates $$ to $$$, 116 units. Complimentary breakfast, nightly dancing and comedy on Tuesdays, restaurant.

Boulder Victoria Historic Bed & Breakfast, 1305 Pine St., Boulder, CO 80302; call 303-938-1300. Rates $$$ to $$$$, 7 units. Guest rooms feature antiques, private baths, afternoon tea.

Briar Rose Bed & Breakfast, 2151 Arapahoe Ave., Boulder, CO 80302; call 303-442-3007, FAX 303-786-8440. Rates $$$, 9 units. English country house with private baths, afternoon tea.

Gold Lake Mountain Resort, 3371 Gold Lake Road, Ward, CO 80481; call 303-459-3544 or 800-450-3544, FAX 303-459-9080. Rates $$$ to $$$$, 17 units. Cabins with outdoor activities ranging from horseback riding to fly fishing, lakeside hot tub and spa.

Hotel Boulderado, 2115 13th St., Boulder, CO 80302; call 303-442-4344 or 800-433-4344, FAX 303-442-4378. Rates $$$ to $$$$, 160 units. Elegant Victorian accommodations, three restaurants and bars, nightly entertainment.

Regal Harvest House, 1345 28th St., Boulder, CO 80302; call 303-443-3850 or 800-545-6285, FAX 303-443-1480. Rates $$$ to $$$$, 270 units. Adjacent to the University of Colorado, complete sports center with two pools, 15 tennis courts, volleyball, bike rental, restaurant and lounge.

BRECKENRIDGE

Beaver Run Resort, P.O. Box 2115, Breckenridge, CO 80424; call 970-453-6000 or 800-525-2253, FAX 970-453-4284. Rates $$ to $$$$, 567 units. Next to Beaver Run Express chair lift, hot tubs, indoor/outdoor pool.

Breckenridge Hilton, P.O. Box 8059, Breckenridge, CO 80424; call 970-453-4500 or 800-321-8444, FAX 970-453-0212. Rates $$ to $$$, 208 units. Deluxe rooms with refrigerators, coffee makers, hot tubs, pool, sauna, restaurant and lounge.

Fireside Inn Bed & Breakfast, 114 N. French St., Breckenridge, CO 80424; call 970-453-6456, FAX 970-453-9577. Rates $$, 9 units. Victorian-era home with hot tub and cable TV, located in historic district.

Hunt Placer Inn, 275 Ski Hill Road, P.O. Box 4898, Breckenridge, CO 80424; call 970-453-7573 or 800-472-1430, FAX 970-453-2335. Rates $$$, 8 units. European-style chalet bed and breakfast, private baths, balconies, fireplaces.

The Lodge at Breckenridge, 112 Overlook Drive, Breckenridge, CO 80424; call 970-453-9300 or 800-736-1607, FAX 970-453-0625. Rates $$ to $$$$, 45 units. Complimentary breakfast, athletic club and spa.

Pine Ridge Condominiums, 400 4 O'Clock Road, Breckenridge, CO 80424; call 970-453-6946 or 800-333-8833, FAX 970-453-0746. Rates $$$, 70 units. Two bedrooms and loft with kitchen, fireplace, balconies, outdoor hot tubs and heated pool.

Ridge Street Inn, 212 N. Ridge St., Breckenridge, Co 80424; call 970-453-4680 or 800-452-4680. Rates $$, 6 units. Circa 1890s Victorian inn with antique furnishings, private bath and cable TV.

Wildwood Suites, 120 Sawmill Road, Breckenridge, CO 80424; call 970-453-0232 or 800-866-0300, FAX 970-453-7325. Rates $$, 36 units. Located two blocks from downtown; hot tub, sauna, massage and complimentary breakfast.

BUENA VISTA

Vista Inn, P.O. Box 1101, 733 U.S. Hwy. 24 North, Buena Vista, CO 81211; call 719-395-8009 or 800-809-3495, FAX 719-395-6025. Rates $$, 41 rooms. Hot tub, game room, continental breakfast.

BURLINGTON

Burlington Inn, 450 South Lincoln, Burlington, CO 80807; call 719-346-5555, FAX 719-346-5555. Rates $$, 112 units. Located near main attractions, restaurant and lounge.

CAÑON CITY

Best Western Royal Gorge Motel, 1925 Fremont Drive, Cañon City, CO 81212; call 719-275-3377 or 800-231-7317, FAX 719-275-3931. Rates $$, 67 units. HBO, heated pool, hot tub, laundry, small pets okay, restaurant and lounge.

CARBONDALE

Carbondale Days Inn, 950 Cowen Drive, Carbondale, CO 81623; call 970-963-9111 or 800-944-3297, FAX 970-963-0759. Rates $$, 69 units. Central location near attractions, shopping and restaurants.

Mt. Sopris Inn, Box 126, Carbondale, CO 81623; call 970-963-2209 or 800-437-8675, FAX 970-963-8975. Rates $$ to $$$$, 15 units. Bed & breakfast on 14 acres overlooking Crystal River Valley, private baths, TV, pool table, swimming pool and hot tub.

CENTRAL CITY

Harveys Wagon Wheel Hotel & Casino, 321 Gregory St., Central City, CO 80427; call 800-WAGONHO, FAX 303-582-5860. Rates $$, 118 units. Comfortable hotel with gaming facilities.

Winfield Scott Guestquarters Bed & Breakfast, P.O. Box 369, 210 Hooper St., Central City, CO 80427; call 303-582-3433, FAX 303-582-3434. Rates $$ to $$$, 2 units. Secluded mountain setting, deck, grill and garden.

COLORADO SPRINGS

Antlers Doubletree, 4 S. Cascade, Palmer Center, Colorado Springs, CO 80903-1685; call 719-473-5600 or 800-222-8733, FAX 719-389-0259. Rates $$$, 290 units. Located downtown, health facility, indoor swimming pool, whirlpool, microbrewery, restaurant and lounge.

Best Western Palmer House, 3010 N. Chestnut, Colorado Springs, CO 80907; call 719-636-5201 or 800-223-9127, FAX 719-636-3108. Rates $$, 150 units. Centrally located, pool, restaurant and lounge.

The Broadmoor Hotel, 1 Lake Ave., Colorado Springs, CO 80906; call 719-634-7711, FAX 719-577-5700. Rates $$$$, 700 units. Mobile five star, AAA five diamond, fitness center, spa, restaurant and lounge.

Colorado Springs Marriott, 5580 Tech Center Drive, Colorado Springs, CO 80919; call 719-260-1800 or 800-962-6982, FAX 719-260-1492. Rates $$ to $$$, 310 units. Indoor/outdoor pools, health club, sauna, whirlpool, restaurant and lounge.

Hampton Inn, 1410 Harrison Road, Colorado Springs, CO 80906; call 719-579-6900 or 800-HAMPTON, FAX 719-579-0897. Rates $$, 112 units. Complimentary breakfast, HBO, indoor pool and hot tub.

Hearthstone Inn, 506 N. Cascade, Colorado Springs, CO 80903; call 719-473-1322 or 800-521-1885, FAX 719-473-1322. Rates $$ to $$$, 23 units. Mobile three star, AAA three diamond bed and breakfast, antique furnished rooms with private baths.

Maple Lodge, 9 El Paso Blvd., Colorado Springs, CO 80904; call 719-685-9230. Rates $$, 16 units. On two wooded acres, family suites with kitchens, heated pool, cable TV, BBQ and picnic area.

Radisson Inn Colorado Springs

North, 8110 N. Academy Blvd., Colorado Springs, CO 80920; call 719-598-5770 or 800-333-3333, FAX 719-598-3434. Rates $$, 200 units. Near Air Force Academy, indoor pool, exercise room and outdoor hot tub.

Room At The Inn, 618 N. Nevada Ave., Colorado Springs, CO 80903-1021; call 719-442-1896, FAX 719-442-6802. Rates $$, 7 units. Bed and breakfast with private baths, whirlpool tubs, fireplaces, outdoor hot tub and afternoon tea.

Super 8 Chestnut, 3270 N. Chestnut, Colorado Springs, CO 80907; call 719-632-2681 or 800-800-8000, FAX 719-475-0606. Rates $, 32 units. Near downtown, cable TV, children under 12 stay free.

COPPER MOUNTAIN

Copper Mountain Resort, P.O. Box 3001, Copper Mountain, CO 80443; call 970-968-2882 or 800-458-8386, FAX 970-968-2308. Rates $$ to $$$$, 750 units. AAA four diamond, golf, athletic club and bicycling.

CORTEZ

A Bed & Breakfast on Maple Street, 102 S. Maple St., Cortez, CO 81321; call 970-565-3906 or 800-665-3906. Rates $$, 5 units. Country charm, private bath and hot tub.

Best Western Turquoise Motor Inn, 535 E. Main, Cortez, CO 81321; call 970-565-3778 or 800-547-3376, FAX 970-565-3439. Rates $$, 46 units. Cable TV, outdoor heated pool, free continental breakfast, children under 12 stay free.

Holiday Inn Express, 2121 E. Main, Cortez, CO 81321; call 970-565-6000 or 800-626-5652, FAX 970-565-3438. Rates $$ to $$$, 100 units. Indoor pool, hot tub, free continental breakfast.

Kelly Place, 14663 County Road G, Cortez, CO 81321; call 970-565-3125 or 800-745-4885, FAX 970-565-3450. Rates $$, 8 units. Adobe-style lodge bordering on 100 acres, hiking, biking and horseback trails.

CRESTED BUTTE

Crested Butte Lodge, P.O. Box A, Mt. Crested Butte, CO 81225; call 970-349-4700 or 800-544-8448, FAX 970-349-2304. Rates $$, 22 units. Indoor pool, sauna, outdoor hot tub, restaurant and bar.

Cristiana Guesthaus, Bed & Breakfast, 621 Maroon Ave., P.O. Box 427, Crested Butte, CO 81224; call 970-349-5326 or 800-824-7899, FAX 970-349-1962. Rates $$, 21 units. European-style lodge, private baths, fireplace, hot tub, sauna and sun deck.

CRIPPLE CREEK

Imperial Casino Hotel, 123 N. 3rd St., Box 869, Cripple Creek, CO 80813; call 719-689-7777 or 800-235-2922, FAX 719-689-0410. Rates $$ to $$$, 29 units. Restored historic hotel, casino, summer melodrama theater, restaurant and bar.

DELTA

Escalante Ranch Bed & Breakfast, 701-650 Road, Delta, CO 81416; call 303-426-0360, FAX 303-426-0366. Rates $$$, 3 units. Working ranch on Gunnison River in Escalante Canyon, canoeing, hiking, biking and rock climbing.

DENVER

Adams Mark Hotel Denver, 1550 Court Place, Denver, CO 80202; call 303-893-3333 or 800-444-ADAM. Rates $$ to $$$, 744 units. Downtown location on 16th Street Mall.

Brown Palace Hotel, 321 17th St., Denver, CO 80202; call 303-297-3111 or 800-321-2599, FAX 303-293-9204. Rates $$$$, 230 units. Prestigious property, four restaurants, afternoon tea, cigar bar.

Capitol Hill Mansion, 1207 Pennsylvania St., Denver, CO 80203; call 303-839-5221 or 800-839-9329, FAX 303-839-9046. Rates $$ to $$$, 8 units. Victorian mansion bed and breakfast, private baths, whirlpool, some private balconies and fireplaces.

Castle Marne-A Luxury Urban Inn, 1572 Race St., Denver, CO 80206; call 303-331-0621 or 800-92-MARNE, FAX 303-331-0623. Rates $$$$, 9 units. Victorian mansion bed and breakfast, antique furnishings, private baths, afternoon teas.

Denver Marriott City Center, 1701 California St., Denver, CO 80202; call 303-297-1300 or 800-228-9290, FAX 303-298-7474. Rates $$$, 613 units. Convenient downtown location close to attractions.

Executive Tower Inn, 1405 Curtis St., Denver, CO 80202; call 303-571-0300 or 800-525-6651, FAX 303-825-4301. Rates $$$$, 337 units. Indoor pool, cable TV, sauna, whirlpool, tennis, restaurant and lounge.

Holiday Chalet-A Victorian Hotel, 1820 E. Colfax, Denver, CO 80218; call 303-321-9975 or 800-626-4497, FAX 303-377-6556. Rates $$, 10 units. Restored brownstone, kitchens, athletic club.

Holiday Inn Denver Downtown, 1450 Glenarm Place, Denver, CO 80202; call 303-573-1450 or 800-423-5128, FAX 303-572-1113. Rates $$, 397 units. Cable TV, outdoor pool, exercise room, pets welcome, restaurant and lounge.

Holtze Executive Place, 818 17th Street, Denver, CO 80202; call 303-607-9000 or 800-422-2092. Rates $$$$, 119 units. European-style hotel, suites with kitchens, breakfast included in rate.

Hyatt Regency Denver Downtown, 1750 Welton St., Denver, CO 80202; call 303-295-1234 or 800-233-1234, FAX 303-293-2565. Rates $$$$, 511 units. Indoor pool, health club, outdoor track, whirlpool, restaurant and lounge.

Loews Giorgio Hotel, 4150 E. Mississippi, Denver, CO 80222; call 303-782-9300 or 800-345-9172, FAX 303-758-6542. Rates $$$$, 197 units. Northern Italian-inspired Mobile four star, AAA four diamond property in Cherry Creek area, health club, restaurant and lounge.

Oxford Hotel, 1600 17th St., Denver, CO 80202; call 303-628-5400 or 800-228-5838, FAX 303-628-5413. Rates $$$$, 81 units. Historic property in the heart of LoDo.

Queen Anne Bed & Breakfast Inn, 2147-51 Tremont, Denver, CO 80205; call 303-296-6666 or 800-432-INNS, FAX 303-296-2151. Rates $$ to $$$, 14 units. Two Victorian homes facing a park, private baths, gardens.

Warwick Hotel, 1776 Grant St., Denver, CO 80203; call 303-861-2000 or 800-525-2888, FAX 303-839-8504. Rates $$$ to $$$$, 194 units. European-style hotel, balconies, pool and health club.

The Westin Hotel-Tabor Center Denver, 1672 Lawrence St., Denver, CO 80202; call 303-572-9100 or 800-228-3000, FAX 303-572-7288. Rates $$$ to $$$$, 420 units. Pool, hot tub, sauna, exercise facilities, cable TV, restaurant and lounge.

DILLON

Mountain Condominium Management Company, P.O. Box 462, Dillon, CO 80435; call 970-468-0556 or 800-525-3682, FAX 970-468-1305. Rates $ to $$$$, 120 units. Studios to three bedrooms with kitchens, fireplaces, private balconies, cable TV, indoor pool and hot tubs.

DOLORES

Dolores Mountain Inn, 701 Railroad Ave., P.O. Box 307, Dolores, CO 81323; call 970-882-7203 or 800-842-8113, FAX 970-882-7011. Rates $$, 30 units. Cable TV, laundry facilities, bike rentals.

Mountain View Bed & Breakfast, 28050 County Road P, Dolores, CO 81323; call 970-882-7861 or 800-228-4592. Rates $$, 8 units. Rooms, suites and cottages situated on 22 acres with pond and creek.

DURANGO

Best Western Rio Grande Inn & Suites, 400 E. 2nd Ave., Durango, CO 81301; call 970-385-4980 or 800-245-4466, FAX 970-385-4980. Rates $$, 138 units. Downtown location near Narrow Gauge Train Depot, free breakfast.

Blue Lake Ranch Bed & Breakfast Country Inn, 16000 Hwy. 140, Hesperus, CO 81326; call 970-385-4537, FAX 970-385-4088. Rates $$ to $$$$, 9 units. Private country estate, gardens, lake and fishing.

Iron Horse Inn, 5800 N. Main, Durango, CO 81301; call 970-748-2990 or 800-748-2990; FAX 970-385-4791. Rates $$, 140 units. Bi-level suites with fireplaces, indoor pool, spa and sauna.

Jarvis Suite Hotel, 125 West 10th St., Durango, CO 81301; call 970-259-6190 or 800-824-1024, FAX 970-259-6190. Rates $$, 22 units. All-suite property, full kitchens and outdoor hot tub.

Landmark Motel, 3030 Main Ave., Durango, CO 81301; call 970-259-1333 or 800-252-8853, FAX 970-247-3854. Rates $$, 48 units. Cable TV, heated pool, whirlpool, sauna, continental breakfast.

Leland House Bed & Breakfast Suites, 721 E. Second Ave., Durango, CO 81301; call 970-385-1920 or 800-664-1920, FAX 970-385-1967. Rates $$ to $$$, 10 units. Restored historic 1927 inn closed to Narrow Gauge Train Depot.

Lightner Creek Inn, 999 County Road 207, Durango, CO 81301; call 970-259-1266 or 800-268-9804. Rayes $$ to $$$, eight units, cozy B&B with terrific charm.

Logwood Bed & Breakfast, 35060 Hwy. 550 North, Durango, CO 81301; call 970-259-4396 or 800-369-4082,

FAX 970-259-4396. Rates $$ to $$$, 6 units. Red cedar log home overlooking Animas River, private baths.

The New Rochester Hotel, 726 E. Second Ave., Durango, CO 81301; call 970-385-1920 or 800-664-1920, FAX 970-385-1967. Rates $$ to $$$, 15 units. Restored 1891 historic hotel close to Narrow Gauge Train Depot, free gourmet breakfast.

Red Lion Inn/Durango, 501 Camino Del Rio, Durango, CO 81301; call 970-259-6580 or 800-547-8010, FAX 970-259-4398. Rates $$ to $$$, 159 units. Located on Animas River, indoor pool, hot tub, massage therapy, exercise room, restaurant and lounge.

Strater Hotel, 699 Main Ave., Durango, CO 81301; call 970-247-4431 or 800-247-4431, FAX 970-259-2208. Rates $$ to $$$, 93 units. Restored Victorian hotel, antique furnishings, private baths, restaurant, saloon and melodrama theater.

Tamarron Resort, P.O. Drawer 3131, Durango, CO 81302; call 970-259-2000 or 800-678-1000, FAX 970-259-0745. Rates $$ to $$$$, 320 units. San Juan Mountain setting with Cliffs golf course.

ESTES PARK

Alpine Trail Ridge Inn, 927 Moraine Route, Estes Park, CO 80517; call 970-586-4585 or 800-233-5023, FAX 970-586-6249. Rates $$, 48 units. Some private balconies, pool and restaurant.

Amberwood, 1889 Fall River Road, Estes Park, CO 80517; call 870-586-4385. Rates $$ to $$$$, 17 units. Cottages and lodge rooms, kitchens, microwaves, cable TV, some fireplaces.

American Wilderness Lodge, 481 W. Elkhorn, Estes Park, CO 80517; call 970-586-4402 or 800-ROCKY MT, Ext. 220. Rates $$, 33 units. Riverside location, balconies, fireplaces, kitchens, TV, heated pool, sauna, hot tubs, pets welcome.

Aspen Lodge Ranch Resort, 6120 Hwy. 7, LPR, Estes Park, CO 80517; call or FAX 970-586-8133. 56 units, package rates only. Log lodge and cabins bordering Rocky Mountain National Park.

Baldpate Inn, 4900 South Hwy. 7, P.O. Box 4445, Estes Park, CO 80517; call 970-586-6151. Rustic lodge and cabins, restaurant. 15 units, Rates $$

Best Western at Lake Estes Resort, 1650 Big Thompson Hwy. Box 1466C, Estes Park, CO 80517; call 970-586-3386 or 800-292-VIEW, FAX 970-586-9000. Rates $$ to $$$$, 58 units. AAA three diamond, great views, kitchens, fireplaces, hot tub.

Black Canyon Inn, 800 MacGregor Ave., P.O. Box 856, Estes Park, CO 80517; call 970-586-3154. Rates $$ to $$$, 25 units. Suites, fireplaces, kitchens, indoor spa and outdoor pool.

Black Dog Inn Bed & Breakfast, P.O. Box 4659, 650 South St. Vrain Ave., Estes Park, CO 80517; call 970-586-0374. Rates $$ to $$$, 4 units. Restored 1904 mountain home, antique furnishings, whirlpool tub, fireplaces.

Brynwood on the River, 710 Moraine Ave., P.O. Box 1929, Estes Park, CO 80517; call 970-586-3475 or 800-279-4488. Rates $$ to $$$$, 28 units. Family resort, river cottages or motel, hot tubs and pool.

Comfort Inn, 1450 Big Thompson Ave., Box 393, Estes Park, CO 80517; call 970-586-2358 or 800-228-5150. Rates $$ to $$$, 75 units. Some balconies, pool, whirlpool and A/C.

Deer Crest, P.O. Box 1768, Estes Park, CO 80517; call 970-586-2324 or 800-331-2324, FAX 970-586-8693. Rates $$, 26 units. AAA three diamond, riverfront setting, refrigerators, microwaves, cable TV, balconies/patios, heated pool.

Holiday Inn of Estes Park, 101 South St. Vrain, Box 1468, Estes Park, CO 80517; call 970-586-2332 or 800-80-ESTES, FAX 970-586-2332. Rates $$ to $$$, 150 units. Holidome, indoor pool, whirlpool, fitness room, restaurant.

Lazy R Cottages, P.O. Box 1996, Estes Park, CO 80517; call 970-586-3708 or 800-726-3728. Rates $$ to $$$$, 14 units. Knotty pine cabins, great views, fireplaces, hot tubs, cable TV, kitchens, grills and picnic tables.

McGregor Mountain Lodge, 2815 Fall River Road, Estes Park, CO 80517; call 970-586-3457, FAX 970-586-4040. Rates $$$ to $$$$, 19 units. Cottages, suites with kitchens and fireplaces.

Ponderosa Lodge, 1820 Fall River Road MR, Estes Park, CO 80517; call 970-586-4233 or 800-628-0512. Rates $$ to $$$$, 19 units. AAA three diamond, riverfront balconies, fireplaces, kitchenettes, HBO.

Rams Horn Village Resort, 1565 Hwy. 66, Estes Park, CO 80517; call 970-586-4338 or 800-229-4676, FAX 970-586-4689. Rates $$ to $$$$. Great views, luxury vacation homes and rustic cottages, pool, hot tubs, some fireplaces.

Romantic Riversong Bed & Breakfast Inn, P.O. Box 1910, Estes Park, CO 80517; call 970-586-4666. Rates $$$ to $$$$, 9 units. Country inn on 27 acres, whirlpool tubs and fireplaces.

Silver Saddle Lodge, 1260 Big Thompson Ave., P.O. Box 1747, Estes Park, CO 80517; call or FAX 970-586-4476. Rates $$ to $$$, 54 units. AAA three diamond, pool, whirlpool, some balconies, kitchens.

The Stanely Hotel, 333 Wonderview Ave., Estes Park, CO 80517; call 970-586-3371.Rates $$ to $$$, 133 rooms. Two restaurants, fine dining with American Continental cuisine.

Streamside… A Village of Cabin Suites, 1260 Fall River Road, Box 2930, Estes Park, CO 80517; call 970-586-6464 or 800-321-3303, FAX 970-586-6272. Rates $$$$, 19 units. AAA four diamond property on 17 acres.

Sunnyside Knoll Resort, 1675 Fall River Road, Estes Park, CO 80517; call 970-586-5759 or 800-586-5212. Rates $$ to $$$$, 15 units. Suites with hot tubs, fireplaces, cable TV, outdoor hot tub and heated pool. No children under 12.

Triple R Cottages, 1000 Riverside Drive, Estes Park, CO 80517; call 970-586-5552, Rates $ to $$$, 7 units. Housekeeping cottages, cable TV, kitchenettes, grills, picnic area and playground.

Valhalla Resort, P.O. Box 1439, Estes Park, CO 80517; call 970-586-3284, FAX 970-586-6361. Rates $$ to $$$$, 22 units. Vacations homes and rustic cottages, fireplaces, cable TV, pool and hot tub.

Wildwood Inn, 2801 Fall River Road, Estes Park, CO 80517; call 970-586-2933. Rates $ to $$$$, 16 units. Condo suites, in-room spas, fireplaces and private decks.

EVERGREEN

Bauer's Spruce Island Chalets, 5937 S. Brook Forest Road, Evergreen, CO 80439; call 303-674-4757. Rates $$, 5 units. All have kitchens, living rooms, private baths and cable TV.

Bears R Inn, 27425 Spruce Lane, Evergreen, CO 80439; call 303-670-1205 or 800-863-1205, FAX 303-670-8542. Rates $$, 12 units. Historic 1924 inn, full country breakfast.

FORT COLLINS

Budget Host Inn, 1513 N. College Ave., Fort Collins, CO 80524-1217; call 970-484-0870 or 800-825-4678, FAX 970-224-2998. Rates $$, 30 units. Cable TV, outdoor hot tub, picnic area, some with kitchens.

Ft. Collins Marriott, 350 E. Horsetooth Road, Fort Collins, CO 80205; call 970-226-5200 or 800-548-2635, FAX 970-282-0561. Rates $$ to $$$, 230 units. Indoor/ outdoor pool, cable TV, restaurant and lounge.

FORT MORGAN

Best Western Park Terrace Motel & Inn, 725 Main St., Fort Morgan, CO 80701; call 970-867-8256, FAX 970-867-8257. Rates $ to $$, 24 units. Small motel and good restaurant.

FRISCO

Best Western Lake Dillon Lodge, P.O. Box 552, 1202 N. Summit Blvd., Frisco, CO 80443; call 970-668-5094 or 970-825-7423 (Denver direct) or 800-727-0607, FAX 970-668-0571. Rates $$ to $$$$, 127 units. Indoor pool and hot tub, ski and bike shop, restaurant and lounge. Near Keystone, Copper Mountain and Breckenridge.

Galena Street Mountain Inn, 106 Galena St., Frisco, CO 80443; call 970-668-3224 or 800-248-9138, FAX 970-668-1569. Rates $$, 14 units. Mountain views, Mission-style furnishings, private baths, cable TV, hot tub, gourmet breakfast.

GEORGETOWN

The Hardy House Bed & Breakfast, P.O. Box 156, 605 Brownell, Georgetown, CO 80444; call 800-490-4802. Rates $$, 4 units. Victorian-era home in historic district, private bath and outdoor hot tub.

GLENWOOD SPRINGS

Hotel Denver, 402 7th St., Glenwood Springs, CO 81601; call 970-945-6565 or 800-826-8820, FAX 970-945-2204. Rates $$$, 60 units. Centrally located, room service, cable TV, restaurant and bar.

Hot Springs Lodge & Pool, 401 N. River Road, Glenwood Springs, CO 81601; call 970-945-6571 or 800-537-7946, FAX 970-945-6571. Rates $$,

107 units. World's largest outdoor mineral hot springs pool, sport shop, restaurant and lounge.

GRANBY

Drowsy Water Ranch, P.O. Box 147H, Granby, CO 80446; call 970-725-3456 or 800-845-2292. Weekly rates $1,005 double, 15 units. Dude ranch with pool, children's program and entertainment.

GRAND LAKE

Grand Lake Lodge, 15500 US Hwy. 34, Box 569, Grand Lake, CO 80447; call 303-759-5848 or 970-627-3937, FAX 303-759-3179 or 970-627-9495. Rates $$ to $$$$, 56 units. National historic landmark, rustic cabins, pool, entertainment, restaurant.

GRAND JUNCTION

Grand Junction Hilton, 743 Horizon Drive, Grand Junction, CO 81506; call 970-241-8888 or 800-HILTONS, FAX 970-242-7266. Rates $$ to $$$, 264units. Outdoor pool and hot tub, tennis courts, volleyball, children's playground, restaurant and sports bar.

Historic Hotel Melrose, 337 Colorado Ave., Grand Junction, CO 81501; call 970-242-9636 or 800-430-4555; FAX 970-242-5613. Rates $, 24 units. Old fashioned hotel, centrally located near restaurants and shops.

The House of Ouray, 760 Ouray Ave., Grand Junction, CO 81501; call 970-245-8452. Rates $ to $$, 3 units. Restored 1905 Victorian, private baths, TV and game room, young adults over 14 welcome.

GREELEY

Greeley Holiday Fairfield Inn, 2401 West 29th St., Greeley, CO 80631; call 970-339-5030 or 800-228-2800, FAX 970-339-5030. Rates $$, 62 units. Indoor pool and spa, deluxe continental breakfast.

Greeley Holiday Inn Express, 2563 West 29th St., Greeley, CO 80631; call 970-330-7495 or 800-HOLIDAY, FAX 970-330-7495. Rates $$, 64 units. Indoor pool and spa, deluxe continental breakfast.

GUNNISON

Holiday Inn Express, 400 E. Tomichi Ave., Gunnison, CO 81230; call 970-642-1288 or 800-GUNNISON, FAX 970-641-1332. Rates $$, 55 units. Indoor pool, whirlpool and fitness center.

Mary Lawrence Inn Bed & Breakfast, 601 North Taylor, Gunnison, CO 81230; call 970-641-3343. Rates $$, 5 units. Renovated Victorian, private baths, full breakfast, children 6 years and older welcome.

IDAHO SPRINGS

Argo Motor Inn, 2622 Colorado Blvd., Box 837, Idaho Springs, CO 80452; call 303-567-4473, FAX 303-567-9736. Rates $$, 22 units. Some rooms with fireplace, oak furniture and creekside patio.

IGNACIO

Sky Ute Lodge & Casino, P.O. Box 340, Iganacio, CO 81137; call 970-563-3000 or 800-876-7017, FAX 970-563-3007. Rates $$, 36 units. Casino, restaurant and lounge.

JULESBURG

Platte Valley Inn, I-76 and U.S. 385, Julesburg, CO 80737; call 970-474-3336 or 800-562-5166, FAX 970-474-3336. Rates $$, 59 units. Heated outdoor pool, cable TV, restaurant.

KEYSTONE

Keystone Resort, Box 38, U.S. Hwy. 6, Keystone, CO 80435; call 800-258-9553, Rates $$ to $$$$, 255 hotel rooms and 800 condos. Package prices available.

LA JUNTA

Quality Inn, 1325 East 3rd St., La Junta, CO 81050; call 719-384-2571, FAX 719-384-5655. Rates $ to $$, 60 units. Room service, satellite TV, hot tubs, outdoor pool, whirlpool, sauna, restaurant and lounge. American food. Rate $

LAKE CITY

The Crystal Lodge, P.O. Box 246, Lake City, CO 81235; call 970-944-2201 or 800-984-1234, FAX 970-944-2503. Rates $$ to $$$, 18 units. Rooms, suites or cottages, pool, spa and restaurant.

LAMAR

Best Western Cow Palace Inn, 1301 North Main, Lamar, CO 81502; call 719-336-7753 or 800-678-0344, FAX 719-336-9598. Rates $$, 102 units. Satellite TV, indoor pool, hot tub, sauna, restaurant and lounge.

LAS ANIMAS

Best Western Bent's Fort Inn, East U.S. 50, Las Animas, CO 81504; call 719-456-0011, FAX 719-456-2250. Rates $ to $$, 38 units. Satellite TV, outdoor pool, restaurant.

LEADVILLE

Apple Blossom Inn, Victorian Bed & Breakfast, 120 West 4th St., Leadville, CO 80462. Rates $$, 8 units. Restored 1879 Victorian, baked goods and tea all day, full breakfast.

Grand West Village Resort, P.O. Box 957, Leadville, CO 80461; call 719-486-0702 or 800-691-3999, FAX 719-486-0766. Rates $$ to $$$$, 4 units. Kitchens, fireplaces, jetted tubs, Cable TV-VCR and laundry.

Historic Delaware Hotel, 700 Harrison Ave., Leadville, CO 80461; call 719-486-1418 or 800-748-2004, FAX 719-486-2214. Rates $$ to $$$, 36 units. Victorian hotel, antique furnishings, hot tub, restaurant.

Leadville Country Inn, 127 E. 8th St., Leadville, CO 80461; call 719-486-2354 or 800-748-2354, FAX 719-486-0300. Rates $ to $$$, 9 units. Private baths, hot tub, complimentary bicycles, gourmet breakfast.

LONGMONT

Briarwood Inn Motel, 1228 North Main, Longmont, CO 80501; call 303-776-6622, FAX 303-772-7453. Rates $$, 17 units. Centrally located, cable TV, kitchenettes, whirlpool spa, patio area and BBQ.

Raintree Plaza Hotel & Conference Center, 1900 Ken Pratt Blvd., Longmont, CO 80501; call 303-776-2000 or 800-843-8240, FAX 303-776-2000. Rates $$, 211 units. Concierge wing and mini-suites with refrigerator, wet bar and coffee maker, pool, gym, restaurant.

LOVELAND

Best Western Coach House Resort, 5542 East Hwy. 34, Loveland, CO 80537; call 970-667-7810, Rates $ to $$, 88 units. Mobil two stars, AAA three diamond, indoor/outdoor pool, whirlpool, tennis, picnic area, restaurant and lounge.

MANCOS

Mesa Verde Motel, P.O. Box 552, 191 Railroad Ave., Mancos, CO 81328; call 970-533-7741 or 800-825-MESA. Rates $, 16 units. Seven miles to Mesa Verde Entrance, AAA approved, A/C.

MANITOU SPRINGS

El Colorado Lodge, 23 Manitou Ave., Manitou Springs, CO 80829; call 719-685-5485 or 800-782-2246. Rates $$, 26 units. Cabins, 1 and 2 bedrooms, A/C, fireplaces, some kitchens, cable TV, children's playground and outdoor pool.

Historic Red Crags Bed & Breakfast, 302 El Paso Blvd., Manitou Springs, CO 80829; call 970-685-1920, Rates $$ to $$$, 6 units. Victorian mansion on two acres, antiques, private baths, fireplaces, outdoor hot tub, herb garden and duck pond.

Western Cabins Resort, 106 Beckers Lane, Manitou Springs, CO 80829; call 719-685-5755 or 800-873-4553. Rates $$ (three night minimum), 11 units. Cabins with scenic views, porches, kitchens, cable TV, heated pool, playground and BBQ.

MONARCH

Monarch Mountain Lodge, #1 Powder Place, Monarch, CO 81227; call 719-539-2581 or 800-332-3668. Rates $$ to $$$, 100 units. Indoor pool, outdoor hot tub, sauna, free ski shuttle, racquetball, massage, mountain biking and horseback riding.

MONTROSE

Best Western Red Arrow Motor Inn, 1702 East Main, Hwy. 50, Montrose, CO 81402; call 970-249-9641 or 800-468-9323. Rates $$ to $$$, 60 units. Cable TV, HBO, whirlpool baths, fitness center with hot tub, pool and playground.

Country Lodge, 1624 East Main, Montrose, CO 81410; call 970-249-4567. Rates $$, 22 units. Pool, redwood deck, hot tub and flower garden, children's play area.

Uncompahgre Lodge Bed & Breakfast, 21049 Uncompahgre Road, Montrose, CO 81401; call 970-240-4000 or 800-397-4257/6862. Rates $$, 8 units. Spacious rooms and private baths.

MOSCA

Great Sand Dunes Country Club and Inn, 5303 Highway 150, Mosca, CO 81146; call 719-378-2356 or 800-284-9213, FAX 719-378-2428. Rates $$$, 15 units. Rustic inn on historic ranch in San Luis Valley, 3,000 bison roaming base of Sangre de Cristo Mountains, golf and dining.

OURAY

Alpenglow Condominiums, 215 5th Ave., Ouray, CO 81427; call 970-325-4972. Rates $$ to $$$, 16 units. Kitchens, private decks, fireplaces, cable TV, hot tub, sauna and BBQ pit.

China Clipper Inn, 525 Second

Street, Ouray, CO 81427; call 970-325-0565 or 800-315-0565. Rates $$ to $$$ 11 units, elegant rooms, many with fireplaces or whirlpools.

Comfort Inn, 191 5th Ave., P.O. Box 771, Ouray, CO 81427; call 970-325-7203 or 800-438-5713. Rates $$, 32 units. Mountain views, cable TV, hot tub and sun deck.

The Manor Bed and Breakfast, 317 Second Street, Ouray, CO 81427; call 970-325-4574, Rates $$, seven units, comfortable rooms with great breakfast.

St. Elmo Hotel, 426 Main St., P.O. Box 667, Ouray, CO 81427; call 970-325-4951, FAX 970-325-0348. Rates $$, 9 units. Restored 1898 hotel, now a bed and breakfast, private baths, restaurant.

Wiesbaden Hot Springs Spa & Lodgings, 625 Fifth St., P.O. Box 349, Ouray, CO 81427; call 970-325-4347, FAX 970-325-4358. Rates $$ to $$$, 21 units. Natural hot springs, vapor cave, outdoor pool, spa with massage, mud wraps, facials and reflexology.

PAGOSA SPRINGS

Davidson's Country Inn Bed & Breakfast, P.O. Box 87, Pagosa Springs, CO 81147; call 970-264-5863. Rates $$, 9 units. Three-story log inn and cabin on a 32-acre ranch, antique furnishings, game room and playground.

Spring Inn, P.O. Box 1799, 165 Hot Springs Blvd., Pagosa Springs, CO 81147; call 970-264-4168 or 800-225-0934, FAX 970-264-4707. Rates $$, 23 units. Ten mineral pools, massage therapy and health club.

PUEBLO

Abriendo Inn, 300 W. Abriendo Ave., Pueblo, CO 81004, call 719-544-2703 , FAX 719-542-1806. Rates $$, 10 units. Historic estate home, now a bed & breakfast, whirlpool.

REDSTONE

Clevehom Manor, 58 Redstone Blvd., Redstone, CO 81623; call 970-963-3463 or 800-643-4837. Rates $$ to $$$$, 16 units. Historic mountain inn, restaurant.

Redstone Inn, 82 Redstone Blvd., Redstone, CO 81623; call 970-963-2526 or 800-748-2524. Rates $$ to $$$$, 35 units. Historic property, two restaurants, health club, pool, views.

RIDGWAY

Chipeta Sun Lodge and Suites, 304 South Lena, Ridgway, CO 81432; call 970-626-3737 or 800-633-5868. Rates $$ to $$$$, nine units. Southwest-style architecture, well located between Ouray and Telluride, spectacular views.

SALIDA

Best Western Colorado Lodge, 352 W. Rainbow Blvd., Salida, CO 81201; call 719-539-2514 or 800-528-1234, FAX 719-539-4316. Rates $$, 35 units. Indoor pool, sauna, hot tub, next to hot springs pool.

Woodland Motel, 903 West First, Salida, CO 81201; call 719-539-4980 or 800-488-0456. Rates $ to $$, 18 units. AAA two diamonds, kitchens, hot tub, BBQ grill, pets welcome.

SILVER CREEK

Mountainside at Silver Creek, P.O. Box 4104, 96 Mountainside Drive, Silver Creek, CO 80446; call 970-887-2571 or 800-777-1700, FAX 970-887-2571. Rates $$ to $$$$, 40 units. Condominiums with ski-in/ski-out to Silver Creek ski area.

SILVERTON

Grand Imperial Hotel, 1219 Greene St., Silverton, CO 81433; call 970-387-5527, FAX 970-387-5527. Rates $$ to $$$, 38 units. Centrally located, restaurant on premises.

The Wyman Hotel, 14th and Greene, Silverton, CO 81433; call 970-387-5372. Rates $-$$, 8 units. Nicely decorated, quiet, clean rooms, breakfast included.

SOUTH FORK

Wolf Creek Ski Lodge, P.O. Box 283, South Fork, CO 81154; call 719-873-5547 or 800-874-0416. Rates $$, 49 units. AAA approved, kitchenettes, restaurant and lounge.

STEAMBOAT SPRINGS

Best Western Ptarmigan Inn, 2304 Apres Ski Way, Steamboat Springs, CO 80477; call 970-879-1730 or 800-538-7519, FAX 970-879-6044. Rates $$, 77 units. Ski-in/ski-out to Steamboat Springs slopes.

Inn at Steamboat Bed & Breakfast, P.O. Box 775084, Steamboat Springs, CO 80477; call 970-879-2600 or 800-872-2601, FAX 970-879-9270. Rates $$, 32 units. Heated pool, fireside parlor, shuttle to ski slopes.

Sheraton Steamboat Resort and Conference Center, 2220 Village Inn CT. Box 774808, Steamboat Springs, CO 80477; call 970-879-2220 or 800-848-8877, FAX 970-879-7686. Rates $$ to $$$, 315 units. Ski-in/ski-out to Steamboat Springs slopes.

STERLING

Best Western Sundowner, Overland Trail St., Sterling, CO 80751; call 970-522-6265 or 800-528-1234, FAX 970-522-6265. Rates $$, 29 units. Hot tub, fitness center, laundry, continental breakfast.

TELLURIDE

New Sheridan Hotel/Colorado Suites, 231 W. Colorado Ave., Telluride, CO 81435; call 970-728-4351 or 800-200-1891, FAX 970-728-5024. Rates $$ to $$$$, 38 units. Restored 1898 downtown hotel, walk to restaurants and shops.

The Peaks at Telluride, P.O. Box 2702, 136 Country Club Drive, Telluride, CO 81435; call 970-728-6800, FAX 970-728-6567. Rates $$$$, 177 units. Luxury resort, spa, ski-in/ski-out, tennis, restaurant and lounge.

San Sophia Inn, 330 W. Pacific Ave., Telluride, CO 81435; call 970-728-3001 or 800-537-4781, FAX 970-728-6226. Rates $$ to $$$, 16 units. Restored Victorian bed & breakfast located in town.

VAIL/BEAVER CREEK

Antlers at Vail, 680 W. Lionshead Place, Vail, CO 81657; call 970-476-2471 or 800-843-VAIL, FAX 970-476-4146. Rates $$, 70 units. Condominiums with great mountain views.

The Christie Lodge, 47 East Beaver Creek Blvd., Avon, CO 81620; call 970-849-7700 or 800-551-4326. Rates $$, 280 units. One and three-bedroom units with mini kichens, fireplaces, balconies, pool, hot tub and restaurant.

Beaver Creek Lodge, 26 Avondale Lane, P.O. Box 2578, Beaver Creek, CO 81620; call 970-845-9800 or 800-732-6777, FAX 970-845-8242. Rates $$ to $$$$, 71 units. Indoor/outdoor pool, health spa, sauna, cable TV, restaurant and sports pub.

Black Bear Inn of Vail, 2405 Elliott Road, Vail, CO 81657; call 970-476-1304, FAX 970-476-0433. Rates $$, 12 units. Handcrafted log inn, private baths, breakfast.

Eagle River Inn, P.O. Box 100, Minturn, CO 81645; call 970-827-5761 or 800-344-1750, FAX 970-827-4020. Rates $$, 12 units. Southwestern-style inn bed and breakfast, evening wine and cheese.

Gasthof Gramshammer, 231 E. Gore Creek Drive, Vail, CO 81657; call 970-476-5626. Mobil two stars, AAA three diamond, balconies, kitchens, fireplaces, cable TV, health spa, restaurant and bar.

Holiday Inn/Chateau Vail, 13 Vail Road, Vail, CO 81657; call 970-476-5631 or 800-451-9840, FAX 970-476-2508. Rates $$ to $$$, 119 units. Heated pool, hot tub, restaurant.

Hyatt Regency Beaver Creek, P.O. Box 1595, Beaver Creek, CO 81620; call 970-949-1234 or 800-233-1234, FAX 970-949-4164. Rates $$$$, 295 units. Year-round resort, spa, ski-in/ski-out, children's programs, restaurant and lounge.

The Lodge & Spa at Cordillera, Box 1110, 2205 Cordillera Way, Edwards, CO 81632; call 970-926-2200 or 800-87-RELAX, FAX 970-926-2486. Rates $$$$, 28 units. Mobile four star golf and nordic ski resort located on 3,466 acres.

Sitzmark Lodge, 183 Gore Creek Drive, Vail, CO 81657; call 970-476-5001, FAX 970-476-8702. Rates $$, 35 units. Balconies, some fireplaces, sun deck, outdoor pool, whirlpool, sauna, restaurant and lounge.

Sonnenalp Resort of Vail, 20 Vail Road, Vail, CO 81657; call 970-476-5656 or 800-654-8312, FAX 970-476-1639. Rates $$ to $$$$, 186 units. European-style resort, Bavarian furnishings, breakfast.

Vail Athletic Club Hotel & Spa, 352 East Meadow Drive, Vail, CO 81657; call 970-476-0700 or 800-822-4754, FAX 970-476-6451. Rates $$$ to $$$$, 38 units. Athletic club, full-service spa, restaurant.

Vail Cascade Hotel & Club, 1476 Westhaven Drive, Vail CO 81657; call 970-476-7111 or 800-420-2424, FAX 970-479-7050. Rates $$$ to $$$$, 289 rooms. European-style resort with all the amenities.

The Wren, 500 S. Frontage Road East, Vail, CO 81657; call 970-476-0052 or 800-345-5415, FAX 970-476-4103. Rates $$ to $$$, 42 units. Condos with kitchens, fireplaces, balconies and outdoor pool.

WINTER PARK

Beau West Bed & Breakfast, 148 Fir Drive, P.O. Box 587, Winter Park, CO 80482; call

970-726-5145 or 800-473-5145, FAX 970-726-8607. Rates $$$, 5 units. Rooms with "Great American West" motifs, private baths.

Gasthaus Eichler, P.O. Box 3303, Winter Park, CO 80482; call 970-726-5133 or 800-543-3899, FAX 970-726-5135. Rates $$, 15 units. European-style lodge with whirlpool baths, cable TV, restaurant.

Iron Horse Resort Retreat, P.O. Box 3123, Winter Park, CO 80482; call 970-726-8851 or 800-621-8190, FAX 970-726-2321. Rates $$ to $$$$, 131 units. Condos with pool, hot tubs, health club, restaurant and lounge.

AIRPORTS

Denver International Airport, 8500 Pena Blvd., Denver, CO 80249-6340; call 303-342-2250.

Regional airports are located in Alamosa, Aspen, Colorado Springs, Cortez, Durango, Eagle/Vail, Fort Collins, Grand Junction, Gunnison, Hayden, Lamar, Loveland, Montrose, Pueblo, Steamboat Springs and Telluride.

ASSOCIATIONS

American Youth Hostels, Rocky Mountain Council, P.O. Box 2370, Boulder, CO 80306; call 303-442-1166.

Association of Historic Hotels of the Rocky Mountain West, 1002 Walnut #201, Boulder, CO 80302; call 303-546-9040.

Bed & Breakfast Innkeepers of Colorado Association, P.O. Box 38416, Dept. T96, Colorado Springs, CO 80937; call 800-83-BOOKS.

Colorado Association of Campgrounds, Cabins & Lodges, 5101 Pennsylvania Avenue, Boulder, CO 80303; call 303-499-9343.

Colorado Dude/Guest Ranch Association, P.O. Box 300, Tabernash, CO 80478; call 970-887-3128 or 970-724-3653.

Colorado Hotel and Lodging Association, 999 18th Street, Suite1240, Denver, CO 80202; call 303-297-8335.

Distinctive Inns of Colorado, P.O. Box 2061, Estes Park, CO 80517; call 800-866-0621.

EMERGENCIES

Dial 911 to reach local emergency services.

GOVERNMENT AGENCIES

STATE AGENCIES

Colorado Division of Wildlife, 6060 Broadway, Denver, CO; call 303-297-1192.

Colorado Geological Survey, 1313 Sherman St., #715, Denver, CO 80203; call 303-866-2611.

Colorado Historical Society, 1300 Broadway, Denver, CO 80023; call 303-866-3682.

Colorado State Parks, 1313 Sherman St., #618, Denver, CO 80203; call 303-866-3437.

Colorado State Patrol, 700 Kipling, Denver, CO 80215; call 303-239-4500.

FEDERAL AGENCIES

Bureau of Land Management, Colorado State Office, 2850 Youngfield St., Lakewood, CO 80215; call 303-239-3600.

U.S. Fish & Wildlife Service, P.O. Box 25486, DFC, Denver, CO 80225; call 303-236-7904.

U.S. Forest Service, P.O. Box 25127. Lakewood, CO 80225; call 303-275-5350.

U.S. Geological Survey, Box 25046 Federal Center, Mail Stop 504, Denver, CO 80225-0046; call 303-202-4200.

NATIONAL FORESTS

Arapaho/Roosevelt National Forests, Pawnee National Grassland, 1311 S. College Ave., Fort Collins, CO 80524; call 970-498-2770.

Boulder Ranger Station, Arapaho/Roosevelt National Forests, 2995 Baseline, Rm. 110, Boulder, CO 80303; call 303-444-6600.

Clear Creek Ranger Station, Arapaho/Roosevelt National Forests, P.O. Box 3307, Idaho Springs, CO 80452; call 303-567-2901.

Grand Mesa, Gunnison & Uncompahgre National Forest Headquarters, 2250 Hwy. 50, Delta, CO 81416; call 970-874-7691.

Pike National Forest Headquarters, 1920 Valley Drive, Pueblo, CO 81008; call 719-545-8737.

Rio Grande/San Juan National Forest Headquarters, 1803 W. Hwy. 160, Monte Vista, CO 81114; call 719-852-5941.

Routt National Forest Headquarters, 29587 W. U.S. 40, Ste. 20, Steamboat Springs, CO 80477; call 970-879-1722.

San Isabel National Forest Headquarters, 1920 Valley Drive, Pueblo, CO 81008; call 719-545-8737.

San Juan National Forest Headquarters, 701 Camino del Rio, Durango, CO 81301; call 970-247-4874.

White River National Forest Headquarters, P.O. Box 948, Glenwood Springs, CO 81602; call 970-945-2521.

U.S. Forest Service Regional Headquarters, 740 Simms St., Lakewood, CO 80025; call 303-275-5350.

National Parks and Monuments

Bent's Old Fort National Historic Site, 35110 Hwy. 194 East, La Junta, CO 81050; call 719-384-2596.

Black Canyon of the Gunnison National Park, 2233 E. Main St., Montrose, CO 81401; call 970-249-7036.

Colorado National Monument, Fruita, CO 81521; call 970-858-3617.

Curecanti National Recreation Area, 102 Elk Creek, Gunnison, CO 81230; call 970-641-2337.

Dinosaur National Monument, P.O. Box 210, Dinosaur, CO 81610; call 970-374-2216.

Florissant Fossil Beds National Monument, P.O. Box 185, Florissant, CO 80816; call 719-748-3253.

Great Sand Dunes National Monument, 11500 Hwy. 150, Mosca, CO 81146; call 719-378-2312.

Hovenweep National Monument, Mesa Verde National Park, CO 81330; call 970-529-4465.

Mesa Verde National Park, Mesa Verde National Park, CO 81330; call 970-529-4465.

Rocky Mountain National Park, Estes Park, CO 80517; call 970-586-1206.

RECREATION

Backpacking

See Government Agencies, Bureau of Land Management or U.S. Forest Service.

BICYCLING

Bicycle Colorado, P.O. Box 698, Salida, CO 81201; call 719-530-0051 or 800-997-BIKE for a free copy of Bicycle Colorado brochure.

Colorado Plateau Mountain Bike Trail Assn., P.O. Box 4602, Grand Junction, CO 81502; no phone. Send SASE for trail map.

BOATING

See Government Agencies, Colorado Division of Wildlife, Colorado State Parks and U.S. Forest Service.

FISHING

See Government Agencies, Colorado Division of Wildlife, Colorado State Parks and U.S. Forest Service.

FOUR WHEELING

Colorado Association of Four-wheel Drive Clubs, Inc., P.O. Box 1413, Wheat Ridge, CO 80034; call 303-343-0646.

GOLF

Colorado Golf Assn., 5655 S. Yosemite, Ste. 101, Englewood, CO 80111; call 303-779-4653.

Colorado Golf Resort Assn., 2110 Ash, Denver, CO 80222; call 303-699-GOLF.

GUIDES/OUTFITTERS/HUNTING

Colorado Outfitters Assn., P.O. Box 1304, Parker, CO 80134; call 303-841-7760.

Northwest Colorado Guides & Outfitters, P.O. Box 770876, Steamboat Springs, CO 80477; call 970-879-0954.

Guest Ranches

Colorado Dude and Guest Ranch Association, P.O. Box 300, Tabernash, CO 80478; call 970-887-3128.

RAFTING

Colorado River Outfitters Assn., P.O. Box 1662, Buena Vista, CO 81211; call 303-369-4632 (Denver direct).

SKIING

Colorado Cross Country Ski Assn., Snow Mountain Nordic Center, P.O. Box 169, Winter Park, CO 80482; call 970-887-2152.

Colorado Ski Country USA, 1560 Broadway, Ste. 2000, Denver, CO 80202; call 303-837-0793 or 303-825-7669 (snow report).

Ski Train, 555 17th St., Denver, CO 80202; call 303-296-4754.

SNOWMOBILING

Colorado Snowmobile Assn., P.O. Box 1260, Grand Lake, CO 80447; call 800-235-4480.

TENNIS

Colorado Tennis Assn., 1201 S. Parker Road #200, Denver, CO 80231; call 303-695-4116.

RESTAURANTS

Information

Colorado Restaurant Assn., 899 Logan St., Ste. 300, Denver, CO 80203; call 303-830-2972

Restaurant pricing

Listings are arranged by city. Cost ratings are based on the restaurant's general price category for single entrées.

$ ....entrées generally priced between $5 and $12

$$.........entrées generally priced between $9 and $22

$$$.......entrées generally priced higher than $18

AKRON

Hearty Rancher, 902 E. First St.; call 303-345-2616. Family cafe, breakfast, lunch and dinner. Rate $

ALAMOSA

True Grits, 100 Santa Fe Ave., at the corner of highways 160 and 17; call 719-589-9954. Fantastic steak and baked potato dinners in an atmosphere full of John Wayne icons. Rate $$

Great Sand Dunes Country Club, 5303 Highway 150, south of Great Sand Dunes National Monument; call 719-378-2356. Best in the San Luis Valley for European food. Rate $$

ASHCROFT

Pine Creek Cookhouse, Ashcroft Touring Center, Ashcroft; call 970-925-1044. Well worth the 12-mile drive from Aspen to savor Elk or trout in a gorgeous setting. You must make reservations. Rate $$$

ASPEN/SNOWMASS

Lucci's, 508 E. Cooper Ave., Aspen, CO 81611; call 970-925-8866. Affordable Italian restaurant, full bar, children's menu, complete wine list. Rate $

Little Annie's, 517 E. Hyman Ave.; call 970-925-1098. Wood walls and the well-worn floor spell comfort. Excellent food, reasonable prices. Rate $

La Cocina, 308 E. Hopkins Ave., Aspen, CO 81611; call 970-925-9714. Fresh, fun New Mexican cooking, local gathering place. Rate $

Explore Bistro, 221 E. Main St., Aspen, CO 81611; call 970-925-5338. Old world bistro within a bookstore, international vegetarian cuisine. Rate $$

Campo De Fiori, 205 S. Mill St., Aspen, CO 81611; call 970-920-7717. Authentic Tuscan and Venetian cuisine. Rate $$

Acme Bar, 320 S. Mill St., Aspen, CO 81611; call 970-925-3775. Comfortable atmosphere featuring regional and seasonal cuisine. Rate $$

Piñons, 105 S. Mill St., Aspen, CO 81611; call 970-925-2021. Fine Colorado cuisine featuring elk, ahi, pork tenderloin and lobster. Rate $$$

L'Hostaria, 620 E. Hyman Ave., Aspen, CO 81611; call 970-925-9022. Elegant, contemporary Italian cuisine. Rate $$$

Baang Cafe Bar, 325 E. Main St., Aspen, CO 81611; call 970-925-9969. Blends French styles and techniques with Asian ingredients. Rate $$$

BLACK HAWK

Black Forest Inn, on Highway 6 in Blackhawk, call 303-279-2333. In the been-there-forever category, serving hearty German dishes with exceptional service for three decades. Rate $$

BOULDER

Flagstaff House, on Baseline Road halfway up Flagstaff Mountain; call 303-442-4640. Wide-ranging gourmet menu in a gorgeous setting, Boulder's best. Rate $$$

Gold Hill Inn, Gold Hill west of Boulder; call 303-443-6461. Gourmet, fixed-price menu in a log cabin setting, very romantic in a western way. Rate $$$

Dot's Diner, 799 Pearl St.; call 303-449-1323. Breakfast burritos, biscuits and gravy, fresh muffins. Breakfast and lunch only. Rate $

Rockies Brewing Company, 2880 Wilderness Place; call 303-444-8448. Brats, burgers and beer. Rate $$

Chautauqua Dining Hall, Chautauqua Park, 900 Baseline Road; call 303-440-3773. Traditional breakfast, lunch and dinner meals with a twist—the dining room and porch overlook the park. Rate $

Lucilee's, 2124 14th St.; call 303-442-4743. Near the Pearl St. Mall, tucked into an old house, Cajun dishes for breakfast and lunch. Rate $

Boulder Wrapsody, 1136 Pearl St., on the Pearl St. Mall; call 303-444-1305. These folks have taken the idea of the wrap to the level of Asian cuisine. Rate $

Jax Fish House, 928 Pearl St.; call 303-444-1811. Seafood and raw bar, menu changes daily based on availability. Rate $$

BRECKENRIDGE

Blue River Bistro, 305 N. Main St.; call 970-453-6974. Nice après ski atmosphere, good pasta, dependable. Rate $$

Cafe Three Eleven, 311 S. Main St.; call 970-453-7656. Healthy gourmet food, sinful desserts, cafe atmosphere on the river. Rate $

Hearthstone Victorian Dining, 130 S. Ridge St.; call 970-453-1148. Continental, steaks, chicken, seafood, wonderful deck overlooking the mountains. Rate $$

Mi Casa Restaurant and Cantina, 600 S. Park St., call 970-453-2071. Family oriented, Mexican restaurant. Rate $

Pierre's River Walk Cafe, 137 S. Main St., call 970-453-0989. Fresh French menu and extensive wine list. Rate $$$

BUENA VISTA

Delany's Depot, 605 Hwy. 24; call 719-395-8854. Very popular because they dish out large portions of good food. Rate $-$$$

BURLINGTON

Mr. A's Interstate House, 415 S. Lincoln St., call 719-346-8010. Nice salad bar and daily specials. Rate $

CENTRAL CITY

Black Forest Inn, on Highway 6 in Blackhawk; call 303-279-2333. In the been-there-forever category, serving hearty German dishes with exceptional service for three decades. Rate $$

COLORADO SPRINGS

Briarhurst Manor, 404 Manitou Ave.; call 719-685-1864. Award-winning restaurant in a landmark setting; the rack of lamb is exceptional. Rate $$$

Howard's Pit BBQ, 3019 W. Colorado Ave.; call 719-473-7427. Traditional chicken and ribs. Rate $

Craftwood Inn, 404 El Paso Blvd.; call 719-685-9000. This is the spot for wild game, as in sautéed caribou and pheasant sausage. Rate $$$

Giuseppe's Old Depot, 10 S. Sierra Madre; call 719-625-3111. Relaxing atmosphere in a renovated train depot, a family favorite, nice salad bar. Rate $

Adam's Mountain Cafe, 733 Manitou Ave.; call 719-685-1430. Natural food doesn't get much better, flavorful breakfasts and Mexican entrees. Rate $

Michelle's, 122 N. Tejon St.; call 719-633-5089. In the must-see category for homemade ice cream and gourmet burgers. Rate $

Red Top, 1520 S. Nevada Ave.; call 719-633-2444. Home of the six-inch-diameter burger in a 1950s setting. Rate $

Dale Street Cafe, 115 E. Dale St.; call 719-578-9898. Among the best in town, great salads and pasta. Rate $$

COPPER MOUNTAIN

Farley's, Snowflake Building; call 970-968-2577. Comfortable après-ski atmosphere, ribs, steak and seafood. Rate $$

Rackets Restaurant, Copper Mountain Racquet & Athletic Club; call 970-968-2882. New Mexican and American dishes in a large comfortable room; a local favorite. Rate $$

CORTEZ

Anasazi Restaurant, 640 S. Broadway; call 970-565-9617. Steaks, seafood and Mexican, comfortable lounge. Rate $$

Gordy's, 801 E. Main; call 970-564-0205. Breakfast, lunch and dinner with a diverse menu. Rate $

CREEDE

Creede Hotel, 120 N. Main St.; call 719-658-2608. Variety of menu selections in a charming Victorian hotel. Rate $

CRESTED BUTTE

Soupçon, 2nd St. and Elk Ave.; call 970-349-5448. Extraordinary French food in the casual atmosphere of a log cabin. Rate $$$

Idlespur, 226 S. Elk Ave.; call 970-349-5026. Broad and delicious menu and brew selections in this woody, raucous, fun brew pub. Rate: Lunch $, Dinner $$

CRIPPLE CREEK

The Imperial Hotel, 123 N. Third Ave.; call 719-689-2922. One of Cripple Creek's oldest buildings, buffet dinner with prime rib. Rate $

DENVER

Jax Fish House, 1539 17th St., LoDo; call 303-292-5767 Seafood and raw bar, menu changes daily based on availability. Among the best in LoDo. Rate $$

Racines, 850 Bannock St.; call 303-595-0418. A breakfast, lunch and dinner institution in a spacious building near downtown. Dependable food, friendly service, local favorite. Rate $-$$

Tommy Tsunami, 1432 Market; call 303-534-5050. Asian specialties with an up-to-date twist in a great room. Rate $$

Dixons Downtown Grill, 1610 16th St.; call 303-573-6100. Wonderfully prepared food in a stylish atmosphere. Pasta and seafood. Rate: Lunch - $, Dinner - $$

Pete's Kitchen, 1962 E. Colfax Ave.; call 303-321-3139. Burgers and gyros cooked up behind a long lunch counter, Denver's definitive greasy spoon. Rate $

Carlos on the Park, 1700 Vine St.; call 303-399-1700. Mexican food in a noisy, neon-lit establishment. Pool room in the rear. Rate $

McCormick's Fish House and Bar, 1659 Wazee St.; call 303-

825-1107. Fresh seafood every day, comfortable paneled, pub atmosphere. Lunch - $, Dinner - $$

Delhi Darbar, 1514 Blake St.; call 303-595-0680. Dependable Indian specialty restaurant. Rate $-$$

Kokoro Restaurant, 2390 S. Colorado Blvd.; call 303-692-8752. Rice bowls, sushi and green tea cheesecake. No tipping, please. Rate $

Palace Arms, 321 17th St.; call 303-297-3111. In the Brown Palace Hotel, top of the line dining, excellent service, continental food. Rate $$$

Ship Tavern, 321 17th St.; call 303-297-3111. In the Brown Palace Hotel, excellent steaks, salads, seafood. Rate $$

Augusta's Westin Hotel, 1672 Lawrence St.; call 303-572-7222. Fine dining in lower downtown. Rate $$$

Wynkoop Brewing Company, 1634 18th St.; call 303-297-2700. The largest brew pub in the country, wide menu selection, great beer. Rate $ to $$

The Fort, 19192 Hwy. 8, Morrison; call 303-697-4771. Perfect for special occasions in a setting with a view of the Great Plains. Buffalo, quail, elk. Rate $$$

Buckhorn Exchange, 1000 Osage St.; call 303-534-9505. Join Teddy Roosevelt and Buffalo Bill Cody to be among the many who have devoured buffalo and elk among the stuffed heads. A Denver must-do. Rate $$$

Strings, 1700 Humboldt St.; call 303-831-7310. An elegant lunch or dinner, nouvelle cuisine, friendly service. Rate: Lunch - $$, Dinner - $$$

Cliff Young's, 700 E. 17th St.; call 303-831-8900. Very elegant dining. Rate $$$

Denver Buffalo Company, 1109 Lincoln St.; call 303-832-0880. Do a little shopping in the trading company before enjoying a great Southwestern meal. Rate $$

Paramount Cafe, 511 16th St.; call 303-893-2000. Nice downtown deli. Rate $

My Brother's Bar, 2376 15th St.; call 303-455-9991. Burgers, fries and beer with classical music. Rate $

Goodfriend's, 3100 E. Colfax Ave.; call 303-399-1751. Salads, seafood, pastas. Try the fish and chips. Rate $-$$

Casa Bonita, 6715 W. Colfax Ave. ; call 303-232-5115. A must-do with children. The food is very basic Mexican, the atmosphere is "Mexican village," including a cliff diver. Rate $

Bistro Adde Brewster, 250 Steele St.; call 303-388-1900. One of the more established continental restaurants in the Cherry Creek area. Rate $$-$$$

Blue Bonnet Cafe and Lounge, 457 S. Broadway; call 303-778-0147. Get in line for Mexican burritos, tacos and enchiladas. Rate $-$$

Bocaza, 1740 E. 17th. Ave.; call 303-393-7545. One of the better burrito-wrap restaurants. Rate $

Little Shanghai, 456 S Broadway; call 303-777-9838. Denver's dependable Chinese restaurant. Rate $

Healthy Habits, 865 S. Colorado Blvd.; call 303-733-2105. Fresh soup, salad bar and dessert bar. Rate $-$$

DOLORES

Ponderosa, Hwy 145 and 8th St.; call 970-882-7910. Family-style restaurant with fresh baked goods, Mexican food and steaks. Rate $

DURANGO

Cyprus Cafe, 725 E. 2nd Ave.; call 970-385-6884. Mediterranean cuisine in a Victorian setting. Rate $$-$$$

Olde Tymer's, 1000 Main Avenue; call 970-259-2990. Burgers, salads and sandwiches indoors and out. Rate $-$$

ESTES PARK

Andrea's, 145 Elkhorn; call 970-586-0886. International cuisine. Rate $$

Baldpate Inn, 4900 Co. Hwy 7; call 970-586-5397. Extraordinarily good soup and salad buffet, homemade bread and desserts. Rate $

Black Canyon Inn, 800 MacGregor Ave.; call 970-586-9344. Continental cuisine with a specialty in seafood. Rate $$ to $$$

Bunny's Buns, 184 E. Elkhorn (on Riverwalk); call 970-586-6918. Cinnamon buns, bagels, croissants and ice cream. Rate $

Cowpoke Cafe, 165 Virginia (Courtyard Shops); call 970-586-0234. Hearty Western food with salad bar. Rate $-$$

Dunraven Inn, 2470 Co. Hwy. 66; call 970-586-6409. Italian specialities and fresh fish. Rate $$

Ed's Cantina, 362 E. Elkhorn; call 970-586-2919. Mexican food, broasted chicken and salad bar. Rate $

Elkhorn Lodge Restaurant, 600 W. Elkhorn; call 970-586-4416. Cowboy breakfasts, steak and trout dinners. Rate $$

Estes Park Brewery, 470 Prospect Village Dr.; call 970-586-5421. Burgers, brats and beer. Rate $-$$

Friar's Restaurant, 157 Elkhorn (Church Shops); call 970-586-2806. American specialities including hazelnut chicken. Rate $-$$

Grumpy Gringo, 1560 Big Thompson Ave., call 970-586-7705. Mexican specialties. Rate $

Inn of Glen Haven, Devils Gulch Rd.; call 970-586-3897. Fine dining, steak and salmon specialties. Rate $$$

La Chaumière, Hwy. 36 between Estes Park and Lyons; call 303-823-6521. Smokehouse specialties, homemade ice cream. Rate $$-$$$

Mama Rose's, 338 E. Elkhorn; call 970-586-3330. Family-style Italian cooking. Rate $

Notchtop Cafe & Pub, Upper Stanley Village; call 970-586-0272. Baked goods and sandwiches. Rate $

Other Side Restaurant, National Park Village; call 970-586-2171. Steaks and seafood. Rate $ to $$

Poppy's Pizza & Grill, 342 E. Elkhorn (Barlow Plaza); call 970-586-8282. Pizza, sandwiches, soup and salad bar. Rate $

The Stanley Hotel, 333 W. Wonderview Ave.; call 970-586-3371. Two restaurants, the Dunraven Grille and the MacGregor Room; fine dining with American Continental cuisine. Rate $$ to $$$

Wild Basin Smorgasbord, 13 miles south of Estes Park on Hwy 7; call 303-747-2545. Chicken and roast beef, soup and salad bar. Rate $

FAIRPLAY

Fairplay Hotel, 500 Main St.; call 719-836-2565. Comfortable and dependable. Rate $

FORT COLLINS

Charco Broiler, 1716 E. Mulberry; call 970-482-1472. Perfectly cooked steaks and homemade pies. Rate $$

Silver Grill Cafe, 218 Walnut St.; call 970-484-4656. Diner feel with booths and counter, cinnamon rolls for breakfast, hamburgers and specials for lunch and dinner. Rate $

FORT MORGAN

Momma's Kitchen, U.S. Interstate 76 at Exit 82, call 303-867-6569. Home cooking, open 24 hours a day. Rate $

FRISCO

Golden Annie's, 603 Main St.; call 970-668-0435. Diverse selection, Mexican, hamburgers, ribs. Rate $-$$

GEORGETOWN

The Renaissance, 1025 Rose St.; call 303-569-3336. Italian veal, chicken, beef, call for hours. Rate $-$$

GLENWOOD SPRINGS

Italian Underground, Good Italian food in a setting full of Glenwood history. Rate $

Glenwood Canyon Brewpub, Lively setting in Hotel Denver, five to seven microbrews accent a mixed menu. Rate $$

Sopris Restaurant, Great ambiance in bright red, Russian-style atmosphere, continental cuisine. Rate $$$

GRAND LAKE

Grand Lake Lodge and Restaurant, Just north of Grand Lake on Hwy. 34; call 970-627-3967. Enjoy fine dining with a fantastic view of Grand Lake in this split-log interior. Rate $$-$$$

EG's Garden Grill, 1000 Grand Avenue (Main St.); call 970-627-8404. Wonderful lunches, dinners and desserts in what can only be described as a festive interior. Rate $-$$

GRAND JUNCTION

Los Reyes, 811 S. 7th St.; call 970-245-8392. Great Mexican food in a clean, quiet atmosphere. Rate $-$$

Starvin' Arvins, 752 Horizon Dr., near Interstate 70; call 970-241-0430. Breakfast, lunch and dinner, more-than-ample servings. Rate $.

Sweetwater's Uptown, 336 Main St.; call 970-234-3900. Northern Italian cuisine in a popular location downtown.

GREELEY

Stetsons at the Ramkota Inn, 701 8th St., call 303-353-8444. Broad menu selection, pleasant, clean atmosphere. Rate $

Rosi's European Cafe. 809 9th St., call 303-352-1126. Soups, salads and sandwiches in a comfortable atmosphere. Rate $

GUNNISON

Gold Creek Inn, East of Gunnison, call for directions; call 970-641-2086. Gourmet dining where you least expect it, in the middle of nowhere, worth the drive, make reservations. Rate $$$

Sidewalk Cafe, 113 W. Tomichi Ave.; call 970-641-4130.

traditional breakfast, soup and sandwich lunches. Rate $

The Trough, 1.5 miles west of Gunnison on Hwy. 50; call 970-641-3724. Think ribs, prime rib, steaks, game and seafood. Rates $$ to $$$

IDAHO SPRINGS

Beau Jo's, 1517 Miner St.; call 303-573-6924 (Denver number). The best pizza in Colorado is served in this fun, wood-lined pizzeria.

KEYSTONE

Alpenglow Stube, atop Keystone's North Peak via gondola; call 970-496-4386. Six course fixed-price meals with Bavarian flair. Rate $$$

Ski Tip Lodge, One mile east of Keystone on Montezuma Road; call 970-468-4202. Choose from meat, seafood or wild game nightly after warming up by the fire. Rate $$$

LA JUNTA

Chiaramonte's, 101 Dalton Ave.; call 719-384-8909. Popular Mexican restaurant.

Copper Kitchen Cafe, 116 Colorado Ave.; 719-384-7216.

LAKE CITY

Crystal Lodge, Two miles south of town on Hwy. 149; call 970-944-2201. AMerican food. Rates $ to $$

LEADVILLE

The Prospector, 2798 Hwy. 91, three miles north of Leadville; call 719-486-2319. Rustic and fun, this fine dining restaurant features fish, ribs and lamb. Rate $$

Golden Burro, 710 Harrison; call 719-486-1239. Three basic meals a day in the heart of town amidst locals. Rate $

MANCOS

Dusty Rose Cafe, 200 W. Grand; call 970-533-9042. Traditional breakfast and lunch, Italian dinners. Rates: lunch $, dinner $$

MANITOU SPRINGS

See Colorado Springs

MESA VERDE NATIONAL PARK

Metate Room, located in the Far View Lodge inside the park; call 970-529-4421. Rate $ to $$

MONTROSE

The Daily Bread, 346 Main St.; call 970-249-8444. Fragrant fresh breads and pastries make this special. Rate $

The Glenn Eyrie, 2351 Townsend Ave.; call 970-249-9263. Elaborate, Austrian-based entree selections in a relaxed setting. Rate $$-$$$

OURAY

Bon Ton Restaurant, 426 Main St., Ouray, CO 81427. Call 970-325-4951. Among the best restaurants for meat and seafood in the region, great herb Salmon. Rate $$

The Piñon Restaurant, 737 Main St., Ouray, CO 81427. Call 970-325-4334. Nice patio in this establishment that ages its own succulent beef. Fun sports bar upstairs. Rate $

Cecilia's Restaurant, 630 Main St., Ouray, CO 81427. Call 970-325-4223. Homemade pastries, great burgers. Rate $

PUEBLO

DJ's Steak House, 4289 N. Elizabeth; call 719-545-9354. Steaks and seafood. Rate $$

REDSTONE

Redstone Inn, 0882 Redstone Blvd.; call 970-963-2526. This is the place jaded Aspenites come to for a getaway. Incredible food and service in a romantic setting. Rate $$$

Cleveholm Manor, 0058 Redstone Blvd.; call 970-963-3463. Elegant dining on most Friday and Saturday evenings, call ahead. Rate $$$

RIDGEWAY

The Adobe Inn, 251 Liddell Drive, Ridgeway, CO 81432; call 970-626-5939. Fun hacienda atmosphere, great margaritas and Mexican food with homemade chips and salsa. Rate $

SALIDA

Country Bounty, 413 W. Rainbow Blvd. (on Hwy. 50); call 719-539-3546. There is something for every taste on this huge menu. Plus great pastries and a gift shop. Rate $-$$

SILVER CREEK

The Inn at Silver Creek, two miles west of Silver Creek at Hwy. 40; call 800-926-4FUN. Basic menu, three meals a day. Rate $-$$

SILVERTON

Gold King Dining Room, in the Imperial Hotel at 1219 Greene St.; call 970-387-5527. Rate $ to $$

STEAMBOAT SPRINGS

Steamboat Brewery and Tavern, Fifth and Lincoln Ave., downtown, call 970-879-2233. Great beer, great sandwiches, great lunches, great dinners. Rates: Lunch $; Dinner $$

Winona's, 617 Lincoln Ave., Steamboat Springs, CO , downtown; call 970-879-2483. Broad breakfast and lunch menu with excellent cinnamon buns and pastries. Rate $

Harwigs/L'apogee; 911 Lincoln Ave., Steamboat Springs, CO, downtown; call 970-879-1980. Two restaurants share the same kitchen and wine list; Harwigs is more casual with an international menu, L'apogée is French in flavor. Rate: Harwig's $$, L'apogee $$$

TELLURIDE

La Marmotte, 150 W. San Juan Ave.; call 970-728-6232. A special restaurant for a special meal, pastas and steaks. Rate $$$

Eagle Bar and Grille, 100 W. Colorado Ave.; call 970-728-0886. A wide menu selection of favorites makes this a dependable spot for a good meal. Rate $$

San Sophia Inn, 330 W. Pacific Ave.; call 970-728-3001 or 800-537-4781. Extraordinary meals served at this inn; nouvelle with a Rocky Mountain twist, fixed-price menu. Rate $$$

TRINIDAD

Nana & Nano's Pasta House, 415 University; call 719-846-2696. Wonderful old-style pasta dinners in a comfortable setting. Rate $-$$

VAIL/BEAVER CREEK

Beano's Cabin, sleigh or horse ride leaves from the Inn at Beaver Creek; call 970-949-9090. After the moonlit sleighride, eat a wonderful meal in an elegantly rustic setting. Highly respected for so long because it deserves it. Rate $$$

Sweet Basil, 193 E. Gore Creek; call 970-476-0125. For Continental lunch or dinner with a view onto the creek. Rate $$

Grouse Mountain Grill, in the Pines Lodge, Beaver Creek; call 970-949-0600. Fine meats and fresh fish in a room with a drop-your-fork view of Beaver Creek. Rate $$$

Hubcap Brewery, Crossroads Shopping Center; call 970-476-5757. Hand-crafted beers and American food like pot pies. Rate $

Terra Bistro, Vail Athletic Club, east of the covered bridge, across from the parking building; call 970-949-5552. Extensive wine list wedded to organic vegetables and free-range game. Rate $$

The Tyrolean, adjacent to the Vail Village Parking Structure; call 970-476-2204. Classic European and American specialties. Rate $$$

WINTER PARK

The Last Waltz, 78336 U. S. Highway 40 (downtown), Winter Park, CO 80428; call 970-726-4877. Consistently voted the locals' favorite, great honey-pecan fried chicken and Mexican. Rate $

Alpeggio's, 78521 U. S. Highway 40 (downtown), Winter Park, CO 80428; call 970-726-5402. Northern Italian cuisine with great sauces, casual atmosphere. Rate $$

The Lodge at Sunspot, top of Winter Park Mountain, call 970-726-5514. Open for dinner from mid-December to early April on Thursdays, Fridays and Saturdays. Four course, fixed-price, including an entrée such as salmon, sea bass, prime rib or filet mignon. Rate $$$

ROAD CONDITIONS

Colorado Dept. of Transportation/State Patrol Recordings; within a two hour drive from Denver call 303-639-1111; statewide call 303-639-1234.

TOURISM INFORMATION

COLORADO STATEWIDE INFORMATION

Colorado Travel & Tourism Authority, P.O. Box 22005, Denver, CO 80222; call 800-COLORADO; internet http://www.colorado.com.

COLORADO WELCOME CENTERS

Colorado Welcome Center at Burlington, P.O. Box 157 48265 I-70, Burlington, CO 80807; call 719-346-5554.

Colorado Welcome Center at Cortez, 928 E. Main St., Cortez, CO 81321; call 970-565-4048.

Colorado Welcome Center at Dinosaur, P.O. Box 207, 101 E. Stegosaurus, Dinosaur, CO 81620; call 970-374-2205.

Colorado Welcome Center at Fruita, 340 Hwy. 340, Fruita, CO 81521; call 970-858-9335.

Colorado Welcome Center at Julesburg, 20934 County Road 28, Julesburg, CO 80737; call 970-474-2054.

Colorado Welcome Center at Lamar, 109 E. Beech St., Lamar, CO 81052; call 719-336-3483.

Colorado Welcome Center at Trinidad, 309 Nevada Ave., Trinidad, CO 81082; call 719-846-9512.

REGIONAL TOURISM ORGANIZATIONS

Clear Creek County Tourism Board, P.O. Box 60, Idaho Springs, CO 80452; call 303-567-4660 or 800-88-BLAST.

Denver Travel Planning Region, 1555 California St., Ste. 300, Denver, CO 80202; call 303-892-1112.

Four Corners Tourism Council, P.O. Box 540, Mancos, CO 81328; call 801-587-2231. (Utah).

Front Range Region, 2440 Pearl St., Boulder, CO 80302; call 800-444-0447 for a free Front Range Adventure Guide.

Northeast Colorado Travel Region, 215 S. Main, Yuma, CO 80759; call 800-777-9075.

Northwest Colorado Travel Planning Region, c/o Summit County Chamber of Commerce, P.O. Box 214, Frisco, CO 80443; no phone.

Pikes Peak Country Attractions Assn., 354 Manitou Ave., Manitou Springs, CO 80829; call 719-685-5894 or 800-525-2250; Internet: ppca@pikes-peak.com.

Poudre Canyon/Red Feathers Lake Tourist Council, Box 178, Red Feathers Lake, CO 80545; call 800-462-5870.

Royal Gorge Attractions Assn., 4218 Fremont County Road 3A, Cañon City, CO 81215; call 719-275-7507.

San Luis Valley Tourism Council, P.O. Box 609, Monte Vista, CO 81144; call 719-852-0281 or 800-835-7254.

South Central Colorado Travel Region, P.O. Box 461, Poncha Springs, CO 81242; call 719-539-2771 or 800-568-8340.

Southeast Colorado Tourism Council, Inc., 302 N. Santa Fe Ave., Pueblo, CO 81003; call 800-338-6633.

Southwest Colorado Travel Planning Region, 1000 Rim Drive, Durango, CO 81301; call 970-247-7066 or 800-933-4340.

CHAMBERS OF COMMERCE/VISITOR BUREAUS

Alamosa County Chamber, Cole Park, Alamosa, CO 81101; call 719-589-3681 or 800-BLU-SKYS.

Antonito/Conejos County Chamber, P.O. Box 427, Antonito, CO 81120; call 719-376-5693.

Aspen Chamber Resort Assn., 425 Rio Grande Pl., Aspen, CO 81611; call 970-925-1940 or 800-26-ASPEN.

Boulder Convention & Visitors Bureau, 2440 Pearl St., Boulder, CO 80302; call 303-442-2911 or 800-444-0447.

Breckenridge Resort Chamber, P.O. Box 1909, Breckenridge, CO 80424; call 970-453-6018 or 800-221-1091.

Buena Vista Chamber, P.O. Box 2021, Buena Vista, CO 81211; call 719-395-6612 or 800-831-8594.

Burlington Chamber, 415 15th St., Burlington, CO 80807; call 719-346-8070.

Cañon City Chamber, P.O. Bin 749, Cañon City, CO 81215-0749; call 719-275-2331 or 800-876-7922.

Carbondale Chamber, 0590 Hwy. 133, Carbondale, CO 81623; call 970-963-1890.

Cedaredge Chamber, P.O. Box 278, Cedaredge, CO 81413; call 970-856-6961.

Central City Public Information, P.O. Box 249, Central City, CO 80427; call 800-542-2999.

Clear Creek County Tourism, P.O. Box 100, Idaho Springs, CO 80452; call 303-567-4660 or 800-88-BLAST.

Colorado Springs Convention & Visitors Bureau, 104 S. Cascade, #104, Colorado Springs, CO 80903; call 719-635-7506 or 800-DO VISIT.

Copper Mountain Resort Assn., P.O. Box 3001, Copper Mountain, CO 80443; call 970-968-2882 or 800-525-3891.

Cortez Chamber, P.O. Box 968, Cortez, CO 81321; call 970-565-3414.

Creede-Mineral County Chamber, P.O. Box 580, Creede, CO 81130; call 719-658-2374 or 800-327-2102.

Crested Butte Chamber, P.O. Box 1288, Crested Butte, CO 81224; call 970-349-6438 or 800-545-4505.

Cripple Creek Chamber, P.O. Box 650, 337 E. Bennett Ave., Cripple Creek, CO 80813; call 719-689-2169 or 800-526-8777.

Delta Chamber, 301 S. Main, Delta, CO 81416; call 970-874-8616.

Denver Metro Convention & Visitors Bureau, 1555 California ST., Ste. 300, Denver, CO 80202; call 800-645-3446.

Town of Dillon, P.O. Box 8, Dillon, CO 80435; call 970-468-2403.

Dinosaur Chamber, P.O. Box 102, Dinosaur, CO 81610; no phone.

Dolores Chamber, P.O. Box 602, Dolores, CO 81323; call 970-882-4018.

Dove Creek Chamber, P.O. Box 613, Dove Creek, CO 81324; call 970-677-2245.

Durango Chamber Resort Assn., P.O. Box 2587, Durango, CO 81302; call 970-247-0312 or 800-525-8855.

Eagle Valley Chamber, P.O. Box 964, Eagle, CO 81631; call 970-328-5220.

Empire Town Hall, P.O. Box 187, Empire, CO 80438; call 303-569-2978.

Estes Park Area Chamber, P.O. Box 3050, Estes Park, CO 80517; call 970-586-4431 or 800-44-ESTES

Evergreen Chamber, P.O. Box 97, Evergreen, CO 80437-0097; call 303-674-3412.

Florissant/Lake George Chamber, P.O. Box 507, Florissant, CO 80816; call 719-748-8000.

Fort Collins Convention & Visitors Bureau, 420 S. Howes #101, Fort Collins, CO 80522; call 970-482-5821 or 800-274-FORT.

Ft. Morgan Area Chamber, 300 Main St., Ft. Morgan, CO 80701; call 970-867-6121; Internet: fmchamber@aol.com.

Fraser Visitor Center, 205 Fraser Ave., Fraser, CO 80442; call 970-726-4118.

Fruita Chamber, P.O. Box 117, Fruita, CO 81521; call 970-858-1000.

Georgetown Visitor Information Center, 613 Sixth St., P.O. Box 444, Georgetown, CO 80444; call 303-569-2888.

Gilpin County Chamber, 281 Church St., P.O. Box 343, Black Hawk, CO 80422; call 303-582-5077 or 800-331-LUCK.

Glenwood Springs Chamber Resort Assn., 1102 Grand Ave., Glenwood Springs, CO 81601; call 970-945-6589 or 800-221-0098.

Golden Area Chamber, P.O. Box 1035, Golden, CO 80402; call 303-279-3113 or 800-590-3113.

Granby Chamber, P.O. Box 35, Granby, CO 80446; call 970-887-2311 or 800-325-1661.

Grand Junction Visitor & Convention Bureau, 740 Horizon Dr., Grand Junction, CO 81506; call 970-244-1480 or 800-962-2547.

Grand Lake Area Chamber, P.O. Box 57, Grand Lake, CO 80447; call 970-627-3402 or 800-531-1019.

Greeley Convention & Visitors Bureau, 1407 8th Ave., Greeley, CO 80631; call 970-352-3566 or 800-449-3866.

Gunnison Country Chamber, P.O. Box 36, Gunnison, CO 81230; call 970-641-1501 or 800-274-7580.

Huerfano County Chamber, P.O. Box 493, Walsenburg, CO 81089; call 719-738-1065.

Idaho Springs Visitor Center, 2200 Miner Drive., Idaho Springs, CO 80452; call 303-567-4382 or 800-882-5278.

Julesburg Chamber, 122 W. 1st., Julesburg, CO 80737; call 970-474-3504.

Keystone Resort Colorado, P.O. Box 38, Keystone, CO 80435; call 970-468-4123.

Kremmling Area Chamber, P.O. Box 471, Kremmling, CO 80459; call 970-724-3472.

La Junta Chamber, P.O. Box 408, La Junta, CO 81050; call 719-384-7411.

La Veta Chamber, P.O. Box 32, La Veta, CO 81055; call 719-742-3676.

Lake City Chamber, P.O. Box 430, Lake City, CO 81235; call 970-944-2527 or 800-569-1874.

Lamar Chamber, P.O. Box 860, Lamar, CO 81052-0860; call 719-336-4379.

Las Animas Chamber, 332 Ambassador Thompson Blvd., Las Animas, CO 81054; call 719-456-0453.

Leadville Area Chamber of Commerce, P.O. Box 861, Leadville, CO 80461; call 719-486-3900 or 800-933-3901.

Limon Town Hall, P.O. Box 9, Limon, CO 80828; call 719-775-2346.

Logan County Chamber, P.O. Box 1683, Sterling, CO 80751; call 970-522-5070 or 800-544-8609.

Longmont Area Chamber, 528 N Main St., Longmont, CO 80501; call 303-776-5295.

Louisville Chamber, 717 Main St., Louisville, CO 80027; call 303-666-5747.

Loveland Chamber, 114 E. 5th St., Loveland, CO 80537; call 970-667-6311.

Lyons Chamber, P.O. Box 426, Lyons, CO 80540; call 303-823-5215.

Town of Manassa, 401 Main, Manassa, CO 81141; call 719-843-5207.

Mancos Visitors Center, P.O. Box 494, Mancos, CO 81328; call 970-533-7434.

Manitou Springs Chamber, 354 Manitou Ave., Manitou Springs, CO 80829; call 719-685-5089 or 800-642-2567.

Meeker Chamber, P.O. Box 869, Meeker, CO 81641; call 970-878-5510.

Montrose Chamber, 1519 E. Main, Montrose, CO 81401; call 970-249-5000 or 800-873-0244.

Nederland Area Chamber, P.O. Box 85, Nederland, CO

80466; call 303-258-3936 or 800-221-0044.
North Park Chamber, P.O. Box 68, Walden CO 80480; call 970-723-4600.
Ouray County Chamber, P.O. Box 145, Ouray, CO 81427; call 970-325-4746 or 800-228-1876.
Pagosa Springs Area Chamber, P.O. Box 787, Pagosa Springs, CO 81147; call 970-264-2360 or 800-252-2204.
Palisade Chamber, P.O. Box 729, Palisade, CO 81526; call 970-464-7458.
Paonia Chamber, P.O. Box 366, Paonia, CO 81428; call 970-527-3886.
Park County Tourism Office, P.O. Box 220, Fairplay, CO 80440; call 719-836-4279.
Pueblo Chamber, Convention and Visitors Council, P.O. Box 697, Pueblo, CO 81002; call 800-233-3446.
Rangely Area Chamber of Commerce, 209 E. Main St., Rangely, CO 81648; call 970-675-5290.
Red Feather Lakes, P.O. Box 184, Red Feather Lakes, CO 80545; call 970-881-2195 or 800-462-5870.
Rifle Area Chamber, 200 Lions Park Cir., Rifle, CO 81650; call 970-625-2085.
Rocky Ford Chamber, 105 N. Main, Rocky Ford, CO 81607; call 719-254-7483.
San Luis Valley Information Center, First and Jefferson, Monte Vista, CO 81144; call 719-852-0660 or 800-835-7254.
Silver Plume Town Hall, P.O. Box 457, Silver Plume, CO 80476; call 303-569-2363.
Silverton Chamber, P.O. Box 565, Silverton, CO 81433, call 970-387-5654 or 800-752-4494.
Snowmass Resort Assn., P.O. Box 5566, Snowmass Village, CO 81615; call 970-923-2000 or 800-332-3245.
South Fork Chamber, P.O. Box 12, South Fork, CO 81154; call 719-873-5512.
Southern Ute Indian Tribe, P.O. Box 550 Ignacio, CO 81137; call 970-563-0100 or 800-876-7017.
Steamboat Springs Chamber Resort Assn., 1255 S. Lincoln Ave., P.O. Box 774408; call 970-879-0880 or 800-922-2722.
Summit County Chamber, P.O. Box 214, Frisco, CO 80443; call 970-668-5800.
Telluride Visitor Services, P.O. Box 653, Telluride, CO 81435; call 800-525-3455.
Trinidad/Las Animas County Chamber, 309 Nevada Ave., Trinidad, CO 81082; call 719-846-9285.
Ute Mountain Ute Indian Tribal Parks, General Delivery, Towaoc, CO 81334; call 970-565-3751 or 800-847-5485.
Vail Resort Assn., 100 E. Meadow Dr., Vail, CO 81657; call 970-476-1000 or 800-824-5737.
Victor Chamber, P.O. Box 83, Victor, CO 80860; call 719-689-2346.
Winter Park/Fraser Valley Chamber, P.O. Box 3236, Winter Park, CO 80482; call 970-726-4118 or 303-422-0666 (Denver direct).
Wray Chamber of Commerce, P.O. Box 161, Wray, CO 80758; call 970-332-5063.

Photography Credits

Courety of the Colorado Historical Society: All black and white archival photos, and p. 70
Ernie Ferguson: 6
Nancy Fleagle: 131
James Frank: 96, front cover
Courtesy of Georgetown Loop: 102
Dan Hudson: 112
David Muench: 2-3, 82-83, 138-139, 154-155
David Muenker: 7, 8, 14, 18 m, 18 r, 27, 34, 56, 59 b, 73 b, 100 t, 101, 110 b, 116-117, 145, back cover
Sherri O'Hara: 44
Jack Olson: 17 b, 19 l, 30 b, 40, 45, 47, 49, 50, 51, 52 l, 52 r, 53, 57 t, 58 t, 58 b, 59 t, 60 t, 61, 63, 65, 68, 71, 78, 84, 85, 86, 88, 89 r, 99 t, 104, 105, 121, 124, 127, 129 t, 135, 146, 157
Jim Osterberg: 17 t, 76
William Panzer: 87, 140
Larry Pierce: 19 r, 26, 43
Dennis & Esther Schmidt 12, 13,18 l,57 b, 161
Patrick Soran/Dan Klinglesmith: 19 m, 30 t, 38, 41, 60 b, 66, 67, 73 t, 74, 79, 81, 89 l, 90, 93, 94, 97, 99 b, 100 b, 103, 109 l, 109 r, 110 t, 113, 115, 118, 123, 125 t, 125 b, 126, 129 b, 132, 134, 141, 143, 148, 149 t, 149 b, 156, 159, 160
Dan Klinglesmith: 32, 36, 133 l, 133 r, 144, 147, 150, 151
Courtesy of the Wynkoop Brewing Co.: 54

Index

About the Authors

Writer and photographer Dan Klinglesmith can trace his Colorado roots back four generations. His great-great grandparents, John and Martha Barrow, came to the "Centennial State" in 1888, settling in Crested Butte. The mining camp was too rowdy a place to raise children so they moved to Hotchkiss, homesteading a few acres outside town on what is still called Barrow Mesa. Born on the Western Slope at Grand Junction, Dan fondly remembers summers spent horseback riding amidst the buttes and valleys that were first settled by his family.

Growing up on the state's Front Range gave Dan a taste of big-city life, and he still calls Denver home. For the last decade, however, the world has become his backyard. Working as a freelance travel writer and photographer, Dan has criss-crossed the globe, penning articles for a wide variety of magazines and newspapers.

Nevertheless, he admits there's no place like home. "Colorado has it all," contends Dan. "It's a state marked with incredible natural beauty, fascinating history and diversions to occupy a lifetime." He adds, "there's no greater joy than writing about the place you love."

Raised and educated in Denver's Capitol Hill, Patrick Soran lives in the very home in which he was born. The house was purchased by his grandparents in 1936 and has served as hearth and home to three generations. Needless to say, Patrick is an enthusiastic advocate of Denver; he loves to pedal its bicycle paths, chat with friends in its urbane coffee shops, walk its tree-lined avenues and, of course, spend autumn Sundays cheering (and crying!) for the Denver Broncos.

Trained as an architect, Patrick designed luxury homes and hotel interiors for 15 years before trading T-square and triangle for computer and camera in 1990. Now he explores the world writing articles about travel, design and personalities for newspapers and magazines across the country.

Patrick is immensely proud to write about his home state. He believes Colorado has terrific wilderness and wildlife experiences, edge-of-the-envelope recreation and exciting cultural and lifestyle opportunities.